The **Essential** Guide to

Jewish Prayer
and Practices

by Andrea Lieber, PhD

ALPHA

A member of Penguin Group (USA) Inc.

ALPHA BOOKS

Published by the Penguin Group

Penguin Group (USA) Inc., 375 Hudson Street, New York, New York 10014, USA • Penguin Group (Canada), 90 Eglinton Avenue East, Suite 700, Toronto, Ontario M4P 2Y3, Canada (a division of Pearson Penguin Canada Inc.) • Penguin Books Ltd., 80 Strand, London WC2R 0RL, England • Penguin Ireland, 25 St. Stephen's Green, Dublin 2, Ireland (a division of Penguin Books Ltd.) • Penguin Group (Australia), 250 Camberwell Road, Camberwell, Victoria 3124, Australia (a division of Pearson Australia Group Pty. Ltd.) • Penguin Books India Pvt. Ltd., 11 Community Centre, Panchsheel Park, New Delhi—110 017, India • Penguin Group (NZ), 67 Apollo Drive, Rosedale, North Shore, Auckland 1311, New Zealand (a division of Pearson New Zealand Ltd.) • Penguin Books (South Africa) (Pty.) Ltd., 24 Sturdee Avenue, Rosebank, Johannesburg 2196, South Africa • Penguin Books Ltd., Registered Offices: 80 Strand, London WC2R 0RL, England

International Standard Book Number: 978-1-61564-138-3
Library of Congress Catalog Card Number: 2011936778

14 13 12   8 7 6 5 4 3 2 1

Interpretation of the printing code: The rightmost number of the first series of numbers is the year of the book's printing; the rightmost number of the second series of numbers is the number of the book's printing. For example, a printing code of 12-1 shows that the first printing occurred in 2012.

Printed in the United States of America

Note: This publication contains the opinions and ideas of its author. It is intended to provide helpful and informative material on the subject matter covered. It is sold with the understanding that the author and publisher are not engaged in rendering professional services in the book. If the reader requires personal assistance or advice, a competent professional should be consulted.

The author and publisher specifically disclaim any responsibility for any liability, loss, or risk, personal or otherwise, which is incurred as a consequence, directly or indirectly, of the use and application of any of the contents of this book.

Most Alpha books are available at special quantity discounts for bulk purchases for sales promotions, premiums, fund-raising, or educational use. Special books, or book excerpts, can also be created to fit specific needs. For details, write: Special Markets, Alpha Books, 375 Hudson Street, New York, NY 10014.

Publisher: *Marie Butler-Knight*
Associate Publisher: *Mike Sanders*
Executive Managing Editor: *Billy Fields*
Executive Acquisitions Editor: *Lori Cates Hand*
Senior Development Editor: *Christy Wagner*
Senior Production Editor: *Kayla Dugger*

Copy Editor: *Krista Hansing Editorial Services, Inc.*
Cover Designer: *Rebecca Batchelor*
Book Designers: *Rebecca Batchelor, William Thomas*
Indexer: *Celia McCoy*
Layout: *Ayanna Lacey*
Senior Proofreader: *Laura Caddell*

Dedication

For Hannah, Sarah, and Leah.

Contents

Appendixes

Introduction

What does an ancient religious tradition like Judaism, which developed thousands of years ago in a world so different from our own, have to offer the twenty-first century? After all, shouldn't the teachings contained in Judaism's classical texts, written in ancient languages like Hebrew and Aramaic with quill and ink on parchment scrolls, be obsolete in our fast-paced, modern world? Yet millions of Jews across the globe today continue to practice Judaism, turning to its ancient wisdom as an ongoing source of inspiration and meaning.

What accounts for Judaism's longevity? How has it remained a vibrant, spiritual wellspring that Jews and non-Jews alike have embraced from generation to generation? These questions have interested me throughout my career, and in the pages of this book, you'll find what I have found to be some of the answers.

Growing up culturally Jewish but not religiously observant, I was curious about Judaism from a young age. When I was about 10 years old, I found a volume of the *Torah,* bound in black leather with gilded lettering on the cover, that had been on my parents' bookshelves for years. Starting at the beginning, I decided to try to read it cover to cover.

The text drew me in. I found it entirely mysterious, yet strangely familiar. I had no idea then that my youthful curiosity was very traditional from a Jewish perspective and that, for nearly 2,000 years, Jews before me had embraced the *Torah* as the path to a meaningful Jewish life.

The truth is that Judaism has a lot to say about how to live in today's complicated world. Although it was born out of an age far simpler than ours, in many ways, human lives of antiquity and human lives in our contemporary age have more in common than you might imagine.

Whether you're nonpracticing and looking to get back to the faith or you're currently very spiritual but looking for a deeper understanding of Judaism, it is my goal in the pages that follow to make Jewish religion and its practices accessible to you. Judaism is a vast ocean of history, traditions, texts, beliefs, and rituals. And I know from personal experience just how daunting it can be to put that first toe in the water.

For starters, there are so many different approaches to Jewish spirituality. How can you know which denomination is right for you?

The use of Hebrew language in Jewish rituals can feel like a barrier to meaningful prayer. How do you open yourself to prayer when it's in a language you don't understand? It's easy to feel uncomfortable in a synagogue, especially if you don't attend regularly. And how can you expect Jewish Sabbath or holiday celebrations to be meaningful if you don't know what they're about?

Perhaps you were raised Jewish but never really understood what the prayers you recited in synagogue truly meant. Maybe you've been engaged in Jewish prayer for years but feel the need to go deeper in your own spiritual practice. Perhaps your sense of Jewish identity is more secular or cultural, and you want to find out what Judaism has to say about prayer and spirituality. Or maybe you've only recently converted to Judaism and want to learn more.

Whatever your background, in *The Essential Guide to Jewish Prayer and Practices,* I provide you with the tools you need to deepen your spiritual connection to Judaism—to help you understand what Jewish prayers, beliefs, and practices are all about and help you see how these ancient traditions can be relevant in your life today.

One thing that sets this book apart from other books about Jewish spirituality is that I write it as a scholar, not as a rabbi ordained in one particular stream of Judaism. This means I'm free to share multiple perspectives as I move through the material. I've explored numerous different Jewish communities, see the beauty of all of them, and am eager to share what I've learned from them with you.

Throughout the book, I focus on the essential basics of Judaism, emphasizing what those traditions, prayers, and beliefs Jews have in common while noting the important practical or philosophical differences you might encounter across the denominations. I don't claim that one particular way of being Jewish is more authentic than another. Wherever you're coming from, consider these pages an invitation to take your own spiritual life to a new level.

How This Book Is Organized

This book is divided into four parts:

To better understand the role prayer and spirituality plays in Jewish life, it's essential to familiarize yourself with a few key concepts in Jewish thought. The chapters in **Part 1, The Foundations of a Meaningful Life,** address the sanctity of human life in the Jewish faith, Judaism's concept of God, and the role of the *Torah* in guiding Jewish spiritual life. This part also helps you appreciate a few unique points of Jewish spirituality.

Part 2, The Path Toward Prayer, introduces you to the form of Jewish prayer—the structure of Jewish worship and the different kinds of prayers that make up Jewish liturgy. You learn practical tips about how to participate in Jewish services, and I introduce you to the different ritual objects commonly used in both private and public prayer.

Part 3, The Practice of Prayer, delves into the most significant prayers and practices in the Jewish prayer book. Starting with daily prayers, the chapters in this part also explain how prayer is different on the Sabbath, the High Holy Days of *Rosh HaShanah* and *Yom Kippur,* and other important Jewish festivals. You also learn how to pray for healing, how to use prayer to remember loved ones who have died, and how Jewish prayer marks other important milestones.

Part 4, Jewish Spirituality in the Synagogue and Beyond, explores the synagogue as a sacred space in Jewish tradition, along with everything you need to know to find a spiritual home. If you're skeptical about finding meaning in synagogue life, the chapters in this part give you some alternative strategies for engaging with Jewish spirituality. From home-centered practices to the Jewish traditions of charity and social justice, there's something for everyone in this final part.

Essential Extras

Throughout this book, you encounter special messages to help you understand Jewish prayer and practices more fully. Here's what to look for:

Look to these sidebars for definitions and explanations of words and phrases that might be confusing or unfamiliar.

Look here for practical advice on how to enrich your own spiritual life using practices described in this book.

Here you'll find uplifting and inspirational quotes from Judaism's classical texts about Jewish religious practices.

You'll also see a fourth, name-changing sidebar that presents anecdotes, important variations in practices, or other extended background information you need to know.

Acknowledgments

Writing *The Essential Guide to Jewish Prayer and Practices* has been an incredible adventure that has helped me grow in so many new ways. Its contents reflect all I have learned as a student, teacher, and seeker of the Jewish faith. What I have accomplished here would not have been possible without an amazing and multilayered network of supportive professionals, colleagues, students, friends, and family.

Above all, I would like to thank my former student Arielle Battat Silverman for remembering me one sunny day in Safed, during a trip to Israel. Without you and your memories of our studies together, I would not have had the opportunity to work on this project.

I am also indebted to Rita Battat Silverman of Leap Over It, Inc., my tireless and talented agent, who believed in this book and cheered me on over every hurdle. Your positive energy got me through some very long hours of writing! Thank you also to everyone at Alpha who worked on this book, especially Lori Cates Hand and Christy Wagner. Thanks also to Kayla Dugger and Krista Hansing.

I owe profound thanks to all my colleagues at Dickinson College, a model liberal arts institution that has supported me and nurtured my intellectual growth for the past 13 years. Thanks especially to the provost, Neil Weissman, and my colleagues in the Department of Religion who inspire me with their ongoing passion for inquiry: Mara Donaldson, Ted Pulcini, Dan Cozort, Nitsa Kann, and Shalom Staub. Thanks also to Yale and Audrey Asbell, whose generosity and vision created the Sophia Ava Asbell Chair of Judaic Studies, which I have been privileged to hold for nearly a decade. I am especially grateful to the Dickinson College Research and Development Committee for a generous grant to support publication expenses.

I must also thank the many students I've taught over the years, both at Dickinson and beyond its limestone walls (you know who you are). Your questions and your curiosity informed every page of this book.

Living in the unique Jewish community of Harrisburg, Pennsylvania, has taught me more about the complexity of Jewish life than any book on my shelf. I am grateful to the community rabbis who have accorded me the respect of a colleague: Rabbi Ron Muroff, Rabbi Peter Kessler, Rabbi Akiva Males, Rabbi Chayim Schertz, Rabbi Jordi Gendra-Molina, and Rabbi Carl Choper.

I am deeply grateful to the leadership and membership of Beth El Temple in Harrisburg, my spiritual home for the past 12 years. Special thanks to Rabbi Eric Cytryn, Michael Schatz, Bob Axelrod, Dr. Alan Schein, and Rick Leiner for the many opportunities to teach, lead, and experiment with Jewish prayer.

Thanks also to the leadership of the Jewish Federation of Greater Harrisburg, David Herman, Jay Steinberg, and Andrea Weikert, who have taught me so much about community collaboration and the meaning of partnership.

The pages of this book are also infused with lessons I've learned over the past 2 years as president of The Silver Academy, a K–8 Jewish community day school in Harrisburg. I feel so privileged to work with a highly talented group of people, professional and lay leaders, educators and administrators, all of them united in a deep commitment to the future of Jewish education in our community.

The list of friends to thank is too long to print, but I do want to acknowledge Shari Dym and Leslie Wiener, who reviewed early drafts of some chapters and provided valuable feedback and advice along the way. Bonni Teplitz Roseman provided assistance in preparing the manuscript for publication.

During the writing process, I had the great pleasure of preparing two amazing young women to become *bat mitzvah*. To Madison Schwab and her parents, Patty and Dan; to Rosie Levi and her parents, Benny and Shaun: thank you for allowing me to be a part of this special time in the lives of your families—so much of what I learned from your daughters is reflected in these pages.

I completed this book surrounded by friends, family, and colleagues at Camp Ramah in the tranquil Pocono Mountains. I can think of no better place to write a book on Jewish prayer. Living each day in a vibrant, spiritual community that takes so seriously the task of nurturing the spiritual lives of Jewish children is truly a blessing. Thank you to Rabbi Todd Zeff, Michelle Sugarman, and all my dedicated colleagues on the teaching staff.

Special thanks go to Rabbi Jay Stein, Senior Rabbi of Har Zion Temple in Penn Valley, Pennsylvania, who read the entire manuscript and provided generous and thoughtful feedback.

I have probably learned the most about what it means to live a meaningful life from my three amazing daughters, Hannah, Sarah, and Leah. I love you all so much and thank you for the joy you bring me every single day with your hugs and your laughter. Your smiles are my inspiration for this book, and I dedicate it to you.

My husband, Ted Merwin, is my partner, my colleague, and my best friend. I could never have completed this work without his patience and understanding. Thank you, Ted, for believing in me every step of the way.

Trademarks

All terms mentioned in this book that are known to be or are suspected of being trademarks or service marks have been appropriately capitalized. Alpha Books and Penguin Group (USA) Inc. cannot attest to the accuracy of this information. Use of a term in this book should not be regarded as affecting the validity of any trademark or service mark.

Siddur Sim Shalom reprinted with permission from *Siddur Sim Shalom: A Prayer Book for Weekdays, Shabbat and Festivals,* © 1985, the Rabbinical Assembly.

Mahzor Lev Shalem reprinted with permission from *Mahzor Lev Shalem,* © 2010, the Rabbinical Assembly.

Quotations from the Hebrew Bible are reprinted from *The JPS Hebrew-English TANAKH,* © 1999, published by The Jewish Publication Society, with the permission of the publisher.

"Prayer Invites" from *Gates of Prayer: The New Union Prayerbook,* by Chaim Sterrn, inspired by a passage by Abraham Joshua Heschel © 1975 Central Conference of American Rabbis and excerpts from *Mishkan T'filah: A Reform Siddur* © 2007 Central Conference of American Rabbis are under the copyright protection of the Central Conference of American Rabbis and reprinted for use by permission of the CCAR. All rights reserved.

Part 1

The Foundations of a Meaningful Life

One thing should become clear to you as you read this book: many paths lead to a meaningful Jewish life. Ultimately, you have to decide for yourself what path makes the most sense for you. The modern denominations of Judaism offer rich, yet competing, interpretations of what it means to live Jewishly, but Jewish practice also varies with respect to where you are in your own life. Your relationship to Jewish tradition changes and grows over time, and it's important to remember that wherever you are on the journey, you have opportunities to connect.

Fundamental principals are shared by the vast majority of Jewish people. As you begin your exploration of Jewish spirituality, I think it's important to cover some basic ground in this regard. What are the key principles at the core of the Jewish faith? What ultimate questions does Judaism seek to answer, and is anything about those answers uniquely Jewish?

The chapters in Part 1 lay the groundwork for a general appreciation of Jewish spirituality and an understanding of Judaism's core values and central beliefs. In the pages that follow, I discuss the sanctity of human life in Jewish tradition and explore different ways of approaching God. In addition, I introduce you to the beauty of the *Torah* as a spiritual focus and the language of blessing that's so central to Jewish piety.

From there, you will be well equipped to delve further into Jewish prayer.

chapter 1

Life Is Sacred

Why Jewish spirituality is "*this*worldly"

The *Torah* as a guidebook for life

How humans reflect the image of God

Becoming sensitive to the power of speech

Connecting to generations past, present, and future

The belief that life is sacred is the cornerstone of Jewish spirituality. In this chapter, I explain where the idea comes from and why it's central to all varieties of Jewish tradition. We explore the concept of "holiness," consider what the Bible means when it says human beings are created in the image of God, and take a look at how these themes can be understood in modern life.

This chapter also provides some strategies for increasing your own daily awareness of life's sanctity, and for learning to see the divine image in those around you.

L'chayim! To Life!

You've probably heard these words exclaimed during a festive toast. *L'chayim* means "to life," and it's the Jewish equivalent of saying "Cheers!" as you lift your glass in honor of a special occasion. Did you ever wonder why Jews cheer for life this way when toasting a special event, whether secular or sacred? I think this simple gesture summarizes Jewish spirituality in a profound way: life is a gift worthy of celebration, because without it, we would be unable to enjoy those unique pleasures and meaningful moments that make it sacred.

Basic to Jewish spirituality is the idea that this life—the one you're living right now, at this very moment—is of supreme importance. If you weren't alive, you wouldn't be able to experience the most profound emotions of love, awe, and gratitude. You wouldn't be able to perform acts of kindness for others, experience growth and change, or engage in meaningful human relationships. You wouldn't be able to do anything to make the world a better place.

Unlike some other religious traditions that see heavenly reward or life after death as the most pressing spiritual priority, for Jews, the way we live our lives in the here and now is of paramount importance. Traditional Jewish theology does imagine a life beyond this one, but it's in the realm of worldly human history that our lives acquire true meaning, and in the arena of the living that the human soul takes shape.

wisdom of the sages

Just to be is a blessing. Just to live is holy.

—Abraham Joshua Heschel, *No Religion Is an Island*

A famous story attributed to first-century rabbi Yohanan ben Zakkai underscores this point. Rabbi Yohanan says, "If you are holding a sapling in hand and someone tells you, 'Come quickly, the messiah has come,' first finish planting the tree and then go to greet the messiah." (*Avot D'Rabbi Natan,* 31b) This short story is a clear example that good works in this world have priority over otherworldly concerns.

The *Torah* as a Roadmap for Life

If life is sacred, how are we supposed to know what to do to live a life that embraces its sacred potential? How do you make the most of this gift you've been given? This is where the *Torah* comes in.

definition

Torah is a Hebrew word that can be translated as "teaching" or "law." In Judaism, *Torah* most commonly refers to the Five Books of Moses, or the *Pentateuch,* which is part of the Hebrew Bible.

Traditional Judaism maintains that the *Torah,* a divinely authored text, revealed in both oral and written form to Moses at Mount Sinai and then passed down and interpreted from generation to generation, is the collection of sacred Hebrew scriptures that stands at the heart of Judaism. It forms the basis of the covenant between God and the Jewish people, an eternal pact that links Jews of every generation, past, present, and future. Jews understand the *Torah* as life's guidebook. It's like a user's manual that has been passed down, interpreted, and reinterpreted through the ages, teaching us how to live through its ancient stories, laws, and poetry.

The *Torah* instructs us about how to bring sanctity into the world through our actions. Sure, it contains teachings about big moral issues like murder, adultery, and theft, but the *Torah* is also concerned about the everyday: how we conduct our business affairs, how we treat a hired laborer, how we welcome guests and neighbors, and how we care for the land we rely on to provide food.

The *Torah* teaches us through precepts called *mitzvot* (*mits-VOTE*), or "commandments." Although the "Ten Commandments" get the most attention, the *Torah* actually contains hundreds of *mitzvot.* Jewish tradition holds that there are 613 in total, 365 positive precepts (Thou shalts …) and 248 negative precepts (Thou shalt nots …).

A Book with Many Names

Christians consider the *Torah* part of their Bible's Old Testament. This terminology is offensive to some Jews because it implies that its teachings are made obsolete by the Christian New Testament. A more neutral term for this body of scripture is the *Hebrew Bible* or *Hebrew Scriptures.*

In the *Torah,* the commandments are a roadmap for the way God wanted the Israelites to live as they established themselves as a new nation and as a community. The rabbinic sages who interpreted the *Torah* for later generations saw these *mitzvot* as a framework for establishing Jewish communities in the future, including our own.

A spiritual Jewish life is framed by the *mitzvot,* and these commandments can be performed only by the living. We love, honor, respect, celebrate, bless, and mourn, and in so doing, we create communities that are what the Jewish sages call *kadosh,* or holy or sacred. They are holy because they manifest the divine presence through human action.

One of the most basic ways you can connect to God in the Jewish tradition is by doing *mitzvot.* Think of them as a vehicle for animating the divine will in the world. If you find it hard to relate to the idea of a "commanding" God, think of the *mitzvot* as a set of sacred obligations or duties. Performing these sacred acts brings *kedushah,* or holiness, into the world.

Definition

The Hebrew words **kadosh** and **kedushah** are usually translated to mean "holy" and "holiness," respectively. Something that is *kadosh,* or holy, is set apart, consecrated, and sanctified to God. Although particular places, objects, and people are holy in Jewish tradition, Judaism places greatest emphasis on creating holiness in *time,* by marking Sabbaths and holy days as set apart from ordinary days.

In the Book of Deuteronomy, Moses addresses the Israelite nation, saying, "Surely, this Instruction [*mitzvah*] which I enjoin upon you this day is not too baffling for you, nor is it beyond reach. It is not in the heavens, that you should say, 'Who among us can go up to the heavens and get it for us ....' Neither is it beyond the sea. No, the teaching is very close to you, in your mouth and in your heart, to observe it."

The *Torah* is not in heaven. It is right here, within your reach. It is not a how-to book for attaining spiritual reward in the afterlife, and it does not contain secrets about what the next life is like. Quite the contrary, it's an accessible book that tells us how to live in the here and now, and how to conduct human life in this world with the utmost sanctity.

Of course, different Jews take different approaches to the *Torah.* Orthodox and Conservative Jews view this spiritual guidebook as the literal word of God and believe each letter is there for a reason. Reform and Reconstructionist Jews believe the *Torah* to be a divinely inspired text, while Jews who come from a more secular or humanistic background might view it as more of a collection of myths that contain moral and ethical teachings.

Regardless of these differences, Jews across the denominational spectrum revere the *Torah* as a key document of Jewish heritage that provides the moral and ethical underpinnings for living in a just society.

What About an Afterlife?

If Jewish spirituality focuses on the sanctity of this life, what does Jewish teaching say about life *beyond* death? It might surprise you to learn that the *Torah* does not mention an afterlife or heavenly reward and punishment. In the biblical world, salvation and punishment take place in the here and now, within human history. Later, the rabbinic sages, influenced by neighboring cultures, developed the concept of a "World to Come" (in Hebrew, *olam ha-ba*), and to this day, the daily prayers recited by both Orthodox and Conservative Jews celebrate God's power to resurrect the dead. Reform and Reconstructionist prayer books, however, have removed this language from the liturgy.

Human Beings and the Divine Image

Another way to think about the *Torah* is to consider it the family album of the Jewish people. Your own family album might begin with baby pictures taken shortly after your arrival, surrounded by adoring relatives and friends. Then come pictures of your toddler years, your first day of school, your graduations—preserving a glimpse of all the key events and people that made you who you are today.

As a family, the story of the Jewish people begins with the patriarch, Abraham. But curiously, the family history recorded in the *Torah* doesn't begin with the story of Abraham. Instead, the *Torah* opens with a legend about the birth of the universe, establishing God as the creator of all life. Before the particular story of the Jewish people gets told, we first have to understand what it means to be human.

Let's take a look at how it all begins.

The Book of Genesis contains two stories about the "birth" of humanity. In one version, the first human beings are created in the image of God: "And God created man in his image, in the image of God he created him; male and female he created them." (Genesis 1:27) In the second version, the first human being is formed from dust and animated with divine breath: "[T]he Lord God formed man from the dust of the earth. He blew into his nostrils the breath of life [*nishmat chayim*], and man became a living being [*nefesh chayah*]." (Genesis 2:7)

Whether you accept these stories as literally true or as myths to be interpreted metaphorically, these verses contain a profound message about the sanctity of human life in the Jewish faith. Jewish spirituality starts with the idea that we are all reflections of the divine image and possess a divine soul. Our likeness to God makes human life inherently precious, connects all of humankind as one family, and has implications for how we must act toward one another.

The Responsibility of Bearing the Divine Image

What does it mean to live a life that reflects the divine image? Jewish sages never imagined that human beings *look* like God in a literal, physical sense. According to Jewish tradition, being created in the divine image means we resemble God in deeper, more substantive ways. In some respects, our divine likeness sets us apart from other living beings, and in others, it connects us to every living thing.

The Power of Speech

Human beings are endowed with the divine gift of speech. Language plays a very important role in the *Torah,* not just because God communicates with humanity through language, but also because it's the tool through which God creates the universe.

In the opening verses of Genesis, we read, "God said, 'Let there be light' and there was light." God speaks, and light spontaneously comes into being. This idea teaches us that language can be a powerful, generative tool and that words can have a life of their own.

Sharing in the divine gift of language, human beings can communicate with one another and with God. We use language to create works of literature, theater, song, and poetry that give expression to our ultimate concerns. We also use language to share intimate moments with a friend.

An important aspect of Jewish spirituality is remembering that our speech is both sacred and powerful. This means we have to use the gift of speech with a sense of the responsibility that comes with it. When we take care to speak respectfully and refrain from gossip and verbal abuse, we reflect the divine image. When we engage in cruel speech (the Jewish sages call it *lashon ha-ra,* or "evil tongue"), we detract from that image.

Reflecting the Divine Image

The simplest tasks can help you connect to the godliness in others. The way you speak and the small choices you make throughout the day are opportunities to reflect the divine image in the world. The next time you catch yourself speaking harshly about a friend or co-worker, for example, make the choice to redirect the conversation, and see how it feels.

The Power of Reason

Human beings are also endowed with a critical mind. Through reason and moral sensibility, we are able to judge between right and wrong, good and bad. Our ability to discern differences and make choices in our lives is also a reflection of God's image within us.

In the Genesis story, God makes order out of chaos by differentiating between day and night, heaven and earth, water and land. When we make healthy moral decisions and use our intellect to make well-reasoned choices, both as individuals and in communities, we draw on the divine gift of a rational mind. An ability to reason distinguishes humans among the animal kingdom and is the cornerstone of civilized society.

When we choose to do a *mitzvah,* we make a conscious decision to act in accordance with God's will. We don't have to—living a life in accordance with the *Torah* is a choice we make over and over again each day. When we make the decision to give charity, tell the truth, or make a blessing, we are using our God-given power to think, assess, and act. And with every choice we make, we have the opportunity to bring *kedushah* into the world.

The Breath of Life

If our capacity for speech and reason distinguish us among the animal kingdom, the breath of life connects us to all that lives. Perhaps the most tangible way to feel the sanctity of life is to become aware of the breath that flows through your body.

I know this might sound more like an Eastern spiritual tradition of meditation or yoga, but like those practices, Judaism also connects breath with life and divinity. I once heard a rabbi teach that God's true name is the sound of breathing that runs through all living things. As in Psalm 150, "Everything that breathes praises God."

Torah Tip

The hectic pace of a busy life can blind us to seeing the sacred in the everyday. The next time you're feeling frazzled, stop and take a couple deep breaths. As you feel the air fill your lungs, think of the divine energy moving through your body. Imagine this breath connecting you to all other living beings. Imagine each breath affirming the miracle of life.

Seeing the Divine Image in Ourselves and Others

Because the sanctity of life is so central to Judaism, it should come as no surprise that many Jews find humanitarian and social justice work a meaningful outlet for their spirituality. If every human being is created in the image of God, then every human being is deserving of respect and dignity. Many of the *Torah*'s commandments focus on caring for those in need out of a basic sensitivity to this principle. Even Jews who are more secular or humanistic in their outlook find a connection to Jewish tradition in the belief in every person's inherent worth.

In today's world, it's so easy to close ourselves off from others, to live a life defined by our own narrow concerns. As we near the end of this chapter, I want to share a few practical strategies for increasing your own awareness that life is sacred.

I feel very strongly that before you can begin to truly see the divine image in others, you must learn to see it in yourself. If you've ever traveled on an airplane, you may have been struck by that moment during the flight attendant's safety presentation when he warns that, in an emergency, you should put on your own oxygen mask before you assist your child.

Well, it's the same with spirituality. Before you can care for the physical or spiritual needs of others, you have to get yourself on solid footing. That means taking the time to turn inward until you truly believe that you reflect the image of God and that through your choices and your actions, you have the power to bring holiness into this world.

So how do you go about cultivating awareness of the divine image in yourself? The discipline of Jewish prayer you read about in the remaining chapters of this book will help you work toward this goal. You'll find that the prayers and meditations in the Jewish prayer book reinforce these very ideas and are still relevant today.

> *Torah*
> *Tip*
>
> One way to develop an appreciation for life is to consider our mortality. Remembering those who have passed on is very important to Jewish spirituality. Our ancestors no longer have the opportunity to perform *mitzvot* or recite prayers, so it's up to us to perform good deeds to honor their memory.

Because Judaism affirms life, it's very important to remember that your body is an important part of this equation. Maintaining a healthy body by eating well and getting adequate rest and exercise is a *mitzvah*—and an essential part of caring for yourself as the bearer of the divine image.

A prayer that appears as part of the morning blessings speaks to this issue beautifully. The words express gratitude to God for the miracle of the human body, without which living a Jewish life filled with prayer and good deeds would not be possible:

> Praised are you, Lord our God, Sovereign of the
> Universe who with wisdom fashioned the human
> body, creating openings, arteries, glands, and organs,
> marvelous in structure, intricate in design. Should
> but one of them, by being blocked or opened, fail to
> function, it would be impossible to stand before you.
> Praised are You, Lord, healer of all flesh who sustains
> our bodies in wondrous ways.

In addition to its placement among the morning blessings, some Jews choose to recite this blessing every time they use the bathroom, to express gratitude for the intricate and intimate functioning of the human body that enables us to sustain life. Imagine having such appreciation and gratitude for your body that every visit to the bathroom is an opportunity for blessing!

Once we learn to view our own selves with the respect we deserve, we can extend that kindness to others. Seeing the divinity in our own souls, we can then recognize that spark in others and learn to respect them as well.

Essential Takeaways

- Jewish spirituality focuses on living a good life in the here and now.
- Commandments (*mitzvot*) are sacred duties prescribed in the *Torah* that guide us in life and connect us with the divine will.
- Jewish ethics are informed by the idea that every human being reflects the image of God.
- The power to communicate through speech is a divine gift to cherish.
- Seeing the divine image in yourself means staying healthy and caring for your body.

chapter 2

Feeling God's Presence

Finding God language that works for you

Understanding the Jewish idea of monotheism

The meaning of *mitzvah*

Insights from Jewish mysticism

To make prayer real, and to make it truly meaningful, you have to figure out what role God is going to play in your spiritual practice. Some people are very open to contemplating God as an active presence in their lives, but for some of us, the notion of a personal relationship with God isn't all that comfortable.

The great thing about Judaism is that there are many different approaches to thinking about God—some that define God as an abstract spirit and some that take a more personal approach. Experiment with the ideas in the following pages to find an approach that speaks to you.

In this chapter, I introduce you to Jewish conceptions of God and share some thoughts about how you can begin to use Jewish tradition to welcome God's presence into your own spiritual practice.

Direct Access

In Jewish practice, no intermediary or middleman stands between you and God. You don't pray to saints or holy individuals, and you don't need rabbis and priests to communicate with God for you. You simply open your heart and mind to God's presence, and the relationship begins. Jewish worship is based on the idea that, when we pray, we stand before God and speak directly to God.

While it can be helpful to know how to pray using formal Jewish liturgy, it's certainly possible to pray without knowing a word of Hebrew or a single traditional blessing or prayer. In fact, there's even a Jewish tradition that singing out a wordless melody—humming a simple tune—can connect you with God if your heart is open enough.

> **wisdom of the sages**
>
> God is waiting for man to seek him.
>
> —Rabbi Abraham Joshua Heschel, *God in Search of Man*

Divine Unity

One of the most central beliefs in the Jewish religion is steadfast devotion to a single God. The very first of the 10 commandments states, "I am the Lord, Your God, you shall have no other gods before me." And the one prayer Jews recite every single day, twice a day, is the *Shema*, an affirmation of God's unity:

> Listen, Israel, the Lord is Our God, the Lord is One!
>
> *Shema Yisrael, Adonai Eloheinu, Adonai Ekhad!*

God is One. It's a simple statement that carries a lot of gravity. But what does it mean? What are we really saying when we talk about divine unity, and what role does this idea play in Jewish prayer?

God Has No Limits

Prayer is a bridge between the finite and the infinite. When we sing out to God in a moment of celebration or gratitude, we forge a connection between our own limited, temporal existence and the infinite reality that is God.

God is eternal and has no physical form. God is not limited by any image or definition and transcends all differences. God has no beginning and no end, but is an infinite force that flows both through the universe and through you during your lifetime. Everything that lives is united in God.

Your breath is the most tangible way to sense God's infinite presence in the world. The breath that animates you also animates all other living beings in the world. There was breath before you came into existence, and breath will continue to give life after you're gone. Breath is a symbol of the part of us that's eternal, unending, and divine, and it reminds us that all life is interconnected. God is this infinite force.

An Exclusive Relationship

Sometimes I think it helps to consider the idea of divine unity in terms of a romantic relationship. When you enter into a committed relationship, all other potential partners are off limits. The same holds true for the relationship between God and the Jewish people. While there may be other deities and divinities out there, Judaism requires that we be loyal to just One.

In the Bible, this idea is expressed in terms of God's jealousy over the worship of idols. In ancient Israel, the neighboring religious cultures expressed their belief in the spirit world through the worship of idols, or material objects that symbolized divinities. When God says, "You shall have no other God but me," God is asking us to look beyond the idols of their time and to worship the One, supreme God who created them all.

This lesson has important implications for our time. In today's society, we may not feel the urge to pray to inanimate statues or trees, but it sure is easy to get caught up in a culture that worships *things*. Whether it's work, money, fame, or the latest technological gadget, the material world is full of objects we pursue with almost religious devotion.

Monotheism, the belief in One God alone, reminds us not to attach ourselves to the false idols of the material world, which are finite and fleeting. Keeping your heart and mind focused on what is abiding and true, as opposed to the ephemeral, serves as a reminder that there's so much more to our life than we can see with our eyes. And awareness of God in this way reminds us that we, too, are holy beings.

The Jewish understanding of God is based on an idea called **monotheism,** or the belief in one, unique God. This is often contrasted with polytheism, or the belief in many gods. Biblical patriarch Abraham is credited with the discovery of monotheism. He recognized the existence of one, singular God at a time when his surrounding cultures were polytheistic.

God Is Beyond Language

If God is infinite, can we ever truly grasp God's essence or know for certain God is real? How do we move from thinking about God as a grand, cosmic force to developing a personal relationship that can be the foundation of prayer? These are big philosophical questions, but they are at the heart of Jewish prayer.

The whole idea of reaching out to God through prayer depends on our ability to suspend our intellectual questions and use the tools we have to express our deepest concerns.

The Book of Genesis presents us with two portraits of God. On one hand, God is the author of the universe—a supreme creator who rules the entire world. On the other hand, these same passages reveal a portrait of God that's close to humankind. This is a God who is intimate and nurturing, breathing life directly into the lungs of the first human beings.

Without End

The *Zohar,* a medieval text of Jewish mysticism, uses the Hebrew term *Ein Sof* to refer to God. *Ein Sof* means "without end."

The Limits of Metaphor

In my own prayer practice, I find it hard to relate to classical images of God. I just can't connect to the idea of God as a patriarch—some stately old man with a long, white beard directing human affairs from his throne on high. But this image of God is everywhere in Judaism, from the Bible to the prayer book. Is there any way to find meaning in it?

Forbidding ideas about God as a threatening, punishing "other" are the greatest barrier to mature, meaningful prayer. It's so important to put those images aside as you seek to deepen your Jewish spirituality. Personifying God can definitely help you feel God's presence, but it's critical not to get trapped by narrow definitions that limit the way you think about the divine presence.

Jewish tradition actually uses many different metaphors to describe God. The most common are terms of royalty and tend to be masculine images: God is King, Lord, Ruler, Judge, or Sovereign. But if we look carefully, we can also find gentler, more intimate names for God. For example, one well-known prayer recited during holidays and festivals uses language that transcends gender:

> *Adonai Adonai,* You are merciful and compassionate, abounding in love and faithfulness, assuring love for thousands of generations, forgiving iniquity, transgression, and sin, and granting pardon.

> *Adonai Adonai, El rahum v'hanun erekh apayim v'rav hesed v'emet. Notzer hesed la'alafim, nosay avon va-fesha, v'hatah v'nakeh.*

In other prayers recited throughout the year, God is described as a loving parent, a guiding shepherd, and an ever-present companion.

In reality, though, God defies description. And to limit ourselves to any one particular way of thinking about God is to lose sight of the all-important principle that God is infinite. In a way, it borders on idolatry!

The different names and titles we use to address God try to describe something ultimately indescribable. If you think about it, it's actually a paradox. Try to remember that the words are simply a gateway, and the language we use to think about God is just a starting point. Prayer opens the doors that help you tap into the richness of your own infinite inner self.

Cultivating Wonder—God Is Awesome

When our ancestors wanted to express their sense of God's awesome power, they used metaphors of kingship and royalty. Kingship and royalty were symbols of power in their time. For them, the idea of God as a sovereign king made sense, and biblical poetry that uses this imagery may have evoked an appropriate sense of awe. But in twenty-first-century democratic America, these images don't really have the weight they once did.

So when I read the words in the prayer book that refer to God as King, instead of reading that image literally, I reach inside myself to retrieve an experience of awe that moves me. I think about standing on a mountaintop after a hike, taking in the majesty of my surroundings. I think about how small I am compared with the enormity of a mountain range, and I am humbled. This scene evokes a sense of awe, wonder, and mystery in me. I imagine this same feeling is what my ancestors meant when they called God "King."

> *Torah Tip*
>
> In Judaism, God is beyond gender. Although many Jewish prayers address God as male, God is not a man. While there may be times in your life when it's comforting to think of God as a "He," at other times, you might seek the comfort of God's feminine presence by thinking of God as "She." At other times, it might help to think of God as a more abstract, genderless energy. The next time you're saying a prayer, try thinking of God as "You." Remember, the words are just a starting point. Use them to open yourself to feeling God's presence. Become aware of your divine breath, and remember that it flows through all human beings, male and female alike.

The ancient authors of Jewish prayers experienced the same feelings of wonder, awe, and humility that we experience today and used metaphors that made sense to them to name it. It's a mistake to take their language too literally. Instead, think of it as an access point, and imagine the emotions that language might have been trying to capture.

For example, a well-known Jewish prayer refers to God as "Our Father, Our King." This central prayer, called *Avinu, Malkeinu* in Hebrew, is recited at the High Holy Days of *Rosh HaShanah* and *Yom Kippur*. It's sung to a wonderful tune and is the highlight of the service for many worshippers.

But thinking about the words too much can create an intellectual barrier to getting into the spirit of the prayer. On one hand, you might read the liturgy as being excessively patriarchal, and this approach, if it bothers you, can shut you off from the possibility of meaningful prayer.

On the other hand, if you approach the words thinking about addressing them to your ideal parent, emphasizing the loving relationship you want to have with a mother, father, or any caretaker, you might find that the prayer opens you to very real feelings of vulnerability and dependence. It doesn't matter what your actual feelings are about your own parents—use the words to provide an access point for entering a deeper relationship with God.

Finding God in the Ordinary

Sometimes the most mundane acts can help you connect with the divine presence. Think about a time when you felt particularly aware of God's presence, and try using that act as a metaphor for God. Here are some examples I turn to from time to time: nursing a baby (God is a loving mother), cooking a meal (God is a nourisher), giving charity (God is generous), receiving charity (God is accepting), teaching a student (God is a teacher), tending a garden (God is a caretaker).

Covenant

One particular metaphor for describing the relationship between God and the Jewish people deserves some special attention. This is the metaphor of covenant, which stands at the heart of Jewish theology. A covenant, or *brit* in Hebrew, is a mutual pact that binds together two parties.

In antiquity, a king offered protection to his subjects and, in return, expected those subjects to abide by an established code of conduct. In Judaism, this same idea gets applied to the relationship between God and the Jewish people.

In the *Torah*, God is a sovereign king who offers protection to his subjects, the Israelite nation, in return for their compliance with a set of legal precepts. So in the Bible, one of the most important characteristics of God is that God is a legislator. God cares how human beings live their lives and provides the laws in the *Torah* as a guidebook for creating a just and holy society. Why law?

If you think about it, it's kind of amazing that the Bible tells the story of the divine-human encounter in this way. The idea is that God becomes known in the world through a divinely revealed moral code. Instead of sharing the "meaning of life" or other unknown secrets of the universe, God enters into human history at Mount Sinai to give a set of ethical precepts to an emerging nation.

> **wisdom of the sages**
>
> To be a member of the covenanted community is to bind ourselves to be partners with God in creating a certain kind of world for ourselves and our progeny.
>
> —Rabbi Neil Gilman, *Sacred Fragments*

If you've ever wondered why Judaism emphasizes action over belief, it has everything to do with the concept of covenant. It's not that beliefs aren't important. But at the end of the day, it's how you act that really matters.

As a Jew, it's your sacred duty to behave ethically, according to the precepts set out in the *Torah* and passed down through the generations. These sacred duties, or religious obligations to God, are called *mitzvot*. Through your behavior, you can fulfill the terms of God's covenant with the Jewish people, which is eternal and everlasting.

Mitzvot

It's a popular misconception that the Jewish God, the God of the Old Testament, is a stern and punishing "God of Law." Christians often contrast this image with the more gentle "God of Love" that appears in the New Testament.

Such an understanding of God is misguided and loses sight of what's really important in the Jewish tradition. If this is the image of God you have in mind, it's critical that you put it aside. Thinking of God as an angry legislator is not at all an approach that will help you deepen your spiritual life. It'll only make you feel guilty!

Mitzvot as a Sacred Obligation

In the Jewish tradition, divine love and divine law are deeply intertwined. This union finds concrete expression in the concept of a *mitzvah* (plural: *mitzvot*). As noted in Chapter 1, *mitzvah* is a complex Hebrew term usually translated as "commandment" or "good deed." But a *mitzvah* is so much more than a unilateral order mandated by God.

Definition

A **mitzvah** (singular; plural *mitzvot*) is an obligatory act prescribed by the *Torah,* or by the rabbinic sages who interpreted the laws contained in the *Torah* for later generations. Although *mitzvah* is often translated to mean "good deed," doing *mitzvot* is about more than just earning brownie points. *Mitzvot* represent the relationship between God and the Jewish people—they are a framework for living in the world with holiness.

The *mitzvot,* as articulated in the *Torah,* are the terms of the covenant between God and the Jewish people. They speak to everyday life and emphasize important humanitarian values: caring for the poor, the stranger, and the widow in your midst; conducting business fairly; and practicing warfare humanely. These commands are a guide for living a life in accordance with the divine will. And when these precepts are enacted by human beings, they give us the power to bring God's presence into the world.

So Jews who accept the *mitzvot* as part of their covenant with God feel an obligation—a sacred duty—to incorporate them into their lives as much as possible. This sense of obligation is not the result of fear or coercion, but an expression of love, commitment, and gratitude. It's about trying to connect to God in a way only human beings can. Try to think of the *mitzvot* as a way to express your commitment to the values and principles you hold most dear. These values connect you to God. When you perform even the most basic *mitzvah,* such as an act of lovingkindness, you reflect God's image in this world.

Jewish tradition holds that a pomegranate is a symbol of the *mitzvot* because, according to legend, it contains 613 seeds—the number of *mitzvot* in Jewish tradition.

Mitzvot as a Spiritual Discipline

So how do you go about cultivating a sense of "sacred obligation" to God? What if you don't feel particularly "commanded" to perform *mitzvot?* What can you do to develop this basic feeling of connection?

Jewish legend says that the soul of every Jew, including those who convert to Judaism, was present at Mount Sinai to witness the revelation of the *Torah*. Our acceptance of the terms of God's covenant was binding upon us before we even entered this world! The *Torah* actually calls the *mitzvot* our communal *morasha*—our communal inheritance.

> **wisdom of the sages**
>
> The covenant extends throughout time to men, women, and children in every generation; to those born Jewish and to those who will become Jewish; to those who stood at Sinai and to those for whom Sinai is but a distant collective memory. It is a demanding idea, but an embracing one.
>
> —Rabbi Miriam Carey Berkowitz, "Women and the Covenant"

This type of feeling doesn't develop spontaneously overnight, and no one feels it all the time. In fact, I find it helpful to think of the *mitzvot* themselves as a kind of spiritual discipline. As a spiritual discipline, *mitzvot* foster an awareness of your sacred obligation to God. You might not necessarily feel divinely commanded to give charity or light candles on *Shabbat,* for example. But as you do them regularly, and as you grow from the experience of doing so, you will deepen your relationship with God.

In some respects, diet and exercise provide a good analogy here. If you start to exercise by moving a little bit each day, it will eventually start to feel "natural." The same is true for *mitzvot.* You have to start doing them, and over time, they will make a difference in your life and in the lives of those around you.

The *mitzvot* are sacred duties that guide us toward living a just and holy life. They are a moral and ethical set of precepts that connects us to God through our actions. Only human beings can perform *mitzvot,* because to do them requires the human faculty of reason. When we choose to act in a particular way, we reject other possible courses of action that are fully open to us. This uniquely human capacity for discernment and choice is one of the ways in which human beings resemble the divine image. The *mitzvot* give us a framework for exercising this faculty in our lives and in the world.

Essential Takeaways

- Jews do not pray through an intermediary. In Jewish prayer, you have direct access to God.
- God is One, and God is infinite.
- If the classic idea of God doesn't appeal to you, don't be afraid to try new metaphors or new names for God.
- Covenant is a pact between God and the Jewish people.
- *Mitzvot,* or "commandments," are sacred obligations.

chapter 3

The Art of Blessing

Gratitude and wonder

Why it's important to recite blessings out loud

The basic structure of a blessing

An overview of some common blessings

Getting creative with your language

It's so easy to rush through life without noticing the small miracles that take place all around us every single day. How often do we gulp down our meals in the car or while watching TV, hardly even tasting the nourishing food on our tongues? Who has time for gratitude? Who has time to experience wonder? It can be such a challenge to slow down long enough to appreciate the abundance of blessings in our lives.

In the Jewish tradition, the art of blessing is a unique and ancient spiritual practice that encourages you to slow down and wake up. Blessings are momentary, spoken prayers that cultivate mindfulness and gratitude in daily life. They are a formula, developed thousands of years ago, to help you deepen your appreciation for the simple gifts of the everyday.

A blessing is the smallest unit of prayer in the Jewish tradition. Taken in combination, blessings are the building blocks of all Jewish liturgy. They can be recited anywhere—in the synagogue, at home, on a hike in the woods, or at the market. In this chapter, you'll see why learning the art of blessing is the foundation of Jewish prayer.

Cultivating Gratitude

From earliest childhood, you were taught to say "Please" when you wanted something and "Thank you" when you received something. It's a script good little boys and girls are expected to memorize and perform at the dinner table, at school, and at their birthday parties. The goal, of course, is to teach manners. But what about gratitude? How do we learn to *feel* grateful? Getting to the heart of gratitude involves taking the script to the next level—when you recite a blessing, you need to say it like you mean it.

Torah Tip

In the *Talmud*, an ancient sage named Rabbi Meir is credited with the saying, "A person is obliged to say 100 blessings every day." (*Babylonian Talmud, Menachot* 43b) This works out to around 1 blessing every 10 minutes of your waking life! Can you name 100 things you're grateful for in a single day? Make a list and hang it on your fridge or bulletin board. Hold on to it for safekeeping, in case you need a little inspiration.

The custom of reciting blessings throughout the day reflects remarkable insight into the human psyche. Although Jews living back in antiquity didn't have nearly the number of distractions we have in our lives today, the ancient rabbis knew that human beings need tangible reminders to help us connect with the divine presence in our world.

Blessings in Judaism are all about cultivating gratitude. It's a way of saying "Thank you" to God for a whole range of human experiences. But does God *need* this social nicety? Of course not! Expressing gratitude out loud, in the form of a blessing, builds awareness and increases sensitivity in your heart. It's a practice that can truly open you to the wonders of the world. In short, blessings are Judaism's language of gratitude.

A Blessing Is an Act of Creation

A basic blessing is a verbal expression of thanks recited out loud. Just as God created the universe through divine speech, when you utter a blessing, it is also an act of creation. Your words create a pause in time that draws your full attention to what you're doing at that very moment. So at the same time that a blessing is an expression of thanks, it's also an exercise in mindfulness.

It's not enough to taste a delicious piece of fruit and think to yourself, *Wow! That was amazing—what a privilege to eat ripe fruit in its season!* A blessing must be spoken aloud. Your lips must move and your breath must utter the words. Although we'll never know if God actually "hears" our blessings or our prayers, one thing we do know is that we, ourselves, can hear them. And that's what really matters.

The Power to Bless

Here's a radical thought: you don't need a rabbi or a priest or any other member of the clergy to recite blessings for you. Judaism is very democratic in this way. Every human being has the power to bless.

Blessing Basics

So how does it all work? What does a blessing sound like, and how do you know when to recite one? More importantly, how do you know what to say?

Blessings fall under three broad categories: blessings of enjoyment, blessings that recognize a unique moment, and blessings recited when you perform a *mitzvah*. Although it might fall into the category of enjoyment, I've given blessings related to eating its own section because food is so central to Jewish culture.

All traditional blessings follow a set formula. The opening words of a blessing invoke the divine presence, bringing God into whatever physical act you are engaged in. I like to think of this part as a "preamble." Then the second half of the blessing, which I call "the body," describes God's connection to the specific thing you're blessing.

The Preamble

To show you how this works, let's look at the special blessing to recite if you're fortunate enough to observe a rainbow. In the biblical legend of

Noah and the flood, God sends a rainbow as a sign of God's promise never to destroy the world. Today when we see a rainbow, it's customary to recite the following blessing, which references that story:

> You are blessed, *Adonai, Eloheinu,* Sovereign of the Universe, who remembers the covenant, is faithful to it, and fulfills promises.

In Hebrew, it goes like this:

> *Baruch Atah Adonai, Eloheinu, Melech Ha-Olam, zocher ha brit, v'ne-eman bi'vrito, v'kayam b'ma-amaro.*

Let's break this down and analyze the structure of the blessing.

The first words are "You are blessed" (*Baruch Atah*). A blessing addresses God in the second person. You call upon the divine presence with the intimacy you'd use to speak to a friend. Take notice that God as a remote, transcendent "other" is not the starting point for the process of blessing.

The next word in a blessing is the divine name, or *Adonai*. The traditional translation of this name is "My Lord." Notice the pronoun *my* and the way it evokes that sense of personal intimacy. In my own prayer practice and in my translation, I prefer to leave this word in Hebrew because I find the image of a "Lord" to be distracting. Instead, when I say, "*Adonai*," I try to imagine God as that powerful force that flows directly through me.

Next in the formula, blessings use another name to refer to God. The word *Eloheinu*, which I also left untranslated, means "Our God." *Eloheinu* is a name that expands our thinking about God from that intimate, personal relationship, to the collective. God is not just my God (*Adonai*), but also the God of our community (*Eloheinu*).

The final phrase we use to invoke God's presence is Sovereign (King) of the Universe—*Melech Ha-Olam*. With this language, the blessing expands the idea of God to include the entire cosmos.

So in a few short words, the formulaic structure of a blessing is a preamble of sorts that brings us many ways to think about God. God can be addressed as "You," God as "mine," God as "ours," and God as "everyone's." In reciting a blessing, you can focus on whatever metaphor speaks to you at that particular moment.

Torah Tip

Traditional Jews consider God's name, as it appears in the *Torah* and the prayer book, too sacred to pronounce, even in prayer. The Hebrew letters that form this name, *Y-H-W-H,* cannot be easily vocalized, so whenever these letters appear in a Jewish text or blessing, it's customary to substitute the name *Adonai,* which means "My Lord" in Hebrew. However, some Jews consider this name for God highly sacred as well and feel it should not be overused. To preserve its sanctity, and to avoid using the divine name in vain, many Jews substitute the Hebrew *HaShem,* which means, "The Name." Decide what feels right for your own blessing practice.

The Body

The body of a blessing is the part that changes according to the occasion. The words that make up this second half are usually built on divine attributes or qualities that connect in some way to the phenomenon you're blessing.

Going back to our example of seeing a rainbow, the body of the blessing emphasizes three divine qualities: God remembers the covenant between God and the Jewish people, God is faithful to that pact, and God keeps promises.

Taken as a whole, then, this blessing is a way to respond Jewishly to a wondrous, natural phenomenon. It's not only an opportunity to stop and express gratitude for its beauty, but it also provides a moment to reflect on God's ongoing relationship with humanity. A rainbow usually appears after a storm. This blessing, then, is a reminder that we can count on the divine presence to remain with us, even through turbulent times.

Blessings of Enjoyment

Have you ever been stopped in your tracks by the fragrance of a newly flowering tree? In my neighborhood, lilacs begin to bloom at a certain time of year, and before I've even noticed their beautiful purple blossoms, I can smell them in the air. Judaism has a special blessing for this experience:

> You are blessed, *Adonai, Eloheinu,* Sovereign of the Universe, who creates fragrant trees.
>
> *Barukh Atah Adonai, Eloheinu, Melech Ha-Olam, boray atzay v'sameem.*

And if it's the first time you're actually seeing blossoms on the tree that year, there's a special blessing for that:

> You are blessed, *Adonai, Eloheinu,* Sovereign of the Universe, who has withheld nothing from this world and who has created beautiful creatures and beautiful trees for us to enjoy.
>
> *Barukh Atah Adonai, Eloheinu, Melech Ha-Olam, she lo khisar b'olamo davar, u-vara vo b'riyot tovot v'ilanot tovim l'hanot ba-hem b'nay olam.*

Literally dozens of blessings sanctify an experience of sensual enjoyment—there's one you recite upon seeing the ocean or upon witnessing a storm, for example. When you see other natural wonders, like a sunrise, shooting stars, or lightening, you say:

> You are blessed, *Adonai, Eloheinu,* Sovereign of the Universe, who has worked wonders of creation.
>
> *Barukh Atah Adonai, Eloheinu, Melech Ha-Olam, osay ma'aseay v'raysheet.*

The idea behind each of these blessings is to acknowledge the divine presence in the natural world and express our gratitude for the pleasures we derive from living within it.

Blessings for Unique Moments

Have you ever had an experience that left you speechless? The blessings for unique moments provide the comfort of a response when you don't quite know what to say. But they also give you a structured way to stop and be present to really experience an important moment in time.

If someone gives you good news, the appropriate blessing is:

> You are blessed, *Adonai, Eloheinu,* Sovereign of the Universe, who is good and who makes good.

> *Barukh Atah Adonai, Eloheinu, Melech Ha-Olam, ha tov v'ha mayteev.*

If you're wearing a brand-new outfit, using your new bike, or doing something really special for the first time, there's an all-purpose blessing to help you focus on the occasion and appreciate its sanctity:

> You are blessed, *Adonai, Eloheinu,* Sovereign of the Universe, who grants us life, sustains us, and has helped us to reach this moment.

> *Baruch Atah Adonai, Eloheinu, Melech Ha-Olam, she-hecheyanu, v'kiy'manu, v'higi'anu la-zman ha-zeh.*

If you see something or someone of extraordinary beauty, like a majestic tree or a newborn baby, you would say:

> You are blessed, *Adonai, Eloheinu,* Sovereign of the Universe, who has such beauty in Your world.

> *Barukh Atah Adonai, Eloheinu, Melech Ha-Olam, sheh-kakha lo b'olamo.*

Each of these blessings recognizes that we can sense God's presence in time, in those unique moments that shape our lives. Uttering a blessing is a way to remember the sanctity of those moments and to try to experience them fully and with complete awareness.

Blessings for Performing a *Mitzvah*

Saying a blessing before you perform a *mitzvah,* or sacred obligation, is a very important part of Jewish prayer. It brings our focus and awareness to the act, so we're not just performing the action mindlessly or without meaning.

Blessings over the performance of commandments typically add another phrase to the blessing formula to remind us that our action is a *mitzvah,* part of our sacred obligation as Jews.

My favorite example is the blessing we recite before lighting candles at the start of the Sabbath. We mark the beginning of the Sabbath with the warmth of Sabbath candles. Immediately after lighting the candles, we cover our eyes, take a moment to focus, and recite the blessing:

> You are blessed, *Adonai, Eloheinu,* Sovereign of the Universe, who has sanctified us with your *mitzvot* and commanded us to kindle the Sabbath lights.
>
> *Barukh Atah Adonai, Eloheinu, Melech Ha-Olam, asher kid'shanu b'mitzvotav v'tzeevanu l'hadleek ner shel Shabbat.*

In these blessings, we express gratitude for the *mitzvot* as an opportunity to shape our lives through divine service.

Torah Tip

When you hear someone else recite a blessing of any kind, you can support them by enthusiastically saying "Amen!" when they're finished. *Amen* literally means "I believe that" or "I agree." When you say "Amen" at the conclusion of a blessing, you are affirming and echoing that person's expression of gratitude.

Blessings over Food

Human beings and animals alike have to eat to survive. Judaism has many dietary practices that transform eating from a basic physical necessity into a spiritual discipline. We learn about these customs in depth in Chapter 17. For now, I want to emphasize the role blessings play in cultivating a spiritual approach to eating.

As Americans, we're more concerned than ever about where our food comes from. Concerns about genetically modified fruits and vegetables, pesticides, hormones, factory farming, and fair labor practices have raised lots of questions about what constitutes healthy eating. The rising popularity of organic and locally produced food is certainly a response to these concerns.

It might surprise you to learn that Jewish tradition has always taught us to be aware of where our food comes from. In fact, the blessings we recite over food require us to take a moment to think specifically about what kinds of food are on our plates, especially about how they were grown or produced.

For example, fruits and vegetables grown in the ground are blessed by acknowledging that they come from the earth. When we eat a salad, made with lettuce, tomato, and cucumber, we say:

> You are blessed, *Adonai, Eloheinu,* Sovereign of the Universe, who creates the fruit of the soil.
>
> *Barukh Atah Adonai, Eloheinu, Melech Ha-Olam, boray pree ha-adamah.*

Fruits that come from trees are blessed accordingly:

> You are blessed, *Adonai, Eloheinu,* Sovereign of the Universe, who creates the fruit of the tree.
>
> *Barukh Atah Adonai, Eloheinu, Melech Ha-Olam, boray pree ha-aytz.*

Baked goods other than bread are blessed with a blessing that acknowledges God for creating all different forms of sustenance. Wine and bread, because they're often used for ritual purposes, each have their own unique blessings.

Reciting a blessing before we eat is an opportunity to reflect for just a moment on what we're putting in our mouths. This is a discipline that teaches us to eat mindfully—grateful for the gift of sustenance and acknowledging the source of our bounty.

Finding the Right Words

In very ancient Jewish practice, not all blessings had a fixed formula. The words of a blessing were spontaneous, free-flowing, and from the heart. At a certain point in history, however, the rabbinic sages thought it was a good idea to fix the language of blessings, to ensure consistency of practice among Jews, who, by their time, had dispersed to many far-off lands. Once Jews started printing prayer books, it was easier to keep track of which blessing to say on a particular occasion.

This shift from spontaneous to fixed blessings has its pros and cons. On one hand, I love the idea of spontaneous blessing. Spontaneity allows you to take in a unique moment without having to worry about whether you know exactly the right blessing to recite for that particular occasion. Instead, just let your gratitude flow and speak from your heart; whatever comes out is your blessing!

A Spiritual Oasis

MISC.

The Hebrew word for a blessing is *b'rachah* (pronounced *beh-rah-KHA;* the *ch* is vocalized with a rough, throaty sound), and most blessings begin with the Hebrew word *baruch* (*bah-RUKH,* again ending in that throaty sound), which means "blessed." Rabbi Joseph Hayim Gikatilla, a medieval Jewish mystic from Spain, noted that these two words are also related to the words *barach* (which means "kneel"), *berech* (which means "knee"), and *b'reychah* (which means "pool"). From this, he taught that reciting a blessing with the proper intention is like kneeling beside a refreshing pool.

On the other hand, fixed blessings mean that those times when you're rendered completely speechless, you still have something to say! And there's something very powerful about using words that have been passed down from generation to generation to mark the same milestones and special moments.

I think it's important to have balance—sometimes it's helpful to have the security of tradition to refine your spiritual sensitivity. Relying on traditional blessings channels your sense of wonder through the wisdom of the ancient sages who composed these words. But sometimes you just want to use your own language to bless an experience or a moment. You might just want to take a deep breath and whisper, "Thank you."

It All Starts with Wonder

There's a passage in the Book of Genesis wherein the patriarch Joseph wakes up from a vivid dream that provided him with all sorts of insight. Upon awakening, Jacob exclaims, "Surely, God was in this place and I, I did not know!" (Genesis 28:16) Jacob "wakes up" to God's presence where he hadn't felt it before.

Blessings help us stay awake to God's presence in the world and help us nurture our sense of wonder. Jacob's exclamation reflects his amazement that God had been in "this place" all along, only he hadn't been able to see it. Blessings help us do the same thing. When we taste that succulent fruit for the first time, instead of just swallowing it, we savor it over a blessing and use it to catch just a quick glimpse of eternity.

> **wisdom of the sages**
>
> Awe is a way of being in rapport with the mystery of all reality. The awe that we sense or ought to sense when standing in the presence of a human being is a moment of intuition for the likeness of God which is concealed in his essence. Not only man; even inanimate things stand in a relation to the Creator. The secret of every being is the divine care and concern that are invested in it. Something sacred is at stake in every event.
>
> —Abraham Joshua Heschel, *God in Search of Man*

It's important not to let your blessings practice become rote or routine. It's easy to fall into a habit of reciting a blessing mindlessly and quickly, without paying attention. While it isn't realistic to think that you'll speak every blessing with the most fervent intention and devotion, it's critical to try to keep yourself attuned to that sense of wonder that pervades this tradition.

The ancient sages knew human life is filled with the potential for holiness. God is everywhere, in everything, and it's up to us to recognize the divine hand in our sacred world. When we utter a blessing—when we recognize our gratitude for a particular gift—we acknowledge and affirm that we are the beneficiaries of God's creation.

Essential Takeaways

- Blessings are the building blocks of Jewish prayer.
- Blessings nurture our sense of gratitude and wonder.
- Blessings must be spoken aloud so you can hear them.
- There's a Jewish blessing for practically everything.
- You can rely on traditional language for blessings, or you can create your own.

chapter 4

The *Torah* as a Spiritual Guide

Why Jews are known as the "People of the Book"

The multiple meanings of *Torah*

The *Torah*'s tradition of interpretation

Worship through *Torah* study

Earlier I introduced the idea that the *Torah* is a divine text—one that plays a critical role in Jewish life. In this chapter, we take a closer look at what it means to lead a spiritual life grounded by the *Torah*. How does this ancient document speak to our contemporary reality, and how can you forge a meaningful connection with the *Torah* in your own life? Is it really anything more than just words on a page?

The *Torah* is at once a family history, a moral and ethical code, and the written terms of the covenant—an everlasting pact between God and the Jewish people. All varieties of Judaism, from liberal to ultra-traditional, share a deep and abiding relationship with the *Torah*. Yet it's precisely the nature of this relationship that differentiates one denomination from another. Orthodox Jews tend to take very seriously the divine authorship of the text and develop customs and practices with this idea at the center. Meanwhile, some of the more liberal forms of Judaism read the *Torah* in its historical context and pick and choose those elements that feel especially relevant today.

You have to decide for yourself what role the *Torah* is going to play in your own spiritual life. As a starting point, let's explore some of the key ways in which the *Torah* has figured in Jewish religious life for centuries. After reading this chapter, you'll understand why Jews refer to the *Torah* as a "Tree of Life."

The People of the Book

Can you imagine a book so compelling that you would read it cover to cover, over and over again, year after year? Have you ever encountered a piece of literature in which, no matter how many times you read it, you always see something new with each fresh read? And if you had such a book, would you be motivated to read just a little bit of it every single day? Would your love for this book be so intense that you might even kiss its binding before putting it away, place it in a special cover, and treat it differently from any other book in your library?

For Jews, the *Torah* is such a work—an ancient text that's remained compelling from one generation to the next—and has been valued in this way over the course of thousands of years. Jews have long been known as the "People of the Book" because of the deep reverence for scripture that pervades Jewish culture and expresses itself in a variety of ways.

People of the Book

The phrase *People of the Book* actually originates in the Qur'an, the sacred scriptures of Islam. The designation refers to both Jews and Christians as adherents of religious traditions that believe in revealed scripture. In early Muslim societies, the phrase had political significance, extending certain privileges and protections to Jews and Christians as a tolerated religious minority. Over time, Jews used it to refer to themselves.

A Divine Text

The *Torah* stands at the center of Jewish religious life. It's an instruction manual for living according to God's will and the starting point for establishing a just and holy human society. Even for Jews who don't practice all the religious customs or rituals of Judaism, the *Torah* is a unique, cultural legacy that's the inheritance of every single Jewish person. As Jews, we don't just read the *Torah*—we engage with it through an active tradition of interpretation that fosters debate, argument, and critique. For many people, the *Torah* is a spiritual anchor, the basis of their connection to God.

Since the Romans destroyed the ancient Temple in Jerusalem nearly 2,000 years ago, Jews have located God's presence in the text of a *Torah* scroll. The Temple had been home to the priestly sacrificial rites that symbolically bridged the distance between humanity and God. But once the Temple could no longer function as God's dwelling place—a place to connect with the divine presence—the *Torah* became Judaism's key spiritual access point. Rabbis, or sages, whose function was to teach and interpret the biblical text replaced priests as the central religious and political authorities in ancient Jewish society.

Today Jews are among the last people on Earth to continue the active practice of reading directly from a scroll. At one point in history, the scroll was an innovative technology for recording, preserving, and transmitting all kinds of stories and information that had previously been transmitted orally. But eventually, the scroll gave way to the newer technology of the codex, which ultimately gave way to the printed book. And if you're reading this book on an electronic device, you may very well be holding the next incarnation of the book right in your hands!

Throughout all these changes in the technology of how texts are preserved, read, and transmitted, Jews have continued the practice of writing and reading the *Torah* in the form of a scroll. Scribal arts are a valued tradition in Jewish religious life and culture, and hand-calligraphed *Torah* scrolls and ritual objects are still being produced today. In fact, if you love calligraphy or the visual arts, your connection to *Torah* may start with an appreciation of its unique artistic form.

Torah Tip

According to Jewish custom, the 613th commandment of the *Torah*—the ultimate *mitzvah*—is the command that every individual should actually write a *Torah* scroll of one's own. This law is derived from Deuteronomy 31:19: "Write for yourselves this song, and teach it to the children of Israel." Jews today can fulfill this *mitzvah* by commissioning a scribe to write a *Torah* for them or by participating in writing or repairing a *Torah* scroll owned by the community.

With all the attention Jews have historically given to books, reading, and commentary, it's no wonder Jewish culture places a high value on literacy. In Judaism, learning scripture is not just for the intellectual elite. Every single person is charged with the ability to read and interpret the text, according to one's ability. In fact, it's an obligation to do so! Let's take a look at the different ways Jews center their lives around *Torah*.

Defining the *Torah*

The word *Torah* can be confusing because it's often used to name a number of different things. The word itself literally means "teaching" or "instruction," although it's sometimes translated as "law."

Torah is also shorthand for the sacred ritual object known as a *Torah* scroll. In this context, *Torah* refers to the first five books of the Bible, handwritten in Hebrew script on parchment sheets and sewn together to form a scroll. The parchment is then wrapped around two wooden dowels to facilitate navigation through the text.

> **wisdom of the sages**
>
> There are 70 faces to the *Torah:* Turn it and turn it, for everything is in it.
>
> —Numbers Rabbah 13:15

The five books included in a *Torah* scroll are Genesis, Exodus, Numbers, Leviticus, and Deuteronomy. When these same five biblical books are printed in a bound volume, they're commonly referred to as the "Five Books of Moses," or in Hebrew, the *chumash* (*khoo-MAAAHSH*). A *chumash* can also be called the *Torah*. Traditional Judaism asserts that these texts were revealed by God to Moses at Mount Sinai and then transmitted to the rest of the Israelite nation.

Viewed from a much broader perspective, *Torah* can also refer to the entire tradition of interpretation that grows out of the Five Books of Moses. Because *Torah* literally means "instruction," it's often used to describe any and all Jewish teaching, whether or not it's actually contained in the *Torah*.

For example, a medieval folktale that illustrates a core biblical principle like giving charity might also be called *Torah*, even though it was composed long after the biblical text. Or a rabbi's sermon that addresses contemporary current events, interpreting them through the lens of a particular episode in the Bible, might also be called *Torah*.

The Jewish mystical tradition understands the *Torah* as infinite, containing truths that cut across time. This concept gives rise to the idea that *Torah* actually includes all interpretations that will ever be derived from it. So the *Torah* is not just the literal letters on the page, or even the fixed stories that make up its narrative; its meaning also expands to include newer texts and teachings that have developed over the centuries.

To this day, a *Torah* scroll is handwritten with a quill and ink on parchment.

But if the definition of *Torah* is so wide ranging, who has the authority to decide what counts as *Torah* and what doesn't? This is a question the different Jewish denominations approach quite differently.

Orthodox and Conservative communities affirm a specific canon of interpretive writings as binding and authoritative. While the definition of *Torah* is still quite flexible in these traditional communities, there is a standard process for interpreting the text, especially when it comes to matters of practical Jewish law.

Reform, Reconstructionist, and Secular Humanist communities have moved away from a strict reliance on a classical and authoritative body of interpretation. As a result, these more liberal denominations leave more room for individual interpretation and personal choice. They don't place as much emphasis on the authority of the *Torah's* classical, rabbinic commentators.

Interpretation and the Oral *Torah*

Although the *Torah* contains stories, poetry, and other kinds of literature, it is, first and foremost, a law code. Another Hebrew word for Jewish law is *halakha*, which is related to the verb for "walking" or "going." The *Torah* sets out a standard of moral and ethical behaviors that are meant to serve as a guide for daily living—a pathway, of sorts. But how can an ancient law code possibly apply to contemporary life? In biblical times, slavery, stoning, and polygamy were accepted normal social practices. Our society is so different today!

Like any written code of law, the *Torah* requires interpretation to flesh out its principles into a practical legal system. For example, we know the *Torah* prohibits murder with the commandment "Thou shalt not kill." But as a legal principle, that statement is much too vague to enforce. What about a case of self-defense? And what about the death penalty or euthanasia? The *Torah* is silent on these very complex questions and other gray areas of the law. As everyone knows, real life is infinitely more complicated than it looks on paper. In order to govern human society by the principles of the *Torah*, it was necessary to develop a system of interpretation to go along with it.

In Judaism, that system of interpretation is called the *Oral Torah*—a body of commentary that breathes life into the *Written Torah* and enables it to remain applicable over time. Jewish tradition maintains that this oral commentary on the *Torah* was also revealed to Moses and the Jews at Mount Sinai, making it binding and authoritative upon the entire community.

Today this process makes it possible for the *Torah* to serve as a practical and spiritual guide for modern life. The written text provides principles and a framework, but it's the tradition of interpretation that makes the *Torah* into an organic document that can be applied in real-life situations and that endures over time.

Think about how many contemporary religious issues have no precedent in the Written *Torah*. Is it appropriate to use a computer on the Sabbath? Is the meat of cloned animals kosher? Is abortion ever acceptable? If the *Torah* is to guide our lives today, we must figure out what it has to say to the unique dilemmas this generation faces. The Oral *Torah*, a fluid and evolving expression of the divine will, is the key to this process.

The Oral *Torah* was originally transmitted by mouth from generation to generation. After the destruction of the second Temple, when Jews were dispersed to diverse regions of the Mediterranean, the Oral *Torah* was committed to writing to ensure its preservation and to encourage consistency of practice among Jews living in different lands.

The two key written texts of Oral *Torah* are the *Mishna* and the *Talmud*. The *Mishna* is a teaching text that compiles Jewish law according to subject. It was written in Hebrew and Aramaic and codified approximately 200 B.C.E. The *Mishna* was an important work because of its practicality—arranging all the laws of the *Torah* by topic made it simpler to use as a reference.

The *Talmud* (also called *Gemara*) is a commentary on the *Mishna* that attempts to expand on the *Mishna*'s treatment of biblical law. The *Talmud* is written principally in Aramaic and represents discussion and debate among rabbinic leaders between the third and sixth centuries.

Together, the *Mishna* and the *Talmud* are part of a body of literature known in Hebrew as *Midrash Halakha,* or Jewish legal discourse.

Another, related genre of interpretation focuses on the narrative dimension of the *Torah*. *Midrash Aggada* is a kind of commentary that fills in the missing pieces of the many stories in the *Torah* that do not focus on practical law. Just as *Midrash Halakha* helps flesh out the details of the *Torah*'s legal teachings, *Midrash Aggada* is a creative, literary response to passages in *Torah* that are ambiguous or unclear. It raises questions such as, "Why is the creation story told twice in the Book of Genesis?" and then seeks to answer them through folk tales and alternative stories.

Definition

Midrash is a Hebrew word that means "seek" or "dig." The process of *midrash* is one of seeking out deeper meanings or digging into the text to find new connections and insights that help us understand the text more fully. *Midrash* is a tradition that keeps the *Torah* alive by raising questions of contemporary relevance. The two principal genres of *midrash* are **Midrash Halakha** (legal discourse) and **Midrash Aggada** (narrative discourse). Although they represent distinct genres of rabbinic commentary on the *Torah,* there's often overlap between them.

Although standard collections of both *Midrash Halakha* and *Midrash Aggada* have been passed down since antiquity, both forms of *midrash* are still being composed today. What's important to understand about the Oral *Torah,* then, is that it represents the lively and ongoing conversation Jews have been having about the *Torah* for centuries. This entire tradition is an important aspect of Jewish spirituality because it reflects the dynamic approach Jews take to scripture.

Study as Spiritual Practice

The ancient rabbis thought of the *Torah* as an orchard, ripe with fruit for the picking. For them, the study of *Torah* was the greatest *mitzvah* and should be prioritized over everything. In the rabbinic imagination, engaging with the text through study brought us closer to God and connected human beings more deeply to divine wisdom.

The Jewish mystical tradition views the *Torah* as a divine text that has four levels of interpretation:

- *Peshat:* This is the literal, plain meaning on the text's "surface."

- *Remez:* This level focuses on the allegorical meaning of the *Torah*.

- *Derash:* This level seeks out the metaphorical meaning of a given text and is related to *midrash*.

- *Sod: Sod* means "secret" and refers to the fourth level of understanding the *Torah's* hidden, mystical truths.

Together, these four levels of interpretation spell *PaRDeS,* which actually means "orchard" or "paradise." This metaphor demonstrates that the work of learning the *Torah* is never complete. Even the most learned sages can continue to deepen their studies as they enter the *Torah*'s orchard in search of its sweet fruit.

These are the deeds which yield immediate fruit and continue to yield fruit in time to come: honoring parents; doing deeds of loving kindness; attending the house of study punctually, morning and evening; providing hospitality; visiting the sick; helping the needy bride; attending the dead; probing the meaning of prayer; making peace between one person and another, and between husband and wife. And the study of *Torah* outweighs them all.

—*Babylonian Talmud*, Shabbat 127a

Many opportunities exist to help you make the study of *Torah* part of your spiritual life. The following sections list a few that I recommend.

Learn Every Day

You don't have to spend hours studying *Torah* every day to reap the spiritual rewards that come with learning. Make a commitment to study just one line of *Torah* a day. Choose a passage from the Bible, or perhaps something from the *Mishna* or even a modern Jewish thinker, and dedicate yourself to reading one line each day. Include this study as part of your daily prayer routine. You can work it into your morning prayers or perhaps before bedtime.

Taking just 3 minutes a day to open yourself to the wisdom of the *Torah* can yield tremendous spiritual payoff!

Find Yourself a Teacher

A famous saying from the *Mishna* goes, "Find yourself a teacher, and acquire for yourself a friend." Because the *Torah* and its commentaries are so vast, it can be extremely helpful to find a teacher to guide you in your studies. Although you don't need a rabbi or an expert to give you access to the texts, learning with someone who has more experience can be really helpful.

Many synagogues and Jewish community centers offer courses for adults wherein you can study a variety of topics related to the *Torah* itself or other aspects of Jewish thought. Try out some classes and see if the teacher can open the text for you in a stimulating way.

Do not say: "When I have free time, I will study," for perhaps you will never have free time.

—Maimonides, *Mishneh Torah* 3:7

If you want to have more of an immersive experience in Jewish learning, there are opportunities to study at unique, short-term institutes devoted to Jewish studies. In Appendix B, I share a number of these opportunities to engage in intensive study over the course of a long weekend retreat or a week-long program. Sometimes it really helps to get out of your regular routine and plunge yourself fully into a study environment.

Many colleges and universities also offer opportunities for introductory Jewish studies. Although university courses are typically secular in their orientation, they can provide valuable background that you can then incorporate into your own spiritual life.

Find a Study Partner

When you think about studying, the image that likely comes to mind is a library where the atmosphere is so quiet, you can hear a pin drop. Maybe there's even a librarian whispering "Shh!" to remind you to keep your voice down.

A Jewish house of study couldn't possibly be more different. In Jewish tradition, a place of learning is noisy, and the air is filled with a cacophony of voices raised in heated discussion and debate.

The *Torah* is best when studied out loud. Sure, you can sit quietly and read the text on your own, but the deepest engagement comes from raising questions together with a partner. This model of study is called *hevruta* in Hebrew, which literally means "partner." The root of the word *hevruta* is related to the word *haver,* which means "friend."

You know how great it can be to read a book with a friend or book group? You get so much more out of a text when you can talk about it and bounce your ideas and interpretations off others. *Hevruta* study is the same way. It can be so stimulating to have a conversation about the *Torah,* out loud, one on one or in a small group. You'll find that you're able to go much deeper into the text, even without a teacher.

A study partner can be anyone—a friend, a relative, your spouse, or even a child. Just pick a text and take turns reading out loud to one another, raising questions as you go. See where your own "Oral *Torah*" takes you!

Hear the *Torah* Chanted

Another opportunity to study *Torah* happens in the synagogue each week on the Sabbath, typically on Saturday mornings, but sometimes Friday nights as well. Hearing the *Torah* chanted in Hebrew can be a wonderful experience. Even if you don't understand Hebrew, you can follow along in an English translation or just sit quietly and take it in. Knowing that the same passages have been read in synagogues around the world for centuries is quite moving and can be a starting place for meditation on the *Torah*.

Saturday morning is also a time when the spiritual leader of the congregation, usually the rabbi, gives a sermon addressing a section of the *Torah* being read that week. Sermons are a great opportunity for learning— rabbis typically work very hard to give congregants something to think about each week to make the *Torah* compelling.

The idea that God's presence can be known through the *Torah* transforms reading from a mundane activity into a religious practice. Interpretation of the *Torah* is a method of study that values dissent, dialogue, and debate. Understanding how important study is in classical Judaism should help you appreciate why literacy in any language is such an important value in Jewish culture. Consider making a commitment to regular study as a starting point for your spiritual practice. Not only will it increase your knowledge of Jewish tradition, but it also can help you lead a more engaged Jewish life.

Essential Takeaways

- The first five books of the Hebrew Bible make up the *Torah*.

- The definition of the *Torah* can also be extended to include all Jewish moral and ethical teaching.

- Traditional Judaism understands the *Torah* to be divinely revealed in two parts, Written and Oral.

- The Oral *Torah* is the tradition of interpretation and commentary on the Written *Torah*.

- Judaism values active engagement with the *Torah* through commentary and discussion.

- The regular study of *Torah,* alone or with a partner, is an important avenue for Jewish spirituality.

Part 2

The Path Toward Prayer

Now that you have a basic understanding of the key themes that shape Jewish spirituality, it's time to focus on prayer. Jewish prayer has a long and rich history. Our prayer book is full of references to an ancient sacrificial cult, in which priests in Jerusalem offered live sacrifices, as well as prayers, upon an altar in the Jerusalem Temple. How could any of it possibly have meaning for us today?

Of course, modern Judaism no longer practices animal sacrifice, but the memory of cultic worship is an important part of the Jewish prayer cycle. Just as the ancient priests drew near to God by offering sacrifices, today we can enter God's presence through offerings of prayer, study, and song. The chapters in Part 2 take you through the overall framework of Jewish prayer practice. Before you begin your own prayer journey, it might help to have a sense of the big picture.

I begin with a brief overview of a variety of prayer techniques from the Jewish tradition. Next, I explore the language of prayer and spend some time thinking about the limits and strengths of praying in a language that's not your native tongue. I also provide an overview of the different ritual objects you'll encounter in Jewish prayer. Once we cover these basics, we'll be ready to move on to look at specific prayers and their meanings.

chapter 5

What Is Jewish Prayer?

The origins of Jewish prayer in sacrifice

To whom is prayer addressed?

The three dimensions of Jewish prayer

Finding a prayer "voice"

If the study of *Torah* opens your mind to Jewish spirituality, then prayer opens your heart. Of course, prayer engages your intellect, too. But in Judaism, prayer is not about learning texts or practicing your Hebrew. Rather, it's about cultivating your awareness, awe, gratitude, and humility. It's about increasing your awareness of God on a daily basis and using that awareness to help you grow as a person.

Sometimes it can be difficult to "claim" the language of prayer. In our very secular culture, the idea of speaking to God might feel weird. You might even be thinking that prayer is only for religious fanatics. But it's not. Anyone can learn to pray, and in this chapter, I help you understand what prayer looks like in the Jewish tradition and how you can embrace it. In trying to deepen your own sense of spirituality, it's so important to let go of your preconceived ideas about what prayer is.

It's also critical for you to take ownership of your own prayer experience. The greatest rabbi, cantor, or synagogue choir cannot make your prayer experience meaningful—only you can do that. In Jewish prayer, the goal is to open yourself to the experience of the sacred. It's about recognizing the grandeur of a reality that's bigger than you are. And it's about taking these insights to heart to become the best "you" possible.

Drawing Near: The Legacy of Temple Sacrifice

In biblical times, the ancient sacrificial cult was the center of Israelite religious practice. The ancient priesthood was responsible for bringing animal and grain offerings to the Temple altar as a way of communicating with God. The performance of sacrifice expressed gratitude to God and also made atonement for transgressions of the community.

In English, the word *sacrifice* implies giving up something. When you make a sacrifice, you give something small in return for something more important. But what you offer as a sacrifice has to be something you care about, or else it wouldn't mean anything. While it's certainly the case that Israelite sacrifice involved "giving up" a sacrificial offering as an expression of gratitude or a request for forgiveness, the Hebrew word for sacrifice actually has a more complex meaning.

In Hebrew, the word for sacrifices is *korbanot,* the root of which means "to draw near" or "to bring close." Offering a sacrifice was a way of coming close to the divine presence. In my mind, this layer of meaning brings out a completely new dimension of the Temple offerings. Sacrifices were a ritual expression—a language of sorts—that brought human beings closer to God. Offerings presented on the altar bridged the distance between the human and the divine realms. And in ancient times, priestly sacrifices were also accompanied by prayer.

> **wisdom of the sages**
>
> Every Jew must always have a fiery love for God in his heart, just like the fire which burns all the time on the altar.
>
> —Rabbi Menachem M. Schneerson, *Likkutei Sikhot Volume 1, Tzav*

Once the ancient Temple was destroyed, however, prayer replaced sacrifice as the Jewish path to God. Alongside *Torah* study, prayer became a key religious institution. Using the Temple cult as a paradigm, the ancient rabbis modeled the prayer service after the different sacrificial offerings that were part of the priestly service. So for every sacrifice prescribed in the Bible, we now have a prayer to take its place. Only instead of having priests recite prayers for the people, the rabbis empowered every individual to bring forward the offerings of his or her lips in prayer.

This paradigm shift gives us a valuable lesson. Today, in the absence of an official priesthood, we are all responsible for our own prayer lives. It's easy to blame the rabbi for being uninspiring, the cantor for singing too high, or the community for being complacent. But looking to someone else to make your prayer experience meaningful is always going to fall short.

The ancient rabbis teach us that the key to developing a meaningful prayer practice is to become your own inner priest. Think of your heart as your altar. You are in charge of making prayer meaningful for yourself. You are the one who makes your prayer genuine. You control the quality of your prayer offerings. You are the only one who can make your heart/altar a fitting dwelling place for the divine presence.

By committing to a regular prayer practice, you can slowly learn to do just that.

Reaching Out to God

One of the first things I think about when beginning my prayer practice is how much I want to feel something. My personal yearning is often simply a desire to allow myself to feel the genuine longing that is the doorway to meaningful prayer. Life is filled with so many distractions. I'm talking about not just the busy chaos of my life, but also the multitude of distractions floating around inside my own head. So many interior demands vie for my attention.

Many days, I just begin with a quiet meditation in which I ask God to help me focus, to help me be open enough to have just a single moment of genuine prayer. I know from experience that just one moment of prayer can be the key to achieving insights that can truly transform your life.

A young woman recites her daily prayers at the Western Wall in Jerusalem.
(Photo by Mikhail Levit/Shutterstock.com)

But to whom is my request directed? Does God really hear prayer? This question presents one of the greatest obstacles to a meaningful prayer life. It's painfully obvious, given all the suffering that exists in our world today, that God doesn't literally "answer" every prayer like a magician granting wishes. So how can I pray to God if I don't know for sure that my prayers will be answered?

This is where it's important to remember our discussion about language and the metaphors we use to think about God. It may be true that God is not literally a "person" who can hear and respond to your individual prayer, but it's essential to remember that your relationship with God is personal.

Whether you think about God as a process, a power, a force, or an energy, in prayer, you enter into a personal relationship with God. That means addressing God as "You." It means opening yourself to God as a parent, friend, or confidante. Why is this so important? Because we can't connect meaningfully with an abstract force or energy. In the words of Jewish philosopher Martin Buber, we have to understand God as a "Thou" rather than an "It" if we want our relationship to grow. And as our relationship with God matures, we also grow closer to becoming the person we want to be.

> **wisdom of the sages**
>
> Great is the power of prayer. For to worship is to expand the presence of God in the world. God is transcendent, but our worship makes God imminent.
>
> —Abraham Joshua Heschel, *Between God and Man*

> Where is God to be found? In the places where He is given entry.
>
> —The Kotzker Rebbe

Expressing Desire

When you're first learning how to pray, it can feel strange to verbalize your innermost desires, even quietly in prayer. Perhaps you've been trained to feel guilty about wanting something more from life, from relationships, or from your career. If this is your experience, consider starting with a written meditation in a prayer journal.

A prayer journal can be a notebook you have lying around or a Word file you maintain on your computer. The next time you have a few private moments, try this exercise: close your eyes and think of two or three things you feel grateful for. Jot them down in your prayer journal. It might help to write, "Dear God, I am grateful for ...."

When you're finished, close your eyes again and think of two or three things you really want. They can be improvements you want to make in your life, or they can be material things. If you start to feel guilty, like you shouldn't want it, push those feelings away. It's okay and completely normal. Jot down your list of desires. It might be helpful to write, "Dear God, I really long for …."

Writing can be a great intermediate step until you're willing to express what you yearn for in words.

Know Before Whom You Stand

"Know Before Whom You Stand." In many synagogues around the world, you'll see these beautiful words inscribed in the sanctuary, usually on the wall where the *Torah* scrolls are kept. This phrase is a powerful reminder of what prayer is all about in Judaism. It captures the intertwined feelings of awe and humility that are the foundation of Jewish spirituality.

On one hand, this phrase reminds us that we are always "before" God—that we live our lives in God's presence, and we are accountable for our conduct and our behavior. But more deeply than that, it also captures the essence of the prayer relationship.

"Know Before Whom You Stand" is a call to awareness. Prayer starts when you become aware of a force in the universe that is greater than you are. But knowledge is not just about awareness. Knowledge is also about intimacy. When I know you, I have a connection to you. You are more than just a stranger passing by on the street. The command to "know" means to be aware, but it also means to be in relation with God. In presenting yourself to God, you are opening yourself to that relationship and allowing God's presence to speak to you. Imagining God as "Whom" also reinforces the idea that the relationship is personal.

"Know Before Whom You Stand" is a humbling image. The metaphor, like so many phrases in Jewish liturgy, is of a subject standing before a royal king. We live our lives in the presence of an awesome power, and this fact is a humble reminder of our own limitations and our finitude.

Rabbi Simcha Bunim of Peshischa used to say, "Every person should have two pockets. In one pocket there should be a note that says, 'For my sake was the world created.' And in the second pocket, he should have a note that reads, 'I am but dust and ashes.' When you are feeling down, you should take out the note that says, 'For my sake was the world created.' And when you are feeling smug, you should take out the one that says, 'I am but dust and ashes.'" (Eighteenth-century Hasidic teaching)

Praise, Petition, and Gratitude

Jewish prayer is both structured and spontaneous. The practice of blessings, the fixed liturgy, and the discipline of daily prayer bring structure to help focus our prayer life. But for prayer to stay real and meaningful, every now and then you have to get beyond the script and reach directly into your heart to express your innermost thoughts.

Whether you're praying from the script of the prayer book or not, Jewish prayer has three main forms: praise, petition, and gratitude. Each works in tandem with the others as a language for communicating with God.

Praise

Halleluyah! This Hebrew word, which literally means "Praise God!" is Judaism's way of saying, "Wow!" It's the simplest phrase used to express a pure feeling of joyous delight. Praise is essential to Jewish prayer. The prayer book is filled with psalms, poetry extolling God's greatness and the beauty and wonders of God's created world.

While prayer acknowledges a whole range of human emotions, Judaism ultimately sees prayer as joyful. Prayer is a celebration of life's beauty, God's grandeur, and our great fortune to be a part of it all. In ancient Temple times, prayers in praise of God were typically accompanied by music, as evidenced in Psalm 150, which is recited daily as part of the morning liturgy.

HALLELUYAH!

Praise God in God's sanctuary;
Praise God in the sky, God's stronghold.
Praise God for mighty acts;
Praise God for God's exceeding greatness.
Praise God with blasts of the ram's horn;
Praise God with harp and lyre.
Praise God with timbrel and dance;
Praise God with lute and pipe.
Praise God with resounding cymbals;
Praise God with loud-clashing cymbals.
Let all that breathes praise *Adonai!*

HALLELUYAH!

—Translation from *Mishkan T'filah, A Reform Siddur*

This psalm is so alive with movement and rhythm. Imagine what it must have been like when our ancestors sang and danced in the Temple court! The energy of this psalm tells us something about what the ideal prayer environment should be like.

Of course, it's not always possible to pray in a state of heightened exaltation all the time. But the emphasis on praise in the prayer book is designed to inspire us and nurture that sense of awe that helps us see all that is good in the world.

Petition

Petition is a form of prayer that originates out of desire. Desire is an experience of longing. The object of your longing can be abstract, like a deeply felt desire for meaning. Or the longing we feel can be for something particular. We might yearn for the healing of a loved one, for greater recognition in our career, or for a more passionate relationship with our partner.

There's so much to yearn for, both in our own private lives and in the world at large. The *siddur* (Jewish prayer book) includes a number of prayers that petition God to bring healing to a broken world. There are prayers for peace; prayers to end hunger and poverty; and prayers for recovery, healing, and health.

Visitors to the Western Wall in Jerusalem insert notes containing prayers of petition in between the stones.
(Courtesy of Jay and Alyson Goodman)

But there's also room to insert our own prayers for well-being and success into the liturgy. Prayer is a vehicle for expressing our deepest desires, for releasing them into the universe so they have a life outside our own hearts.

In this respect, prayer can help us see the difference between where we are and where we hope to be. And the discipline of prayer can help us do the inner spiritual work that enables us to grow into the people we hope to become. If we long to be better people, to be more kind, to be more generous, to be more forgiving, our prayers are the place to express that desire. And as we express it, we come closer to actualizing our dreams—not because God intervenes and "makes" us better, but because the work of prayer is a discipline that refines our souls and helps us focus on our most important goals.

Torah Tip My friend Leslie teaches seventh grade in our synagogue's religious school. When she teaches about the three dimensions of prayer, she likes to use a metaphor the kids can relate to: when you want something from your parents, you typically use a three-fold strategy to get it. First, you butter them up with flattery (praise). Then you beg them for whatever it is you want (petition). When they give it to you, you tell them, with enthusiasm, that they are the greatest (praise)!

Here is one of my favorite prayers of petition. It's said at the conclusion of the *Amidah,* a meditative prayer recited silently by individuals and then repeated by the entire congregation. Many wonderful melodies bring it to life. The following translation is from *Siddur Sim Shalom,* the prayer book of the Conservative Movement, which takes its name from this particular passage.

> Grant peace to the world (*sim shalom*), with
> happiness, and blessing, grace, love, and mercy for
> us and for all the people Israel. Bless us, our Parent,
> one and all, with Your light; for by that light did You
> teach us *Torah* and life, love and tenderness, justice,
> mercy, and peace. May it please You to bless your
> people Israel in every season and at all times with
> Your gift of peace.

This is a petitionary prayer that longs for peace, love, and light. It beseeches God in the second person, using the personal "You" throughout. It also acknowledges peace as a divine gift. If only we longed for peace with the same intensity with which we long for our own personal desires.

Gratitude

As I discussed in Chapter 3, so much of Jewish spirituality is about cultivating a deep sense of gratitude. It's so easy to take our riches for granted. When was the last time you felt truly grateful for a meal, for your salary, for the love of family and community? Jewish prayer reminds us each day that we are the recipients of multiple gifts and that we should approach each one with mindfulness of our fortune.

Prayer is a vehicle to call out to God with a heartfelt "Thank you!" The following prayer is a good example of the kind of sentiments expressed everywhere in Jewish liturgy. This prayer is part of the blessing recited at the conclusion of a meal. Note that we give thanks not just for the food we have eaten, but for the historic ways in which God has nurtured us through the millennia:

> We thank You, *Adonai,* our God, for the pleasing,
> good, and spacious land which You gave to our
> ancestors and for liberating us from Egyptian
> bondage. We thank You for the covenant sealed
> in our flesh, for teaching us Your *Torah* and
> your precepts, for the gift of life and compassion
> graciously granted us, for the food we have eaten,
> for the nourishment You provide us all of our days,
> whatever the season, whatever the time.
>
> —*Siddur Sim Shalom,* Grace After Meals

I once heard a rabbi give a sermon about the idea that it's never too late to say "Thank you." No matter how much time has elapsed since you received a gift or a favor, saying thanks is always appreciated and always brings you closer to the person who gave it to you.

What gets in the way of our ability to give thanks? Usually, it's a sense of entitlement, which, justified or not, can really distance you from the experience of gratitude. Or sometimes we just don't take the time to stop and think about the good fortune in our lives. It's easy to go through life with a "glass half empty" mentality because there's always more we need and want. But Jewish prayer insists that we take a "glass half full" approach to prayer—at least part of the time—to be grateful and to express that gratitude in the words of our prayers.

Finding Your Prayer Voice

Remember the section in Chapter 1 where I talked about the divine breath that flows through every one of us? In Psalm 150, quoted earlier, the final verse is "Let all that breathes praise God." Learning to breathe fully and deeply is a critical piece of your prayer practice. Whether you prefer silent meditation, ecstatic singing, joyful dance, or contemplative *Torah* yoga poses, getting in touch with your breath is the key to finding your authentic prayer voice. And as the psalm indicates, breath has been a source of prayer for millennia.

Whether you're alone or together with a *minyan,* Jewish prayer combines singing, speaking, reading, chanting, and silence. A prayer service typically has a rhythm to it that develops by alternating these various styles of prayer, and you may find that you prefer certain parts of the service over others.

For example, you might love communal singing and feel really moved by it. But silent meditation might feel uncomfortable to you, and you might get impatient waiting for those parts to be over. Having these preferences is completely normal, and in time, you'll come to learn what form of prayer engages you most deeply.

Slow Down

Sometimes when you visit a very traditional synagogue, you'll notice people speeding through the Hebrew prayer book as quickly as possible. After all, if you have to pray three times each day, it can be tempting to get it over with quickly. But racing through your prayers may cause you to lose focus on your breath. If you find yourself racing to finish, it might be time to put down the prayer book and focus instead on the words written on your own heart. What do you need to say to God today?

Whatever your preferred style of prayer, take a moment to think about your prayer voice. We all have different voices we use to communicate in different contexts. I have the tender voice I use with my children, the authoritative voice I use when I'm lecturing in a classroom, and the honest voice I might use with my husband when we need to discuss something important. What voice will you use to address God?

When I started college, I was very quiet in class. I had lots of ideas in my head, but I was too afraid to let them out in class discussions. I just couldn't figure out how to formulate my thoughts into sentences and get them past my lips. I remember feeling afraid to be wrong, afraid to seem stupid, and wanting very badly to sound intelligent. But I just couldn't get past those internal censors. My fears were an obstacle to my full participation in my courses. I just couldn't find my voice.

Over time, of course, I developed the confidence to speak up. I still have those internal censors that make me insecure sometimes, but as I've matured, I've learned how to override them. Today, as a college professor, when I have students who are very quiet in class, I encourage them to take risks by writing down their ideas on a note card or posting to a class blog. It takes practice, but everyone is capable of bringing their voice to the table.

There's a lesson here about learning how to cultivate your prayer voice. The hardest part is getting past those internal censors that are telling you prayer is pointless, there's no one listening, or you have nothing to say. While it can be extremely challenging, you must try to strip away the layers of self-consciousness that keep your prayer voice muted. You have to trust yourself, open your heart to God, and just let it flow. Use the words of the prayer book as a script to get you started. Close your eyes, focus on the power and beauty of your own breath, and see where the process takes you.

Music and Prayer

Like Psalm 150, many passages in the Book of Psalms mention the use of musical instruments in worship. It's clear that in ancient times, prayer was accompanied by instrumentation. Today, however, traditional Jewish communities do not use musical instruments in synagogue on the Sabbath or on holidays. This custom has two explanations.

One reason we refrain from using musical instruments is that it is an expression of mourning for the destroyed Temple. Until another Temple is built and the priesthood is reinstated, our joy in worship is diminished.

Another explanation is that if a musical instrument were to break while in use on the Sabbath or on a holiday, we would be tempted to fix it. Repairing a broken string or other part of an instrument would be prohibited on the Sabbath, so rabbis determined that instruments should not be used at all.

But even without instruments, traditional Jewish prayer services are very musical. Prayers are sung a capella, and a talented prayer leader tries to get everyone in the room to sing along.

Many liberal congregations do use musical instrumentation as a way to inspire prayer and encourage participation among the congregation. Some Jewish congregations use an organ during worship, a practice influenced by Christian custom. Some synagogues incorporate an entire band into their worship services, featuring keyboards, percussion, and brass and string instruments. In less-formal settings, a guitar or drums might be used for simple accompaniment. In synagogues that choose to use musical instruments, the desire for enhanced prayer is prioritized over the *halakhic* prohibitions.

Song, Silence, and Tears

For me, singing is the most natural way to express myself in prayer. Alone or with a group, when I sing, I feel breath moving through me in a powerful way. The melody of prayer helps me put aside self-consciousness and focus my attention on God. There's something so freeing about raising my voice in song.

Singing alone, I find that song helps me turn inward and deepen my experience of prayer. Singing with a *minyan*, I feel part of something larger than myself. The beauty of singing in a group is that every voice adds something unique to the sound of prayer. The traditional liturgy tells us to imagine that we are all part of a heavenly chorus, offering praise before the divine throne!

The melodies of Jewish prayer also have the power to evoke strong memories. Many of the tunes used today are quite ancient and are still sung in synagogues all over the world. It can be an amazing experience to enter a synagogue in another country, where you might not know the language but are able to join right in the prayer service because the *niggun* melodies are the same ones you know from childhood.

Definition

A ***niggun*** (*nee-GOON;* plural *niggunim, nee-goon-EEM)* is a melody without words. These are catchy, repetitive tunes that anyone can sing along with. Hasidic Judaism popularized the use of *niggunim* in public worship to encourage participation. Even if you don't know any Hebrew, you can sing along with a *niggun.* Because they're repetitive, they can be learned quickly and easily. Because they're wordless, they can be adapted to any part of a prayer service.

Silent meditation is also an integral part of Jewish prayer that you can use to deepen your practice. We all have days when the words on the page of the prayer book just don't move us. Jewish tradition acknowledges that sometimes it's important to stop singing, stop speaking, and just close your eyes and feel the rhythm of your heart and the rise and fall of your breath.

Silence can be an important gateway to deeper prayer, and if you can tolerate it, allowing yourself to experience silence can be very moving. In my own prayer practice, silent meditation often brings me to tears. And although Jewish prayer is largely a joyful experience, for it to be truly authentic, you have to be able to experience a full range of emotions when you pray.

I am so grateful for those times when my prayer moves me to tears. One of my earliest teachers, Rabbi Marshall T. Meyer, of blessed memory, taught me the value of tears in prayer. He used to say that "Tears are the *mikveh* [ritual bath] of the soul." Tears help purify our hearts, cleanse our souls, and open the doors to true spiritual growth.

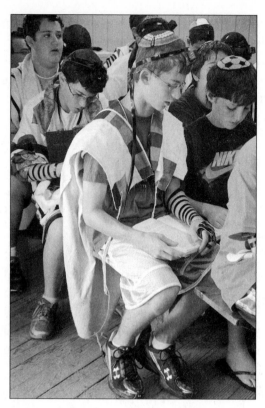

A young man recites morning prayers in *tallit* and *tefillin*.
(Photo by Jess Borba, courtesy of Camp Ramah in the Poconos)

Essential Takeaways

- Meaningful prayer is your responsibility—don't expect anyone else to make it great for you.
- Cultivating a sense of both awe and humility is an important part of Jewish prayer.
- The three main types of Jewish prayer are praise, petition, and gratitude.
- Singing can help you open to genuine prayer, but don't underestimate the power of silence.

chapter 6

The Language of Jewish Prayer

Why Jewish prayer services are in Hebrew

Making prayer meaningful in any language

Praying with a *siddur*

Going beyond the words on the page

Prayer is its own language. It's a vehicle for communication when we want to reach out to God. But what's the best way to express yourself when it comes to Jewish prayer? Do you have to know Hebrew to pray authentically as a Jew? Is it acceptable to pray in English?

While it's true that Hebrew is the traditional language of prayer in Judaism, Jewish prayer is possible in any language. Meaningful prayer comes from the heart and reflects our innermost aspirations and dreams. Prayer is so much more than the words we speak. It incorporates the movement of our bodies through unique choreography and postures. It taps into our innermost intentions and demands the alignment of our hearts and minds with our actions.

The goal of this chapter is to help you appreciate the importance of language in Jewish tradition and the central place it holds in Jewish prayer.

Hebrew as the Language of Jewish Prayer

Hebrew is the *lashon kodesh*, the "sacred tongue" of the Jewish people. The *Torah* and much of the *siddur* (Jewish prayer book) were composed in Hebrew, which is the language God used to communicate with the ancient prophets. Hebrew is the traditional language of Jewish prayer.

Torah Tip

Because speech is one of the divine gifts given to humanity, Judaism holds high ethical standards for how we use it. Gossip, or "hateful speech" (in Hebrew, *lashon ha-ra,* meaning "evil tongue"), is a serious moral transgression. Slander, or "spreading a bad name" (*motzi shem ra*), is also strictly prohibited. And embarrassing someone in public by using speech with cruelty is tantamount to the sin of murder.

According to the Jewish mystical tradition, the letters of the Hebrew alphabet are actually the building blocks of creation. Reading the *Torah* on its most esoteric level, the ancient practitioners of *kabbalah* believed God used Hebrew letters as tools to bring the universe into existence. According to this tradition, Hebrew letters have a unique, sacred power because they are the basic elements of divine speech.

There's certainly something very special about being able to pray in Hebrew. Hebrew connects Jews over time and space and fosters a powerful sense of Jewish religious continuity that transcends both history and geography. Saying the prayers in the original Hebrew links you to the generations of Jews before you who have recited these same words over the centuries.

In addition, wherever you travel, you'll find that Hebrew is the language of Jewish prayer in Jewish communities. So whether you're in Athens or Krackow or Shanghai, the language of Jewish prayer is the same. I once visited a synagogue in Thessaloniki where no one spoke English. I could not communicate at all with the people I met, but I was able to sing along with their prayer. After the service, we figured out that we could communicate in Hebrew!

Hebrew Evolves

The Bible and much of the *siddur* were composed in ancient Hebrew. Although Jewish services use ancient Hebrew for the language of prayer, this classical form of Hebrew is no longer in use as a spoken language.

In the 1880s, scholar Eliezer Ben Yehuda developed a modern version of Hebrew, based on the legacy of biblical Hebrew. Thus, the Hebrew language spoken today in the contemporary State of Israel is related to but not exactly the same as biblical Hebrew.

An analogy might be the relationship between Old English and the English language the way it's spoken today in the United States. You can probably understand Old English, but some key grammatical differences would make it sound awkward if you used it in daily conversation.

Learning Hebrew Through Prayer

But what are you supposed to do if you don't know Hebrew? Does it really make sense to pray in a language you don't understand? Isn't it more important to know what you're saying, as opposed to singing some meaningless syllables? The truth is that, in Judaism, you can pray in any language—it doesn't have to be Hebrew. (I'll talk about that more in the next few pages.)

However, becoming familiar with some key phrases in the Hebrew language can definitely help you connect more deeply to Jewish prayer. Learning Hebrew can also enhance your experience of synagogue services. Even the most beautiful and poetic translation of a Hebrew text cannot capture its meaning precisely. Something always gets lost in translation.

If it's not realistic for you to spend a lot of time learning a whole new language, consider learning a few words from some of the key prayers. Even incorporating a little bit of Hebrew can enrich your prayer experience and help you connect to Judaism's ancient liturgy.

Certain central prayers might make a good starting point. The *Shema,* Judaism's affirmation of monotheistic faith, is just six words long and is pretty easy to learn. You can also learn to understand some other short Hebrew chants without too much extensive study. If you add a few Hebrew words to your repertoire every few months, you'll really build your prayer fluency over time.

Praying with Authenticity in Any Language

It's essential to appreciate the importance of Hebrew language to Jewish prayer, but it would be very wrong to suggest that it's the only authentic language for communicating with God.

Jewish tradition values a concept called *intention,* or *kavanah.* Having the proper intention in a moment of prayer means understanding the words you're speaking and really focusing on their meaning for inspiration. This principle is so important that some authorities have argued that if a person doesn't understand Hebrew, he or she shouldn't use it for prayer at all! After all, how can you truly bare your soul in prayer using a language you can't communicate in?

Praying with *kavanah* demands that you know what you're saying and what you're praying for on some level. *Kavanah* is about going deep into your heart to be the truest self you can be in a moment of prayer. It means stripping away all the layers of pretense and self-consciousness for even just a single, solitary moment that's real and authentic.

The truth is that, as central as Hebrew is, it can be an obstacle to authentic prayer if it makes you feel like an outsider. If you're distracted trying to pronounce Hebrew words or you're feeling self-conscious because you're afraid of how you sound, you cannot be fully present in your prayer practice.

This is when it's a good idea to put aside Hebrew and check out the meanings of the prayers in English. It can be a great exercise, regardless of how fluent you might be in the Hebrew language. Following along in English during services can help you learn a few key phrases and give you a sense of the overall themes of the Jewish prayer service. Even if you just read silently in English while the service progresses in Hebrew, you will get so much more out of it than if you try to stumble through the Hebrew.

Even if you're fluent in Hebrew, it's a good idea to shake things up every now and then by experimenting with language. My classical Hebrew is pretty good, but from time to time, I like to check out the English translation provided in the *siddur.* Sometimes I catch an insight in the translation I hadn't noticed in the Hebrew. And other times, I just need to hear the English because it speaks to me where I am.

Definition

A **siddur** (*see-DOOR;* plural *siddurim, see-door-EEM*) is a book that contains the order of the Jewish liturgy. It's related to the Hebrew word *seder,* which means "order." In traditional communities, the *siddur* is printed entirely in Hebrew. A prayer book that prints the English translation directly over the Hebrew is called an "interlinear" *siddur.* These can be especially helpful if you're trying to learn to pray in Hebrew but want to have a literal translation of each word readily accessible. Other types of Hebrew-English *siddurim* usually have English on one side of the page and Hebrew on the other side. Because Hebrew reads from right to left, a *siddur* often seems to open "backward." This is typical of Hebrew books in general.

So you shouldn't feel that your prayer is less authentic just because English is more accessible for you than Hebrew. Praying in English, or whatever your native language is, can have its advantages for everyone.

However, even if you don't know Hebrew, there's one important advantage to praying in the original language, even if you don't understand the words. While intention is an important discipline in Jewish prayer, sometimes *kavanah* comes through the heart and not through the mind. Praying in Hebrew can help cultivate *kavanah* of the heart, regardless of your level of fluency.

When we pray in English, it's easy to get bogged down and distracted by the translations in the *siddur.* What happens when we come across something in the prayer book that we don't agree with or that feels uncomfortable? A classic example might be the various metaphors used to describe God—if you don't relate to God as a male King, reciting those words in English can be quite alienating.

When you pray in Hebrew, even if you don't understand all the words, you shut off the intellectual censors that distract you from genuine prayer. Vocalizing the ancient words and melodies, together with a congregation or alone, can take you outside your own head. The Hebrew words can serve as a mantra of sorts to focus your meditation and deepen your prayer practice.

Even if you don't understand the language, you can still offer a genuine prayer.

Keva and *Kavanah:* Fixed and Spontaneous Prayer

Jewish prayer presents something of a paradox. On one hand, prayer demands *kavanah*—focused intention and concentration that comes from the heart. *Kavanah* is spontaneous, because it requires you to follow your heart's lead and be in the moment.

On the other hand, Judaism also values a commitment to something called *keva*—the recitation of scripted prayers that are to be recited at fixed times. As we said earlier, the obligation to pray according to a fixed schedule is a key part of the discipline of Jewish prayer practice.

So how do we accomplish both at the same time? The truth is, it's a balancing act. Part of developing a mature prayer routine is learning to infuse the discipline of fixed prayer with meaning from our hearts. This doesn't mean that we'll feel something just because the liturgy tells us to do so. It also doesn't mean that we'll find the perfect scripted prayer to describe an emotion we feel at a given moment. But we do our best to move between *keva* and *kavanah* toward an increasingly meaningful prayer routine that can help us grow.

Becoming Familiar with the *Siddur*

You can find the script of Jewish prayer services for every occasion in a *siddur.* Some *siddurim* are comprehensive and include the entire liturgy for the Sabbath, weekdays, and certain festivals. Others focus just on prayers for the Sabbath, or just on prayers for the weekdays. A completely separate collection of liturgy, called a *machzor,* is used during the High Holy Days of *Rosh HaShanah* and *Yom Kippur*.

While it's clear that prayer existed during the time of the ancient Temple, the *siddur* is a product of ancient rabbinic culture. The outline of the prayer services as we know them today are written down in the *Mishna,* but the first known written *siddurim* date to the ninth century C.E. in the Jewish diaspora community of Babylonia. Before there were written prayer books, individuals either knew their prayers by heart or listened to a prayer leader recite the liturgy publicly.

Today the *siddur* is an important aid in the spiritual life of any Jewish person. The *siddur* becomes a personal script for moving through the prayer service, and its pages are an invitation to encounter Jewish prayer the way it has been formulated for centuries.

In crafting Jewish prayers, the rabbis blended passages from the *Torah* with psalms and excerpts from the prophets. Over time, they added more passages from the *Mishna* and *Talmud,* along with other liturgical poems written in different places and different eras. The *siddur* is truly a diverse anthology of Jewish literature, combining many different genres from many different times and places.

Torah Tip

Many traditional Jews, especially women, recite passages from the Book of Psalms to pray for healing and protection outside the regular cycle of fixed liturgy. The Hebrew word for Psalms is *Tehillim,* and their authorship is traditionally attributed to King David.

While the basic outline of the *siddur* is the same overall, some variation exists among Jewish communities. In Orthodox communities, there are differences between Ashkenazic and Sephardic customs when it comes to some aspects of the *siddur.*

In liberal denominations, the *siddur* is an evolving document, and changes to the liturgy are often incorporated in response to pressing issues of the time. For example, some Conservative and Reform *siddurim* have added gender-inclusive language to the text of the classical Hebrew prayers, out of a need to align the liturgy with egalitarian principles. Reconstructionist *siddurim* include a number of alternative blessings that remove classical references to Jews as "the chosen people," because this principle is not consistent with the movement's theology.

It's important to discover a *siddur* that speaks to you. Do you find the English readings and translations compelling? Is it easy to navigate? Is it comfortable to hold? You want to find a *siddur* that helps you enter prayer easily—one you look forward to opening each day.

Although you can use any *siddur* right off the synagogue shelf, it's nice to have your own so that you can pray at home. Many *siddurim* today have helpful annotations and commentaries to aid your understanding of the prayers and how to recite them. Most *siddurim* have a section detailing the different blessings that might be recited at home, so it can be your trusty guide for *Shabbat* and holiday observances around the table.

 Prayer books are the greatest resource for prayers of the past. But any moment of life can provide an opening to prayer. Prayer can be planned, but it can also be immediate. It can meet the need of regular habit as well as the sudden yearning to reach out.

—Rabbi David Wolpe, *Teaching Your Children About God*

Going Beyond Words on a Page

Whatever language you use, the ultimate goal of prayer is to reach outside yourself and connect with the divine presence. And the truth is, the deepest dimension of prayer is beyond language, anyway. Experience of God is what scholars of mysticism call "ineffable." Words simply cannot describe the mysterious intensity of a true encounter with a transcendent reality.

Language is so important to Jewish prayer, but it's important to regard it as a starting point. If you feel that language is a barrier to your engagement with prayer, try focusing on some of the nonverbal aspects of Jewish prayer.

The Body as a Vehicle for Expression

In many Jewish prayers, we use our bodies to communicate through movement and choreography. The most dramatic posture adopted during prayer is bowing. At several points in the regular prayer services, it's customary to bow at the knee or at the waist for a brief moment. Bowing is a sign of humility and respect. On the High Holy Days, it's customary for the prayer leader to make a full prostration during a high point of the service. Many of the liturgical texts talk about submitting ourselves to God's will and to the precepts of the *Torah,* and it can be very powerful to express this idea with our bodies.

Many traditional Jews rock back and forth on their feet during prayer. This meditative practice aids concentration during the rhythmic recitation of the liturgy. Fervent swaying can be an expression of intense devotion and a sign that a person is really "into" his or her prayer session. It can also simply be performed out of habit.

During the recitation of the *Shema,* it's customary to cover your eyes with one hand to help you concentrate on the text of the prayer. Some Jews also have the custom of kissing the *tzitzit* every time the word *tzitzit* is mentioned in the third paragraph after the *Shema.*

At the start of the *Amidah,* some Jews take three steps backward and three steps forward to signal their withdrawal from the everyday world and their approach before the divine throne in prayer. At the conclusion of these prayers, it's customary to take three steps back again, as if withdrawing from before a respected teacher, and bow in all directions while reciting a prayer for peace.

Praying Without Words

A *niggun* is a repetitive, wordless melody anyone can sing along to. Sometimes singing a *niggun* or simply humming along with melodies during a service opens the door to a meaningful prayer experience.

I know from my own prayer practice that sometimes I've just had enough of words. I don't want to talk; I don't want to read; I just want to breathe and be in the moment. At times, I just want to sway and listen to the community sing out the beautiful, ancient melodies.

In these moments, I venture away from the page of the *siddur* and turn inward to read what's in my heart. It's important to understand that even this moment of personal introspection can be understood as Jewish prayer.

A Note on Jewish Languages

Ancient Hebrew was long ago the spoken language of the Jewish people, but it was eventually replaced as the spoken vernacular in Jewish communities throughout the diaspora. In fact, as a result of their many migrations, Jews have prayed in hundreds of different languages throughout their long history.

In the few centuries prior to the Common Era, the Hebrew Bible was translated into Greek because it had become the popular spoken language of Jews during the Hellenistic period. In ancient Judea, Jews spoke Aramaic, which is a dialect of Hebrew. In fact, some of the prayers we still recite today are in Aramaic. Aramaic is also the language of parts of the *Mishna* and the *Talmud.*

Jews developed many other Jewish languages as well, based on the languages spoken in the communities where they lived. The most well-known examples are these:

- *Ladino* is also known as Judeo-Spanish and is a romance language spoken by Jews of Spanish descent.

- *Yiddish* is a form of Judeo-German spoken by most Jews in Eastern and Central Europe prior to World War II.

- *Judeo-Arabic* is a form of Arabic written with Hebrew characters. Maimonides wrote his famous *Guide for the Perplexed* in this language.

While Hebrew remained the language of sacred study, it's certain that Jews have expressed their desire to connect with God in many different tongues throughout the ages. Rest assured that your prayers are authentic, no matter what language you speak.

Essential Takeaways

- Hebrew is the traditional language of Jewish prayer, and learning it can deepen your appreciation of Jewish services.
- If you don't understand Hebrew, it's perfectly okay to pray in English.
- Jewish prayer tries to balance *kavanah* (spontaneity) with *keva* (fixed prayers).
- The *siddur* is the Jewish prayer book that contains the fixed liturgy.
- Physical gestures and movement of the body are important aspects of prayer language.

chapter 7

Prayer as a Sacred Obligation

Praying in private and in public

Praying with a prayer quorum, or *minyan*

Who counts in a *minyan?*

Tips for getting motivated

In Judaism, daily prayer is the foundation of a spiritual discipline. In the same way daily exercise helps keep you in shape for those times when you really need to perform physically, daily prayer in the Jewish tradition helps you stay in shape "spiritually" so that when you really need prayer, it's part of your toolkit to help you manage life's challenging moments.

But a commitment to daily prayer is not just about you. The obligation to participate in public worship ensures that a community is always there to support those who need to pray for healing, celebrate joyous milestones, or mourn losses. In this chapter, you discover the spiritual value of obligatory prayer.

Public Versus Private Prayer

Traditional Judaism marks the rhythm of each day with a fixed liturgy. This liturgy includes prayers that are to be recited at specific times of the day, either in public or in private. In Judaism, prayer is an obligation—three times each day, we must slow down, take a break from whatever we're doing, and open our hearts to God. In Chapter 9, I take a closer look at the basic meaning behind these daily prayers, but for now, I want to focus on what it means to view prayer as a *mitzvah.*

Whether praying at home in private or in public at synagogue, every Jew prays as an individual. We may be reciting the same prayers as our neighbors, and a prayer leader, choir, or cantor may be guiding and inspiring us through the worship service, but our prayer is always our own. We don't need any intermediary to communicate with God for us. Prayer is always a direct and personal conversation between you and the Infinite God.

> **wisdom of the sages**
>
> While praying, listen to the words very carefully. When your heart is attentive, your entire being enters your prayer without your having to force it.
>
> —Rebbe Nachman of Breslov

Some Jews make the choice to pray privately. Prayers can be recited at home or even first thing in the morning at the office. Parents of young children, very often women, routinely say their prayers at home because they're unable to get to the synagogue for public worship on a daily basis.

Private prayer practice can be very meaningful because it goes at your own pace, and you can sing the melodies you love. You can use the time to meditate quietly without the distraction of other congregants. You can even pray in your pajamas! When you're learning how to pray, private prayer can give you the freedom you need to experiment with different prayer books, postures, and other variations in Jewish practice.

Public prayer has different advantages. In a synagogue setting, every person in attendance adds something unique to the prayer service. Praying in a communal setting can also inspire you when you're not feeling motivated. Certain prayers and blessings can only be recited in public worship, so praying publicly can give you the sense of having the "full experience" of the liturgy that can sometimes be lacking when you pray on your own.

In any setting, prayer is personal. But if it's personal, what's the value of sticking to a traditional prayer routine? Why can't you just pray how you want, where you want, when you want? This is where the wisdom of Jewish tradition comes in. If prayer were not an obligation, would we really make time for it on a daily or even weekly basis?

It can be so hard, in the midst of our chaotic lives, to take a break from what we're doing at home or at work to make prayer a priority. But according to the Jewish sages, those moments when we are required to stop what we're doing and connect with our sense of wonder and gratitude are critical for staying connected to God in our day-to-day lives.

Don't be afraid to get creative. Although it's preferable to stay in one place and focus entirely on your daily prayer, sometimes you can stay connected throughout the day by unconventional means. I have a friend who used to say her daily prayers on the treadmill, with her headphones playing inspiring melodies. One of my teachers kept a CD in his car so he could pray during his daily commute. A growing trend is a form of prayer called "*Torah* yoga," a practice that incorporates yoga postures and breathing exercises into a Jewish prayer service.

Prayer as Communal and Personal Responsibility

What does it mean to make a commitment? When we commit to something, it becomes a priority for us. When we commit to someone, they become a priority for us. That means putting this thing, practice, or person before other demands on our time. It means sticking with it or with them, even during times of hardship. Commitment is challenging because it requires choices that aren't always easy. But the upside is that the experience of making tough choices, and suffering their consequences, really helps us grow as people.

In Judaism, prayer is obligatory. Jewish tradition requires us to pray not because God needs our prayers, but because we do. The personal commitment we make to regular prayer feeds our souls. It cultivates our spiritual discipline and helps keep our focus on what really matters in life. In the same way our bodies need food for physical energy, our spiritual selves need prayer. When you make a commitment to prayer, you are making a commitment to yourself.

Ultimately, a Jew may be truly called a Jew when he/she is part of circles of belonging—to family, community, the nation and the world of humanity. It is when the Jew consciously realizes his/her place in the midst of these concentric circles of responsibility uniting the individual with the world, that the inner nature of the Jewish story can be fulfilled properly.

—Steve Israel, "Connecting to Community"

Minyan: A Symbol of Community

Jewish prayer serves important communal needs as well, and a rich Jewish life necessarily involves moving beyond your own spiritual needs to support the needs of the community. This is where the idea of a *minyan* comes in. A *minyan* is a prayer quorum that symbolizes the Jewish people as a whole. It's the foundation of Jewish communal prayer. When people are headed to synagogue, they might say, "I'm going to the *minyan*," meaning they're going to fulfill their obligation to daily prayer as part of a prayer quorum.

A **minyan** (plural *minyanim*) is defined traditionally as a quorum of 10 adult Jewish men required to recite obligatory prayers in public worship. The liberal denominations of Judaism, including most Conservative congregations, today include Jewish women in the *minyan*. The word *minyan* is derived from the Hebrew word for "counting."

If Jewish prayer is so individualized and personal, why is a *minyan* necessary? In a nutshell, a *minyan* takes the idea of personal commitment to Jewish prayer to the next level. In its ideal form, a *minyan* is a community of individuals who have made the commitment to support one another by their presence. A *minyan* is the heart of a spiritual community.

Many Jewish lifecycle events are celebrated in synagogue in the context of a prayer community. Marking important milestones like birth, *bar* and *bat mitzvah*, conversion, engagement, marriage, and death in a community deepens our experience of them. And because they often involve public reading of the *Torah* or the recitation of special prayers that emphasize God's holiness, every one of them requires a *minyan*.

To live a Jewish life to the fullest, we need community and the community needs us. Perhaps the best example of how this works is evident in the practices that surround mourning the death of a loved one.

When an immediate family member dies, it's customary for mourners to recite a prayer known as the *kaddish* (*KAH-dish*) every day for 11 months and each year on the anniversary of the person's death. This prayer, which does not mention death at all, is a responsive prayer that affirms God's holy presence in the world and can be a tremendous source of comfort to those mourning a loss. The process of reciting a year of *kaddish* is an important part of the Jewish mourning process. According to traditional Judaism, the *kaddish* must be recited in the presence of a *minyan*. It cannot be recited in isolation. If there is no *minyan*, if 10 Jewish adults are not present in the prayer quorum, a mourner cannot perform this basic ritual.

MISC.

Which Prayers Require a *Minyan?*

The prayers and rituals that traditionally require a *minyan* are *kaddish*, the call to prayer (*barechu*), the *kedushah* (a series of blessings praising God's holiness), the repetition of the 18 Benedictions (the *Amidah*), the priestly blessing, public reading from the *Torah* or the prophets, the seven wedding blessings (*sheva b'rachot*), certain passages in the Grace After Meals (*birkat ha-mazon*), recitation of the 13 attributes of God, and the blessing for surviving illness or danger (*birkat ha-gomel*).

Participating in a *minyan* is an important act of kindness. You can make the difference in whether a mourner can fulfill this important *mitzvah*. Judaism is set up this way to affirm our need for community during the mourning process.

If you know that other people are counting on you to complete the *minyan*, it's added motivation to make the effort to be in synagogue. Your regular attendance at a *minyan* binds you in a meaningful way to the other participants because you share important ritual moments together. When a *minyan* truly becomes a community of purpose, a community bound together by commitment to Jewish prayer, it becomes a sacred community.

Who Counts?

A traditional *minyan* requires the presence of 10 adult Jewish males. Sounds simple, right? It's actually a very complicated issue, and one that gets a lot of attention in the Jewish community today. As you explore different congregations, it's important to be aware that there's quite a bit of disagreement among Jews today regarding who "counts" as Jewish.

The classical definition, according to Orthodox Jewish law, understands Jewish identity to be conferred according to *matrilineal* descent. This means a person is considered Jewish if they were born of a Jewish mother. Alternatively, someone who was not born to a Jewish mother can become Jewish through a formal conversion to Judaism under the supervision of an Orthodox rabbi.

Conservative congregations also hold to a standard of defining Jewish identity by matrilineal descent. However, when it comes to conversion, those who converted under the supervision of either Conservative or Orthodox rabbis are accepted as Jewish without question.

Reform and Reconstructionist communities have adopted a broader, more inclusive definition of what it means to be Jewish. In these more liberal congregations, rabbis accept either matrilineal or patrilineal descent. So if you have one Jewish parent, regardless of whether it's your mother or father, you are considered Jewish. In these communities as well, it is possible to become Jewish through a process of conversion supervised by a rabbi of any denomination.

Now, don't worry! No one is standing at the entrance to the synagogue waiting to grill you about your lineage or your conversion process. Synagogues are typically welcoming and eager to include guests of any background. But when it comes to active participation in the service, being invited up to the *Torah,* or being "counted" in the *minyan,* you should be aware that some communities are less inclusive than others. Depending on where you're coming from, this is something to keep in mind as you visit different synagogues.

Minyan Stand-Ins

According to some Rabbinic authorities, a *Torah* scroll, or a minor holding a *Torah* scroll, can be counted as part of the *minyan*. Another tradition is that the divine presence can be counted as part of the *minyan*. This practice comes in handy when only nine people show up for services that day!

Accounting for Gender

If a *minyan* is a symbol of the Jewish people, how do we make sense of the fact that traditionally, and in contemporary Orthodox practice, only men "count" in the prayer quorum? This is one of the more divisive issues within the Jewish community at large, and it's the central issue that divides some of the liberal denominations from the more traditional ones.

All Jews, both men and women, are expected to pray daily. However, in the *Talmud,* the ancient rabbinic sages who interpreted Jewish law ruled that women are exempt from performing any commandments that have to be performed within certain time parameters. Daily prayers, which have to be recited at particular times of the day, fall into this category. Their reasoning was that women would be too busy with the demands of their household to be expected to drop everything to run to the synagogue in time.

This exemption (which also applied to minors) meant that only men are charged with the duty to pray three times daily. Consequently, the rabbis ruled that only persons who are obligated to pray in a *minyan* could be counted in a *minyan*. As a result, in traditional denominations of Judaism, the synagogue is something of a man's domain. Women attend and participate in synagogue worship, but their presence there isn't mandatory. In traditional communities, the home becomes the place where a woman can express her spirituality. (We look at home-centered piety in Chapter 17.)

Minyan or No *Minyan?*

Some Reform and Reconstructionist congregations no longer require a *minyan* as a necessary condition for reciting *kaddish* or any of the traditional prayers. The justification for this practice stems from the idea that an opportunity for prayer should not be limited by the number of people who are or are not present. For the people who do show up, prayer will be meaningful regardless of whether there's a quorum.

A recent innovation in some modern Orthodox communities is special prayer groups for women, in which women lead services and read aloud from the *Torah* scroll. These prayer groups are not considered a *minyan*, so they don't recite some of the blessings that require a prayer quorum. However, they do give women the experience of public, communal prayer and provide opportunities for spiritual leadership that women wouldn't otherwise have.

The more liberal denominations of Judaism (Reform, Reconstructionist, and the vast majority of Conservative synagogues) do not maintain such strict gender roles when it comes to public prayer. In these *egalitarian* communities, men and women count equally in the *minyan* and participate fully in leadership roles during services. In these liberal communities, rabbis have made the decision to revisit the traditional ruling about who can count in the *minyan*. In doing so, they bring contemporary ideas about gender equality to their interpretation of Jewish law.

Egalitarian refers to congregations that include both men and women in the *minyan*. A congregation in which women are not included is *non-egalitarian*.

There's a great deal of variation in the practice of egalitarian communities. Some allow women some privileges of participation, but not all. For example, in some synagogues, women count in the *minyan*, can lead prayers, can read from the *Torah*, and can even serve as rabbi. In other synagogues, women might be able to lead prayer but do not count in the *minyan* and cannot read from the *Torah*.

If you're interested in worshipping in an egalitarian community, be sure to inquire about a synagogue's philosophy concerning women's inclusion, and ask specific questions about what women can and cannot do.

At morning *minyan* in an egalitarian Conservative community, men and women pray together.
(Photo by Jess Borba, courtesy of Camp Ramah in the Poconos)

As you search for your own prayer community, you'll have to figure out what feels right for you. Perhaps you're the kind of person who finds the traditionalism of Orthodox practice a comforting refuge from the "anything goes" attitude of liberal American culture. Or maybe it makes more sense for you to worship in a community that embraces feminism and egalitarianism.

Wonderful opportunities exist for you to enrich your spiritual practice in every Jewish community, regardless of its denominational affiliation. One of the great things about becoming "literate" in Jewish prayer is that you can learn to feel comfortable in any synagogue. You'll need to find a place that allows you to develop and grow in your spiritual practice and eventually becomes a place you'll think of as your "spiritual home."

What If I Don't Feel Like Praying?

I know what you might be thinking at this point. *Isn't it contradictory to say that prayer is an obligation? Shouldn't prayer be spontaneous and come right from the heart, genuine every single time?* This might be the ideal, but it's certainly not the reality for most of us. Just because we're obligated to pray doesn't mean we actually feel like praying.

Acquiring the spiritual discipline to pray the required prayers three times every day requires a lot of practice and a great deal of training. We all have days when we don't want to go to the gym, but we go anyway, and we feel better for our efforts. It's the same with daily prayer. I once heard a rabbi explain it well: she said Judaism requires us to pray daily so that when we really need to communicate with God, we have the skills and tools at our disposal to do so.

Torah Tip

Look forward to your prayer time. Think of it as a date with a really special friend you wouldn't even consider putting off. When other demands pull at you, remember that you come first. Even just a few moments of meditation will fortify you to tackle your "to do" list.

Making a commitment to prayer is a critical step in deepening your spiritual life. Promising yourself that you will do one thing and stick to it helps cultivate a feeling of sacred duty that's so crucial in Jewish prayer practice. Consider getting started by finding one short prayer or blessing you really connect to, and make a commitment to say it every day. You might try it first thing in the morning or perhaps right before you go to bed. If making a daily commitment seems too daunting at first, think about making a weekly commitment and grow from there.

Praying regularly is a lot like riding a roller coaster. There are peaks, valleys, and occasional 360-degree loops. Sometimes the curves sneak up on you, and the ride can change in an instant. Reading a book like this, it's probably easy to imagine that some people experience the rush of transcendent prayer every single day. The truth is, it's very rare.

When I attend services or recite the daily prayers on my own, if I find just one moment during the entire service when I feel genuinely present and open to connection, I am satisfied. And this is where praying daily comes in as an important spiritual discipline. It's so hard to just walk into a Jewish service out of the blue and feel something. It's kind of like starting one of your workout routines with a half-marathon.

By becoming familiar with the rhythm of the liturgy and its subtle changes from day to day, week after week, and over the course of a year, the prayer service begins to speak to you in new ways. Making daily prayer a part of your life helps you cultivate this sensitivity to the rhythm of Jewish prayer.

wisdom of the sages

Prayer invites God's Presence to suffuse our spirits,
God's will to prevail in our lives.
Prayer may not bring water to parched fields,
Nor mend a broken bridge,
Or rebuild a ruined city.
But prayer can water an arid soul,
Mend a broken heart,
Rebuild a weakened will.

—Mishkan T'filah, *A Reform Siddur*

When I'm really focused during prayer, I feel a connection to the transcendent so easily. Something in the texts or the melodies speaks to me, and I'm able to open up and really be in there. These are wonderful, intense, and insightful moments of profound feeling and reflection. When prayer is like this, it's not hard to accept it as an obligation.

But at other times, it's not so easy. I feel distracted, self-conscious, and distant, and I don't connect with much of anything. In these moments, the words of prayer feel empty and the prayer book feels awkward and uncomfortable in my hands. At times like this, the obligation to pray can feel like drudgery.

Please keep in mind that these moments are completely normal, and they are part of the spiritual discipline that is daily prayer. In my experience, they happen more frequently than I'd like to admit, but I try to think of these times as opportunities for spiritual growth. The important thing is to stick with it.

When I'm feeling less than motivated, it might be an indication that I need to do something a little different—try a new setting or tune or find some inspirational reading. Instead of praying the formal text on the page of the prayer book, sometimes I use prayer time just to be silent, take in some deep breaths, and meditate. A teacher once told me that when you're having trouble opening yourself to prayer, you should "yearn to yearn." Long for the blessing of genuine, heartfelt prayer, and you might just receive it.

Essential Takeaways

- Daily prayer is an important spiritual discipline in Jewish tradition.
- Whether public or private, prayer is always personal.
- A *minyan* is a quorum of 10 adult Jews (traditionally, 10 adult Jewish males).
- Liberal Jewish communities do include women in a *minyan.* These congregations are called egalitarian.
- Start slowly, and stick with it. Begin with a commitment to reciting one prayer daily, and build from there.

chapter 8

Dressing for Jewish Prayer

The role of ritual garments in Jewish prayer

Different approaches to head coverings

The meaning of *tallit* and *tefillin*

What it means to dress modestly

Jewish prayer is an interior experience. It's all about opening your heart and letting go of that sense of self-consciousness that tends to prevent you from moving to a deeper spiritual plane. So it may seem contradictory to devote a whole chapter to something as superficial as dressing for prayer, but in Jewish practice, a number of very important customs are related to dress and can actually enhance your prayer experience.

Prayer involves your entire body. The ritual practices described in this chapter involve tangible objects that you wear. They are not clothes, but rather tools to help you mark sacred moments, increase your focus, and add beauty to your prayer life.

Head Covering

For Jews, covering the head is a sign of modesty and a reminder that the divine presence is always "above" us. Although practices vary among the denominations, it's generally considered an appropriate sign of respect for adults to put on a head covering in any religious setting, especially in the synagogue. Whenever it's necessary to recite a blessing or invoke God's name for any purpose, a head covering is there to remind you of God's presence.

Head covering practices raise some interesting gender issues in the Jewish community. Among traditional Jews, it's customary for men to wear a head covering at all times, but especially upon entering a house of worship, during religious study, and when eating a meal. In more liberal communities, the custom is typically to wear a head covering only when performing religious acts in the synagogue. In these liberal communities, women often cover their heads in synagogue as well.

In traditional communities, women wear head coverings, too, but for different reasons than men. It's complicated, but I'll break it all down for you in this section.

Kipah/Yarmulke

In Hebrew, the religious head covering generally worn by men is called a *kipah* (*kee-PAH*). A *kipah* is round and looks a little like a beanie. Another name for a *kipah* is *yarmulke* (*yah-muh-kuh*), which is a Yiddish word that derives from the Aramaic *yirei malka*, which means "in fear of the king." This etymology really captures the sense of reverence a *kipah* seeks to express.

Kipot (pural: *kee-POAT*) come in a wide variety of materials and sizes. They can be crocheted in bright colors or made of a solid material like leather, nylon, or satin. Some are only about 6 inches in diameter, and others take up most of the head. It's not uncommon to see young boys wearing a *kipah* featuring a cartoon character or sports team logo. Some might have a Hebrew name stitched into the needlework.

Special *kipot* for women are also readily available, made from more "feminine" materials like beads, crystals, wire, and lace. One of the favorite *kipot* in my collection is made of cotton with a hot pink and purple tie-dye pattern. What a great souvenir from a *bat mitzvah* celebration!

Kipot, traditional head coverings worn by men and some women, come in a wide variety of sizes and designs.

Some Jews choose to wear a *kipah* all the time. Remember the tradition of reciting 100 blessings per day I discussed in Chapter 3? Well, in theory, we should be continually engaged in acts of blessing and, therefore, it makes sense to have our heads covered at all times. However, many Jews wear a *kipah* only during formal synagogue prayer or when participating in a ritual meal on the Sabbath or a holiday.

Wearing a *kipah* is also significant because it tells the world you're Jewish. So if you make the decision to wear a head covering at all times—at work, at the market, at the gym—it's kind of like wearing a big sign that says, "Hey, I'm a practicing Jew!"

Torah Tip

If you forget your *kipah,* most synagogues have "loaner" *kipot* on hand for you to borrow, along with some bobby pins to secure it in place.

What's important to understand about making this public statement is that it comes with certain responsibilities. Wearing a *kipah* as an outward sign of your Jewish identity means you'll be judged publicly as a Jew. It means you're representing the Jewish people in everything you do. So wearing a *kipah* can also serve as a reminder to yourself to uphold the highest standard of behavior, both in private and in public.

Women and Hair

Some women choose to wear a head covering in synagogue for the same reasons men do—to express reverence for God above them, as an indication of humility, or as a public expression of their Jewish commitment. However, a whole other set of issues comes into play for women in more traditional communities.

In Orthodox Judaism, a woman's hair is considered sensual and erotic. It's an integral part of her beauty, and after she's married, tradition holds that it's inappropriate for other men to see it. It's customary, then, after marriage, for observant, Orthodox women to cover their hair at all times in public. As an expression of modesty, traditional women wear a scarf, hat, or even a wig that fully covers the hair.

If Orthodox women have to cover their own hair out of modesty, why is it okay to wear a wig? Isn't that sort of hypocritical? I hear this question a lot.

Jewish mysticism teaches that a woman's own hair, whether long or short, is deeply sensual. No matter how beautiful a wig might be, it does not contain the level of holiness and sensuality of a woman's real hair. Therefore, according to this tradition, wearing a wig does not provoke the same level of arousal that a woman's own hair could.

Hats

Hats are also a perfectly acceptable form of head covering for both men and women across the denominations. Many women might cover their hair in synagogue but not in other parts of their lives, so a hat can be convenient.

Women who choose to wear hats in synagogue after they're married might not have their entire hair covered. It's really a personal choice. Popular styles of hats include berets and straw hats with a wide brim. Synagogues often have a lacey head covering available for women. These look like a doily and can be folded in half and affixed to the hair with a hairpin. The name for this type of head covering is *kofa*.

Some men (and women in liberal communities) who don't want to draw attention to themselves by wearing a *kipah* might wear a baseball cap or other hat as a way of observing this *mitzvah* in a more subtle fashion.

Many traditional Jewish men wear dressier hats with a *kipah* underneath it, sometimes just on the Sabbath, but sometimes all week long. This is the custom among ultra-Orthodox Jews. In fact, among *Hasidim,* the type of hat a man wears (a fedora versus a *shtreimel,* for example) is an indication of the particular Hasidic sect he belongs to.

On the Fringe

One of the most beautiful ritual garments in the Jewish tradition is the *tallit (tah-LEET),* or *tallis (TAH-liss).* This prayer shawl is a four-cornered garment that is distinguished by the *tzitzit,* or fringes, attached to each corner.

The custom of wearing a *tallit* derives from a passage in the Book of Numbers:

> Speak to the Israelite people and instruct them to make tzitzit for themselves on the corners of their garments through all the ages; let them attach a cord of blue to the tzitzit of each corner. That shall be your tzitzit; looking at it, you shall recall all of God's commandments and observe them and not be seduced by your heart or led astray by your eyes. Thus shall you be reminded to observe all My commandments and to be holy to your God. (Numbers 15:38–41)

The *tzitzit* are a tangible reminder of our sacred duty to obey God's *mitzvot*. We are to look at them and remember our commitment. Instead of following our eyes and hearts, we look at the *tzitzit* to focus our attention on God. In traditional communities, the command to wear *tzitzit* applies only to men, although in the liberal movements, women wear them as well.

The knots of the *tzitzit* are a reminder of the *mitzvot* that bind us to God.

Tallit Katan and Tallit Gadol

The *tallit* comes in two forms:

An undergarment known as a *tallit katan* (small *tallit*) is worn underneath street clothes at all times. This is an intimate garment that expresses a deep level of commitment to the principles of the *Torah*. I think it is such a beautiful idea to bring God into the very act of dressing each day.

A *tallit katan* is customarily worn by both men and boys. However, women can wear one, too. Some people choose to wear the *tallit katan* with the *tzitzit* tucked into the clothes so that it's a more private expression of piety. Others wear the fringes hanging out so they can be seen throughout the day and serve as an outward reminder, as described in Numbers.

A *tallit gadol* (big *tallit*) is worn over the clothing during daily prayer. This type of *tallit* can be long and flowing or worn more like a scarf draped neatly over the neck. A *tallit gadol* is commonly made of silk, wool, or linen and is traditionally white adorned with stripes of black or blue. A trend in more contemporary *tallitot* (plural: *tah-lee-TOAT*) is to use colorful fabrics painted with scenes from Israel or embellished with delicate embroidery.

Your choice of *tallit* is an important form of individual religious expression. It's a deeply personal garment that typically is worn only by you. Although most synagogues have *tallits* for public use, it's really nice to have your own. You can purchase a *tallit* in any Judaica store or synagogue gift shop, or from one of many online vendors in the United States and Israel. You can choose from literally hundreds of designs and styles. Wearing a *tallit* that was passed down to you from a relative or that you received as a gift on a special occasion also can be quite special.

Torah Tip

A *tallit* is a simple garment you can even make yourself. To make a *tallit*, you first need a piece of fabric that you absolutely love, cut into a rectangle large enough to wrap around your shoulders. It can be as long and flowing as you like, or on the smaller side if that's your preference. You also need a strip of complementary fabric to make the *atara*, the collar that drapes across the back of your neck. With some reinforcements for all four corners and string for tying the *tzitzit* on each corner, you're set.

How to Put on a *Tallit*

A *tallit* is generally worn only in the daytime. The act of putting on a *tallit* is one of the first things you do to enter the mind-set of prayer each morning. This is the blessing to recite when putting on the *tallit*:

> Praised are You, *Adonai* Our God, Sovereign of the
> Universe, whose *mitzvot* add holiness to our life and
> who gave us the mitzvah to wrap ourselves in *tzitzit*.

Barukh Atah Adoanai Eloheinu, Melech Ha-Olam,
asher kid'shanu b'mitzvotav v'tzeevanu l'hee-tah-tef
ba-tzeet-tzeet.

As you recite this blessing, it's customary to hold the collar of the *tallit,* the *atara,* in your hands and kiss the fabric before you wrap the *tallit* around your body. When I put on my *tallit,* I like to savor the moment a little bit by wrapping the *tallit* over my head, closing my eyes, and meditating for just a second on my transition into the realm of prayer.

A young man prepares for morning prayer by wrapping himself in his *tallit.*
(Photo by Jess Borba, courtesy of Camp Ramah in the Poconos)

As soon as I put on my *tallit,* I'm in prayer time—the realm of the sacred. For me, the *tallit* symbolizes the creation of my own private sanctuary. As I begin my prayers, I sometimes run my fingers through the *tzitzit* as a way of bringing my attention to the *mitzvot*. The *tallit* I wear pretty regularly was a gift to me from some friends in my synagogue, and every single time I wear it, I feel grateful. If I don't have it on, I feel like something is missing.

I find *tzitzit* to be a very profound symbol of the Jewish faith. *Tzitzit* are made up of thin, loose strings carefully wound and knotted according to a precise pattern. Each tassel has five sets of knots and several inches of string that hang loosely to form the "fringe." In my mind, the knots symbolize my commitment to God's *mitzvot,* while the loosely hanging strings represent my freedom to choose my own course of action. When I look at the *tzitzit,* I remember that I am both free and bound in my relationship to God.

Torah Tip

Resist the urge to let synagogue become a fashion show. It's important to dress neatly and respectably, but it's also important to be comfortable. On the Sabbath or holidays, men often wear a dress shirt, jacket, and tie with slacks, or a suit. If you're attending daily *minyan* during the week, dress is entirely casual. In traditional synagogues, it's customary for women to wear skirts or dresses below the knee, with a top that covers your shoulders and is not too low cut. In more liberal synagogues, pants and pants suits are perfectly acceptable.

Ties That Bind: The *Mitzvah* of *Tefillin*

You've already learned a lot about Judaism's emphasis on sacred duty and the *mitzvot*. *Tefillin* is an ancient Jewish practice, still widely observed today, that takes the concept of a binding commitment to the *Torah* to the next level. If you've only ever been to synagogue on the Sabbath or on holidays, it's possible that you've never been exposed to the practice of wearing *tefillin*.

Tefillin are a pair of small leather boxes that contain passages from the *Torah* handwritten on parchment. One box is worn on the arm, and the other is affixed to the head. Each box is bound to the body with long leather straps that wind around the arm and head, respectively. The word *tefillin* is related to the Hebrew word *tefilah,* which means "prayer."

It's a traditional custom for Jewish men to wear *tefillin* during weekday morning prayers. *Tefillin* are not used on Sabbaths and holidays, so unless you attend a *minyan* on weekday mornings or grew up in a home where men prayed daily, this practice may be unfamiliar to you. I know I'd never seen anyone wearing *tefillin* until I was in graduate school and there happened to be a fire drill during the morning prayer service at the Jewish seminary where I was studying. Whether *tefillin* is familiar or new to you, in this section, you learn what this very unique *mitzvah* is all about.

The Origins of *Tefillin*

Leather *tefillin* boxes were found among the treasures discovered with the Dead Sea Scrolls, an ancient library of texts and artifacts dating all the way back to the first centuries of the Common Era. This remarkable discovery is evidence that *tefillin* is a very ancient ritual practice in Judaism.

The *mitzvah* of *tefillin* is based on four biblical passages in the *Torah* that use similar language. Two are from the Book of Exodus:

> And it shall be for a sign for you upon your hand, and for a reminder between your eyes, that the *Torah* of the Lord may be in your mouth; for with a strong hand did the Lord bring you out of Egypt. (Exodus 13:9)

> And it shall be for a sign upon your hand, and as a symbol between your eyes; for with a mighty hand did the Lord bring us forth out of Egypt. (Exodus 13:16)

Two more passages appear in the Book of Deuteronomy. These passages make up part of the *Shema,* one of the most important prayers in Jewish liturgy:

> And you shall bind them as a sign upon your arm, and they shall be as a symbol between your eyes. (Deuteronomy 6:8)

> You shall put these words of mine on your heart and on your soul; and you shall tie them for a sign upon your arm, and they shall be as a symbol between your eyes. (Deuteronomy 11:18)

Now, these biblical texts don't actually use the word *tefillin*, and they're not completely clear in what they mean by binding a "sign" or a "symbol" on the body. But the rabbis, whose teachings make up the Oral *Torah*, interpreted these verses in a very particular way. In their view, the *Torah* here commands that the very passages from the Written *Torah* should be bound to the arm and to the forehead. This is how the ritual of *tefillin* developed.

Four passages from the *Torah* are written on a single piece of parchment and tucked inside a leather box worn on the arm, called the *tefillin shel yad* in Hebrew. Those same passages are written on a separate piece of parchment and inserted in individual chambers called *batim* inside the *tefillin shel rosh*, the leather box worn on the head.

Tefillin are wrapped tightly around the arm, hand, and middle finger.
(Courtesy of Hank Arkin)

In antiquity, *tefillin* were probably considered an amulet of sorts. One of the translations you'll find for *tefillin* is *phylacteries,* a name that suggests they provided protection. Originally, it was the custom for Jewish men to wear *tefillin* throughout the day, but eventually the practice was limited to morning prayers only.

Because wearing *tefillin* is a *mitzvah* that has to be performed by a specific time in the day, women are traditionally exempt from the obligation to wear them. However, many women in both Orthodox and more liberal communities have made the commitment to wear *tefillin* during their daily prayers.

Tefillin's Meaning

Tefillin are rich with symbolism. As a ritual object, they literally bind the *Torah* to the human body, affirming our commitment and steadfast devotion to God's *mitzvot*. They are a physical reminder of our obligation to live according to the moral code revealed in God's *Torah*.

The *tefillin* also forge a symbolic link that unites our mind, our hearts, and our hands. The idea here is that, in binding ourselves to the *Torah,* we are aligning our hearts and minds with our actions in service of God.

I like to think of *tefillin* as a kind of spiritual antennae—putting them on each day helps us tune in to God's frequency and helps us connect in a tangible way to the divine presence in our lives.

Buying and Caring for *Tefillin*

Purchasing a pair of *tefillin* is a major commitment. They are handmade using expensive materials and can cost more than $1,000 for a very high-quality pair. The more ornate the script and the thicker the leather, the higher the cost. This is an investment that also needs to be maintained well, because if they fall into disrepair, *tefillin* are no longer considered kosher or fit for ritual use. You might have an older pair that has been passed down from a relative—perhaps your father or grandfather received them as a *bar mitzvah* gift. You can take older *tefillin* sets to a scribe to have them checked out, to see if all the texts are still intact. Small fixes can be repaired easily, but in many cases, it's worth it to invest in a new pair.

Tefillin are two leather boxes that contain handwritten passages from the Hebrew Bible. They are bound to the arm and the head with long leather straps.
(Photo by Mordechai Meiri/Shutterstock.com)

How to Put on *Tefillin*

Some call it "wrapping *tefillin*," and others say "laying *tefillin*." But no matter how you describe it, putting on *tefillin* can feel extremely awkward at first. As with any new ritual practice, as you grow into it, it will become second nature.

If you're interested in trying out a pair of *tefillin*, find someone to help you get started. Getting the knots right and wrapping the straps correctly can be a challenge if you're working on your own. It's particularly tough to juggle your *tallit,* the prayer book, and the *tefillin* straps. It helps to have a friend or teacher there to guide you until you can put them on independently.

Here are some basic instructions to help you understand what's involved in wrapping *tefillin*. When the time comes for you to try a pair for yourself, I recommend finding someone to work with you. If you don't have access to a mentor, some great instructional videos are accessible online. You'll find a few good links in Appendix B.

When it comes to wrapping the *tefillin,* there are subtle differences in custom. Some Jews have the practice of wrapping clockwise, some counterclockwise. Some wrap just once around the upper arm, some three times. Some have a slightly different custom when it comes to the finger wrap. However, in spite of these variations, the basic practice is the same for all Jews. It's up to you to figure out what feels comfortable and, most important, what feels meaningful.

Here's how it works:

First, you place the *tefillin shel yad* on your weaker arm right on the peak of your bicep and tighten the strap so it fits snugly. Then angle the box in so it points toward your heart, and recite the following blessing:

> Praised are You, *Adonai* our God, Sovereign of the Universe, whose *mitzvot* add holiness to our life and who gave us the *mitzvah* to put on *tefillin.*

> *Barukh Atah Adoanai Eloheinu, Melech Ha-Olam, asher kid'shanu b'mitzvotav v'tzeevanu l'ha-nee-akh t'fillin.*

Then wrap the leather strap three times around your upper arm, seven times around your forearm, and once around your hand to hold it in place. The straps should be tight enough that they leave a subtle mark on your skin, but not so tight that they cut off your circulation.

Then place the *tefillin shel rosh* on your head, with the box pointing straight out at your hairline. The strap should go around the back of your head, and the straps should hang down on each side of your neck.

Then recite the following blessing:

> Praised are You, *Adonai* our God, Sovereign of the Universe whose *mitzvot* add holiness to our life and who gave us the *mitzvah* of *tefillin.* Praised be God's glorious sovereignty throughout all time.

> *Barukh Atah Adoanai Eloheinu, Melech Ha-Olam, asher kid'shanu b'mitzvotav v'tzeevanu al mitzvat t'fillin. Barukh shem k'vod malkhuto l'olam va-ed.*

After that, the strap is wound three times around your middle finger—once in the upper part of the finger above the knuckle, once in the lower part of the finger, and once between the two. As you wind around the finger, recite:

> Thus says *Adonai:* I will betroth you to Me forever.
> I will betroth you with righteousness, with justice,
> with love and with compassion. I will betroth you
> to Me with faithfulness, and you shall love the Lord.
> (Hosea 2:21–22)

> *V'ayrastikh lee l'olam, v'ayrastikh li b'tzedek,*
> *u-v'meeshpaht, u-v'hesed, u-v'rahamim, v'ayrastikh li*
> *be-emunah v'yada-at et Adonai.*

The marriage symbolism in this final gesture is quite striking. When we put on our *tefillin,* we affirm that our commitment to God and the *Torah* is like a marriage. It is an everlasting bond. What a profound sentiment! The fact that Jews have been putting on *tefillin* in this manner for so many centuries truly speaks to the power of this ancient practice.

Essential Takeaways

- A *kipah* or a *yarmulke* serves as a reminder that God is above us at all times.
- Some traditional women cover their hair as a sign of modesty.
- Modesty in dress can be a meaningful way of expressing Jewish piety.
- A *tallit* is a prayer shawl that aids concentration. *Tzitzit* are attached to each corner and serve as a reminder of the *mitzvot.*
- *Tefillin* are ritual objects that literally bind the *Torah* to our bodies.

Part 3

The Practice of Prayer

Jewish prayer is time sensitive. It encourages us to mark the passage of time with awareness and gratitude. With subtle changes to the rhythm of the liturgy that differentiates morning from evening, Sabbath from weekday, and spring holidays from fall holidays, Jewish prayer teaches us to approach the calendar with mindfulness and connects us to the intricate cycles of the natural world.

I think this is one of the more remarkable aspects of Jewish wisdom. In the 1950s, the great thinker Abraham Joshua Heschel said, "Judaism is a religion of time, aiming at the sanctification of time." Could this message be any more relevant than it is right now? We never seem to have enough time—but the cycle of Jewish prayer tells us to slow down, be in the present, and appreciate the uniqueness of each particular moment.

The chapters in Part 3 take you through Judaism's most important prayers. Each chapter focuses on a particular time frame. I start by looking at the way prayer structures the passing of a single day. After that, I explain how prayer changes each week during the Sabbath. From there, I examine the rhythm of a year as we go over the central prayers of the most important Jewish holidays. Finally, I look at life as a whole by reviewing some of the important prayers that accompany life's milestones. At every step, I help you understand what the most important prayers mean.

chapter 9

The Rhythm of Daily Prayer

The set times for daily prayers

Waking up to prayer

Affirming belief in one God in the *Shema*

What the most central daily prayers are all about

In everyday life, we all have rituals that help us move through the day. Think of your morning workout, your first cup of coffee, a lunch date with a friend, an afternoon break to take a quick look at the news, etc. These short breaks punctuate your day, give you a sense of routine, and mark the passage of time from morning, to afternoon, to evening. Before you know it, it's time to start all over again the next day!

In Judaism, prayer sets a pace for your day. There are specific prayers to recite the moment you wake up in the morning and others to say just before you go to sleep at night. In between, the cycle of daily Jewish prayer gives you the opportunity to take a step back and be in the moment. It's your time to make yourself aware of time.

The fixed times of daily prayer actually hearken to ancient Israelite religion, when sacrifices were offered three times daily in the Temple. Long after the Temple and priesthood disappeared, the rabbis established prayer as a means to connect with God in place of those sacrifices. The three main services are *shaharit* (morning), *mincha* (afternoon), and *ma'ariv* (evening).

In this chapter, we spend some time reviewing the meaning of these central prayers in the daily liturgy. I go over the basic structure of the services, highlight some key passages, and give you a sense of what the cycle of the day looks like through the lens of prayer.

The Gift of Awakening

Even the simple act of waking up each day is cause for celebration in Jewish tradition. The ancient rabbis established special blessings to welcome the dawn because they didn't take awakening each day for granted.

In Jewish tradition, sleep is closely associated with death. In fact, the *Talmud* states that sleep is actually one sixtieth of death. After all, every night when we retire, there's no guarantee we'll wake up again the next day.

In the rabbis' imagination, sleep was a time of uncertainty, straddling life and death. Some authorities believed the soul actually ascends to the heavens each night while we rest and is returned to us each morning. In this sense, each morning we rise anew is like a mini-resurrection or rebirth.

After a night like that, greeting a new day is no small matter. Here are just a few exercises to help you wake up Jewishly each morning. The idea behind these practices is to rev your spiritual engine and focus your mind right away on the higher purpose of your existence.

As soon as you become conscious in the morning (right around the time you check the clock to be sure it's time to get up), it's time to recite *modeh ani*. This blessing is a prayer that thanks God for restoring your soul following a night of sleep:

> I am grateful to You, living, enduring Sovereign,
> for restoring my soul to me in compassion. You are
> faithful beyond measure.
>
> *Modeh ani l'fanekha, Melech khai v'kayam. She-*
> *heh-khe-zarta bee nishmatee, b'hemlah rabah*
> *emunatekha.*

This prayer, like many others throughout the morning blessings, emphasizes the interconnection of soul and body and expresses gratitude for the gift of life granted to us each day.

Orthodox Jews have the custom of washing their hands before they set their feet on the floor in the morning. This practice is called *negel vasser* (Yiddish for "nail washing"), or *netilat yadayim* in Hebrew ("elevating the hands"). According to the Code of Jewish Law, one should not walk more than 2 cubits before washing one's hands in the morning.

This practice has a number of different reasons behind it. Because night is linked to death, washing is a symbolic cleansing from impurities associated with death. And just as the priests washed before performing rites in the ancient Temple, it's customary to wash hands before prayer. Finally, because our hands might have had contact with intimate parts of the body, it's customary to cleanse them before engaging in prayer.

Here's how it works: before going to sleep at night, find a large basin or bowl and a cup that can hold about a pint of water. You can also purchase a special hand-washing cup designed for this ritual. Fill the cup with water, place it inside the basin, and set the whole thing underneath your bed within arm's reach. When you wake up in the morning, reach underneath your bed. Take the cup and pour water over your right hand and then your left, and repeat this pattern two more times. Then recite the blessing for washing:

> Praised are You, *Adonai* our God, Sovereign of the
> Universe, whose *mitzvot* add holiness to our life and
> who gave us the *mitzvah* to wash the hands ritually.
>
> *Barukh Atah Adoanai Eloheinu, Melech Ha-Olam,*
> *asher kid'shanu b'mitzvotav v'tzeevanu al n'teelat*
> *yadayim.*

Now, it's appropriate to attend to your bodily needs, like going to the bathroom, washing your face, or brushing your teeth. If you forget to wash right when you get out of bed, it's okay to wash up at the first possible moment. After that, it's time to get dressed and start your day!

Making the Mundane Meaningful

Because Jewish mysticism associates the right hand with kindness and the left hand with judgment, traditional Jews dress by clothing themselves right to left. This means putting on the right sleeve before the left and the right pants leg before the left. However, when it comes to tying the shoes, it's customary to tie the left shoe first, as a reminder that *tefillin* are (generally) worn on the left arm.

Giving Thanks

Ideally, you'll want to move right from this wake-up ritual into your morning prayer routine. It's helpful to have a special place in your home for prayer, even if it's just a quiet spot in the corner of the living room. In Jewish tradition, we don't have altars in the home, but it can be nice to pray near a bookshelf containing a prayer book, a *chumash,* and other inspirational texts. If you pray wearing a head covering, *tallit,* or *tefillin,* you'll want to find a spot where you can keep these items handy.

Many Jews wait to eat breakfast until after they've finished their morning prayers. In fact, to maintain your focus each day, it's a great idea to avoid checking email, flipping on the morning news, or getting involved in a distracting conversation until you're finished with your prayers.

However, if your mornings are anything like mine, this is an ideal that may not seem all that realistic. As soon as I get up, it's a race to get my kids dressed, fed, and out the door. Only after my family has left for the day can I think about engaging in meaningful prayer.

It's so important to avoid holding yourself to unrealistic expectations. The key is to do what you can to give yourself some focused prayer time each morning. Maybe it would help you to get out of the house once a week to attend a morning *minyan.* Or perhaps you can wake up just a few minutes before the kids and have a moment of quiet meditation before the chaos begins. Take what you can from the practices I describe here. Bringing just a little bit of mindfulness into your morning routine helps fortify you for the day ahead.

Grateful for the Gift of the Body

The morning blessings continue with the practice of putting on your *tallit* and your *tefillin*. (For more information about these practices, check out Chapter 8.)

The next set of blessings expresses gratitude to God for the miracle of the human body, without which, living a Jewish life filled with prayer and good deeds would not be possible:

> Praised are You, *Adonai* our God, Sovereign of the Universe, who with wisdom fashioned the human body, creating openings, arteries, glands, and organs, marvelous in structure, intricate in design. Should but one of them, by being blocked or opened, fail to function, it would be impossible to exist. Praised are You, Lord, healer of all flesh, who sustains our bodies in wondrous ways.

Torah Tip

In addition to its placement among the morning blessings, some Jews choose to recite the blessing of gratitude for the body every time they use the restroom, to give thanks for the intricate and intimate functioning of the human body that enables us to sustain life. I think it's just amazing that Judaism uses prayer to acknowledge the wonders of our biological makeup!

Next, we express gratitude for the gift of *Torah* by studying a brief passage from the Bible or the rabbinic canon.

Grateful for the Gift of the Soul

As a parallel to the prayer for the gift of the body, we also express thanks for the gift of our soul in a beautiful piece of liturgy that is among my favorites:

> The soul which You, my God, have given me is pure. You created it, You formed it, You breathed it into me: You keep body and soul together. One day You will take my soul from me, to restore it to me in life eternal. So long as this soul is within me,

> I acknowledge You, *Adonai* my God, my ancestors'
> God, Master of all creation, Sovereign of all souls.
> Praised are you, *Adonai,* who restores the soul to the
> lifeless, exhausted body.

Both before and after this blessing, take a moment to feel the divine breath pulse through you. When I meditate on this blessing, I like to think of the breath as energizing and life-giving. When I can say this prayer with proper intention and focus, it really helps me feel gratitude for the sacred gift of life.

In the remaining sections of the morning blessings, we give thanks for all the privileges of being alive—physical faculties, material comfort, and spiritual gifts.

These morning blessings were originally recited at home (and are still recited at home by many Jews, especially women). Today all these blessings also are included in the *siddur* as a prelude to the morning service and are recited communally in the synagogue. Regardless of where you say them, they're a beautiful way to transition into your day.

Psalms of Praise

If the blessings of the morning are your spiritual wake-up, then the next section of the morning prayer service, the Psalms of Praise (*P'sukei d'Zimra*), is your warm-up. Psalms of Praise is a collection of psalms and liturgical compositions that sing God's praises—literally. The Hebrew word *zimra* means "song," and the passages in this section were meant to be sung with gusto.

You know how your preworkout warm-up gets your heart pumping and your muscles limbered up? A warm-up is absolutely essential if you're going to challenge yourself physically. Well, it's also important if you're going to challenge yourself spiritually. The hymns in this section of the prayer service get your heart pumping and give your voice increased clarity.

Check out the lyrics to one of my favorites, excerpted from Psalm 33:

> Sing to *Adonai,* you righteous ones.
> It is fitting for the upright to praise God.
> Praise *Adonai* on the harp;
> Sing God songs with the ten-stringed lute.
> Sing to God a new song:
> Play sweetly with shouts of joy.
> For the word of *Adonai* holds true,
> And all God's deeds endure.
> God loves righteousness and justice;
> The earth is filled with God's love.

Like many of the psalms, this one is alive with the spirit of music. Ideally, your prayer during *P'sukei d'Zimra* should embody this spirit of joyous praise.

The "righteous" and "upright" mentioned in Psalm 33 refer to all who gather together to pray, not to a special, limited category of people.

—Rabbi Jules Harlow

If you're praying alone, choose one or two passages in this section to sing and focus on in your prayers. If you're comfortable singing out all by yourself, more power to you. If this is hard for you, try reciting the text quietly, hearing the melody in your head. Hum along or sway as you mouth the words.

If you're praying in a *minyan,* you have the advantage (hopefully) of a group of people to sing with. In public worship, the Psalms of Praise can be one of the most inspiring dimensions of the service if you're fortunate enough to have a prayer leader to draw you in.

The *Shema* and Its Blessings

If there's one prayer that's fundamental to Judaism, it's the *Shema*. The *Shema* affirms a Jew's belief in the unity of God. It is recited twice every single day, once in the morning and once at night. The *Shema* is supposed to be the last prayer a person recites before death, and there are many folktales about Jewish martyrs who have died with the *Shema* on their lips.

Because the *Shema* is so central, you don't just rush into it. A number of blessings lead up to and surround the recitation of the *Shema*.

First comes the formal call to prayer, known as the *Barechu*. This is a responsive prayer in which the prayer leader recites a blessing in praise of God and the congregation responds, acknowledging the presence of a community. Next are blessings that celebrate God as creator and as revealer of the *Torah*.

It is the dominant custom to recite the *Shema* from a seated position. If you wear a *tallit*, it is customary to gather together all the *tzitzit* in preparation for the *Shema*. This act symbolizes the hope that one day all Jews throughout the diaspora will be united as one people. Holding the *tzitzit* also helps you concentrate on the *mitzvot*. Before reciting the *Shema*, it is also customary to close your eyes and meditate on the idea of divine unity.

In its basic form, the *Shema* consists of two lines. The first is recited out loud:

> Hear, O Israel! *Adonai* Our God, *Adonai* is One.
>
> *Shema Yisrael! Adonai Eloheinu, Adonai Echad.*

The second line is recited silently among traditional communities and aloud in Reform and some Reconstructionist communities:

> Blessed is the one whose glorious Kingdom is eternal.
>
> *Baruch Shem Kavod Malchuto l'Olam va'Ed.*

The full *Shema* includes three biblical passages in the recitation, two from Deuteronomy and one from Numbers. As a whole, these passages focus on articulating a commitment to God's commandments and to teaching the *Torah* across the generations.

The most well-known passage is the first one, and it's usually recited aloud in congregational worship. I think it's extraordinary in the way it sets out a complete framework for what Jewish spirituality is meant to look like:

> Love *Adonai* your God with all your heart, with all
> your soul, with all your might. And these words
> which I command you this day you shall take
> to heart. You shall diligently teach them to your
> children. You shall recite them at home and away,
> morning and night. You shall bind them as a sign
> upon your hand, they shall be a reminder above your
> eyes, and you shall inscribe them upon the doorposts
> of your homes and upon your gates. (Deuteronomy
> 6:4–9)

Doorpost *Mezuzahs*

MISC.

A *mezuzah* is a small piece of parchment handwritten with this biblical passage from Deuteronomy. The parchment is inserted into a decorative case, and it's customary to post one on every doorway in a Jewish home, except for bathrooms. Some Jews post a *mezuzah* only on the front door to their home. It's a tradition to kiss the *mezuzah* whenever you pass one in a doorway. You touch your fingers to your lips, kiss your fingers, and then touch the *mezuzah.*

The *Shema* is the core affirmation of Jewish monotheism, and the paragraphs that follow it express a steadfast commitment to the terms of the biblical covenant. Notice the way the passage cited earlier places a high priority on teaching the next generation to value the *Torah*. This is one of the primary reasons education is such a core value in Jewish communities today. Teaching our children is a *mitzvah!* It's a divinely ordained biblical command!

If we want to be able to teach our children about the *Torah,* it's imperative that we educate ourselves as well. The *Shema* calls us all to prioritize the study of *Torah* so we can be sufficiently literate to pass on something meaningful to the next generation.

When you're praying on your own, try this exercise as a way to deepen your appreciation for the *Shema:*

- Prepare for the *Shema* as you normally would, with your eyes closed and *tzitzit* in your hands, if that's your practice.

- Take in a very deep breath, and let it out slowly.

- Take in another breath, and as you exhale, sing the word *Shema* very slowly, so the word lasts for your entire breath.

- Breathe in again, and sing the word *Yisrael* in the same way, taking the time to sing slowly and mindfully.

- Repeat this exercise with each of the words in the first line of the *Shema.* Try it with the second line, if you can.

Use this extended chanting of the *Shema* to focus on the idea of One-ness. Imagine you're connected in your breath to every living being, and the unity that unites you is God.

The Prayer: Silent Devotion and the *Amidah*

The high point of the morning service is the *Amidah,* or "standing prayer." The rabbinic sages called this compilation of blessings "The Prayer" because it represents the culmination of worship in any given service. It's also called the *shmoneh esrei* (*SHMO-neh ES-ray*), or "Eighteen Benedictions," because it contained that many blessings in its original form. Today, this prayer actually contains 19 blessings!

When we pray alone, we recite the blessings of the *Amidah* silently. While our prayer is silent, it's customary to move our lips as we mouth the words, in memory of Hannah, a figure from the book of 1 Samuel, who prayed her heart's desire in silence so intently that the high priest assumed she was drunk.

We stand for this prayer as a subject appearing before the divine throne. Some people recite this prayer in bare feet, and others believe it's important to wear shoes. Prayer begins with a series of bows that acknowledge your respect for and subservience to God.

The first words we utter are a plea to God that we can be open to genuine prayer:

> Eternal God, open my lips that my mouth may
> declare your Glory.
>
> *Adonai s'fatay tiftakh u-fee yageed t'heelatekha.*

The formal text then invokes the memory of the biblical patriarchs Abraham, Isaac, and Jacob as our spiritual ancestors. In more liberal communities, the biblical matriarchs are included, too. When I recite the *Amidah,* I like to imagine myself standing with a line of my own ancestors behind me, supporting me in my spiritual journey and making my existence possible today.

Although I can't trace my ancestry all the way back to Abraham and Sarah, I like to think back as far as I can. Sometimes I even include spiritual mentors who aren't part of my biological family, but who have influenced me and mentored me throughout my adult years. This is a powerful exercise that really brings the text of the prayer book to life for me.

The *Amidah* is the point in the prayer service where *keva* and *kavanah* meet. There's a script of blessings we're required to recite, but before concluding our prayers, we're able to offer the prayers of our hearts in a spontaneous moment of reflection. This is your private time with God to express your deepest longing and most passionate desire.

Transitional *Kaddishes*

MISC.

A *kaddish* is an Aramaic prayer that praises God with poetic and flowery language. There is a reader's *kaddish*, a half *kaddish*, a full *kaddish*, Rabbi's *Kaddish*, and mourner's *kaddish*. The principal role of the *kaddish* is to mark a transition from one part of the service to the next. I like to think of it as a tab on an index that helps you know when you're moving on to something new.

Afternoon and Evening

While the morning prayer service is the most elaborate, prayers in the afternoon and evening are also obligatory. These prayer services are often combined for the sake of convenience. Getting to a *minyan* three times each day would be very difficult to manage around a job and your many other responsibilities. It's hard enough gathering a *minyan* twice a day in many communities!

Most times of the year, then, the afternoon service is pushed as late as possible into the day so it can be recited just before sunset. After sunset, it's acceptable to move on to the evening service. In many communities, it's customary to study a traditional text during the window separating the afternoon and evening prayers.

Mincha

The afternoon service is called *mincha* in Hebrew. During the week, this is a brief service that starts with just one psalm and moves straight into the *Amidah*. It's followed by a number of other psalms and then a full *kaddish*.

On *Shabbat* afternoons, the *Torah* is read during *mincha,* which lengthens the service quite a bit.

Ma'ariv

Imagine what nighttime was like before electricity. If you've ever experienced the darkness of the deep woods or the desert, you know it's a darkness that's far more intense than what we experience in cities and suburbs when night falls. For the ancients, evening was an hour of uncertainty and of coming darkness. *Ma'ariv* is a special collection of prayers that brings comfort to the darkness.

Ma'ariv begins with a formal call to prayer and recitation of the *Shema.* Following the evening *Shema,* there's a special blessing to pray for a peaceful night:

> Help us, our Parent, to lie down in peace; and awaken us to life again, our Sovereign. Spread over us Your shelter of peace, guide us with Your good counsel. Save us because of Your mercy. Shield us from enemies and pestilence, from starvation, sword, and sorrow. Remove the evil forces that surround us, shelter us in the shadow of Your wings, You, O God, guard us and deliver us. You are a gracious and merciful Sovereign. Guard our coming and our going, grant us life and peace, now and always. Praised are You, *Adonai,* eternal guardian of Your people Israel.

The service continues with a third recitation of the *Amidah,* followed by a few hymns and a mourner's *kaddish.*

Bedtime

The theme of asking protection from the night continues in the prayers recited at bedtime. These prayers begin with a plea for restful sleep:

> Praised are You, *Adonai* Our God, Sovereign of the Universe, who brings sleep to my eyes, slumber to my eyelids. May it be your will, *Adonai* my God and God of my ancestors, that I lie down in peace and that I arise in peace. Let my sleep be undisturbed by troubling thoughts, bad dreams, and wicked schemes. May I have a night of tranquil slumber. May I awaken to the light of a new day, that my eyes may behold the splendor of Your light. Praised are You, *Adonai,* whose glory gives light to the entire world.

This prayer is followed by a full recitation of the *Shema,* accompanied by a number of other psalms that focus on peace.

I can't think of a more beautiful way to end the day. These bedtime prayers are among the first we teach to our children, to help them end their day with love and trust in God. And as the sun rises, the whole cycle takes place all over again!

Essential Takeaways

- Jewish daily prayer is structured around three main services: *shaharit* (morning), *mincha* (afternoon), and *ma'ariv* (evening).
- Services are modeled after the daily sacrifices that were offered in the ancient Temple.
- There are unique rituals to sanctify waking up each day and going to sleep each night.
- The *Shema* is one of the most important prayers in Judaism because it affirms belief in God's unity.
- The high point of every prayer service is the *Amidah,* also known as "The Prayer" or the "Eighteen Benedictions."

chapter 10

The Flavor of *Shabbat*

The origins and meaning of the Sabbath

How to prepare for the Sabbath at home

Prayers and rituals for the Sabbath table

Why *Shabbat* is not your average weekend

Shabbat (*shah-BAHT*) is one of Judaism's greatest gifts to Western civilization. Did you know the whole concept of a weekly day of rest comes from the Hebrew Bible? The command to "remember the Sabbath day and keep it holy" is one of the 10 commandments. It's among the most important principles set forth in the *Torah* as part of a framework for a healthy and just human society.

The Jewish Sabbath is welcomed at sundown on Friday evening and ends just after dark on Saturday night. For many Jews, *Shabbat* is a time to take a break from the activities that dictate our lives during the week: the carpool, the shopping, the phone, the email, the internet, the video games, and the TV. For others, it's a day for relaxing and focusing on home and family. Regardless of how you observe it, *Shabbat* is a time for being in the moment and a time to enjoy life free from the distractions that occupy you all week long.

The Sabbath is an essential component of Jewish spirituality. For Jews, *Shabbat* is much more than just a "day off." It's the very heart of Judaism. It's a day built around sacred practices and prayers that help us recharge both physically and spiritually. It's a day for connecting with our families, our communities, and God. In this chapter, you learn how *Shabbat* is observed according to Jewish custom, plus get a few tips on how you can bring a little *Shabbat* into your home each week.

A Sanctuary in Time

Imagine for just a minute what life would be like without a weekend. What would our society look like if we didn't have the opportunity to take a break from the demands of our working lives? If you've ever felt overworked, you know that when you don't get the rest you need, you suffer the consequences on so many levels.

For one, you become very tired physically. And when you're physically exhausted, the quality of your work isn't what it could be. This is true no matter what your profession. Whether you're a student, a corporate CEO, a factory worker, or a stay-at-home parent, you know you need to rest to perform at your best.

But overwork also has spiritual consequences. Without a moment to step off the treadmill of your busy life, it's so easy to lose sight of your greater purpose. What's your life all about, anyway? What are your priorities, your goals? Are you making any progress toward them? Who has time to consider such lofty questions when you're caught up in the daily grind?

Shabbat is a time when we not only rest our bodies, but also refresh our souls. In taking a break from the pressures of the week, we give ourselves the time to turn inward and assess where we are spiritually.

The meaning of the Sabbath is to celebrate time rather than space. Six days a week we live under the tyranny of things of space; on the Sabbath we try to become attuned to holiness in time. It is a day on which we are called upon to share in what is eternal in time, to turn from the results of creation to the mystery of creation; from the world of creation to the creation of the world.

—Abraham Joshua Heschel, *The Sabbath*

I find it remarkable that the *Torah,* an ancient law code authored so many thousands of years ago, acknowledges this basic human need for rest. How amazing to think that human beings living in biblical times had some of the same physical, emotional, and spiritual needs as we do in the twenty-first century!

And according to the *Torah,* not just human beings need structured rest. The creation of the Sabbath on the seventh day actually represents the high point of God's creative process. The *Torah* tells us that rest is integral to divine labor—the act of creation would not be complete without it. In observing *Shabbat,* we extend this cycle of work followed by rest to all beings.

Shabbat in the *Torah*

The institution of the Sabbath day has its origins in the Bible. It's a very ancient practice, although it's hard to know exactly how the Sabbath might have been observed in biblical times. Let's take a look at some of the key passages that explain where the idea of *Shabbat* came from.

The first mention of the Sabbath is found in the opening chapters of Genesis, when the seventh day is set apart as "holy":

> On the seventh day God finished the work that God
> had been doing, and God ceased on the seventh
> day from all the work that God had done. And
> God blessed the seventh day and declared it, "holy,"
> because on it God ceased from all the work of
> creation that God had done. (Genesis 2:1–3)

The seventh day is different from the six days that came before it. If the first six days are devoted to divine labor through which the world came into being, the seventh day is devoted to rest.

Later, in the book of Exodus, God commands the Israelites to remember the Sabbath and maintain its holiness by refraining from labor:

> Remember the Sabbath day and keep it holy. Six days you shall labor and do all your work, but the seventh day is a Sabbath of the Lord your God: you shall not do any work—you, your son or daughter, your male or female slave, or your cattle, or the stranger who is within your settlements. For in six days the Lord made heaven and earth and sea and all that is in them, and God rested on the seventh day; therefore *Adonai* blessed the Sabbath day and made it holy. (Exodus 20:8–11)

Shabbat is a day for remembering the act of divine rest by doing it, not just thinking about it. Imagine what a revolutionary social practice it must have been to give slaves and animals a complete rest from work on one full day each week! When we imitate divine rest and extend that privilege to those who work in our midst, we help create a world that's more peaceful and more just.

This idea is also found in another biblical passage from the Book of Deuteronomy. Here the command to keep the Sabbath day is linked to the memory of the Israelites' experience of slavery:

> Observe the Sabbath day and keep it holy, as *Adonai* your God has commanded you. Six days you shall labor and do all your work, but the seventh day is a Sabbath of *Adonai,* your God; you shall not do any work—you, your son or your daughter, your male or female slave, your ox or your ass, or any of your cattle, or the stranger in your settlements, so that your male and female slave may rest as you do. Remember that you were a slave in the land of Egypt and *Adonai* your God freed you from there with a mighty hand and an outstretched arm; therefore *Adonai* your God has commanded you to observe the Sabbath day. (Deuteronomy 5:12–15)

So observing the Sabbath day is not just a personal practice, but a communal one. It's not just about a lot of laws, rules, and prohibitions, but also about promoting a society that values both freedom and commitment.

Shabbat is integral to Jewish spirituality because it helps frame the way we live our lives. As human beings, we must labor in order to live. *Shabbat* comes as a reminder, though, that our lives are not just about labor and productivity. To live a life filled with holiness, we must maintain a healthy balance between work and rest as we strive for material comfort, so there's also room for our spirit to thrive.

The Sabbath as a Day of Rest

What does it mean to practice rest in a way that sets the Sabbath apart and makes the day a holy, spiritual experience?

The rabbinic commentaries on the *Torah* contain extensive discussions about the kinds of work prohibited on the Sabbath. There's no way for me to cover it thoroughly here, but in this section, I give you a thorough overview of what's involved in making *Shabbat* a meaningful day of rest, according to traditional authorities.

Observing *Shabbat* is a lifestyle. If you want to start living it, it's important to start small and build gradually. It's also important to keep in mind that the rules of keeping *Shabbat* sound more complicated on paper than they are in practice. With a little preparation, it's actually very simple to make *Shabbat* a part of your spiritual life.

Defining Sabbath Rest

In American culture, a day off is a day free from the responsibilities of work. You might use your day off to run errands, go on an outing with the family, or check out the big game on TV with your friends.

In Jewish tradition, *Shabbat* is observed quite differently. This is because the concepts of "work" and "rest" are understood in ways that depart radically from the way we think of them in mainstream American society.

Because *Shabbat* is first mentioned in the opening chapter of Genesis, it's tied very closely to the theme of creation. So many of the prayers recited over the course of the Sabbath emphasize God's delight in the created universe and celebrate its beauty. On *Shabbat,* we are to reassess and realign our relationship with the natural world. Therefore, according to the ancient rabbis, "work" is defined as any activity that alters nature in any way.

The *Torah* suggests that our experience of *Shabbat* should mirror God's rest described in Genesis. In trying to understand what this idea could mean, the ancient rabbis drew an analogy between God's creation of the universe and the tabernacle that the Israelites built in the wilderness. In their mind, the tabernacle, which was a dwelling place for God, was like a microcosm of the universe.

Now, here's where it gets a little complicated. Drawing on this parallel between the tabernacle and the cosmos, the rabbis identified 39 types of labor that were used in the construction of the tabernacle and deemed that they should be avoided on the Sabbath. These include carrying (in a public place), burning, extinguishing, writing, erasing, cooking, washing, sewing, tearing, knotting, planting, harvesting, weaving, and unraveling. Today these prohibitions extend to activities like driving, using electricity, and engaging in commerce.

The ultimate goal on *Shabbat* is to let the world be—to reduce our impact on the environment in concrete ways by avoiding activities that change the natural world. Engaging in Sabbath rest means disengaging from tasks that demonstrate our mastery over nature. In a word, *Shabbat* is not your typical weekend.

The Sabbath Unplugged

So how does a person in today's world go about observing *Shabbat?* In contemporary times, as they have throughout the ages, Jews view *Shabbat* as a day to "unplug" and be in the present moment. The prohibition against work as defined by the rabbis restricts us from doing many mundane activities. *Shabbat* is a day when there's no driving, no cooking, no cleaning, no laundry, and no shopping. It's a day when we don't answer the phone, text our friends, or spend hours checking email.

On *Shabbat,* we put away the latest technologies of social networking and spend time with friends and family the old-fashioned way. We talk and learn from each other face to face. We enjoy festive meals together. We don't rush off to the mall, the game, or ballet class; instead, take time for things we never seem to fit in during a busy week.

Although technology has made our lives easier in so many ways, *Shabbat* reminds us that we're not chained to our cell phones and our computers. I spend so many hours a day staring at a computer screen or driving my kids around in the car. Although it's hard to do without these conveniences sometimes, I'm grateful for the freedom *Shabbat* brings me. Taking a break on *Shabbat* reminds me that I can control my relationship to technology; it doesn't control me 24 hours a day, 7 days a week.

Shabbat can be hard for families with young children. How can you keep your kids busy without the TV, computer, or electronic gaming console to occupy their time? Aren't they (and you) going crazy by the end of *Shabbat?*

It does take some getting used to, but there are so many benefits to setting aside one day a week for your kids to unplug. On *Shabbat,* Jewish kids get a chance to discover alternative sources of entertainment.

Encourage your children to curl up with a great book or magazine, or set them up with a board game, a 5,000-piece puzzle, or a deck of cards. Let them play outside or come up with a "show" for the adults. Better yet, sit down with them and play a board game that takes hours to finish. Having lots of family playtime is one of *Shabbat's* greatest payoffs.

A great way to introduce *Shabbat* into your life is to try to unplug for 25 hours and see how it feels to live without those distractions. You'll be amazed at how liberating the experience can be. At first, choose just one technology—the phone, the computer, the gaming console, the TV, or the car—and add more over time. Think of it not as a period of deprivation, but rather as a gift of freedom you give yourself each week.

The Sabbath as a Taste of World Peace

Shabbat is also a time to put aside arguments or concerns that distract you from celebrating the day. In our house, as soon as I light the *Shabbat* candles, I let go of all the stress of the week. If the kids are fighting or I'm upset about something, the glow of the *Shabbat* candles washes it all away. On *Shabbat*, I try to let go of the small annoyances that stress me out, and instead focus on feeling grateful for all the gifts I'm fortunate to enjoy.

Shabbat Shalom

Shabbat Shalom! This is the customary way to greet someone on the Sabbath. It literally means "Sabbath peace." *Shalom* means "peace" and is used on its own to say both "Hello" and "Good-bye." *Shalom* comes from a root meaning "whole" or "complete." *Shabbat Shalom* expresses the hope that your *Shabbat* will be peaceful and bring you complete rest.

The ancient rabbis talked about *Shabbat* as a "taste of the messianic era" because, on it, we act as if the world is perfect and complete. We bring peace to our homes; enjoy bountiful, festive meals; and are sustained without engaging in labor or commerce. If you've ever wondered about the Jewish idea of heaven, *Shabbat* gives you a glimpse of what it's all about!

Preparation Is Everything

Preparation for *Shabbat* is probably the most important aspect of the day. To be truly free from the cares and concerns of the week, you must take time prior to *Shabbat* to be sure you're in a proper frame of mind.

In fact, the Sabbath liturgy talks about welcoming *Shabbat* each week as a bride or a queen. Think about how you'd prepare to welcome royalty into your home. You'd want the house to be spotless, the table to be perfect, your clothes to be special, and the food to be plentiful. That's pretty much the way we prepare to greet the "*Shabbat* Queen." When *Shabbat* arrives, we want everything to be just right.

Many Jews prepare for *Shabbat* by cleaning the house thoroughly and getting the table set long before guests arrive. Even if you aren't having guests or making an elaborate meal, it's a good idea to locate all the things you will need for your *Shabbat* celebration at home and ensure you have all the necessary ritual items at hand.

Because it's customary to refrain from cooking on the Sabbath, observant Jews prepare their food for *Shabbat* before sundown on Friday evening. This doesn't mean it's necessary to consume cold food on the Sabbath. On the contrary, it's common to have elaborate, hot meals for both Friday night dinner and Saturday lunch.

Traditional Jews keep their food warm on hotplates, in slow cookers, or on a very low setting in the oven. Long-cooking stews and casseroles are often served on *Shabbat* because they remain tasty when heated overnight.

Kindling *Shabbat* Lights

On Friday evening, candles are typically lit at home, although some communities have the custom of lighting them in the synagogue as well. Traditionally, it's an obligation for women to light candles on Friday evening, welcoming the light of *Shabbat* into the home. If no women are present, the men must light them.

Torah Tip

Shabbat candles are lit no later than 18 minutes before sundown. Because sunset varies by geographical region, Jewish calendars often include candle-lighting times for major cities. To find candle-lighting times for your location, consult a Jewish calendar and choose the city closest to you. If you don't have a Jewish calendar, you can find candle-lighting times online. Or check your local newspaper's weather section, where sunrise and sunset times are listed. If sunset falls at 8:15, for example, light the candles at 7:57.

Two candles are lit on *Shabbat*. One is symbolic of the biblical command to "remember" the Sabbath day, and the other symbolizes the command to "observe" the Sabbath day. Some families light additional candles for each child in the household, so a family with three children might light five candles altogether—the two standard candles, plus one for each child.

Here's how candle lighting works: set up your candles and candlesticks someplace where they'll be safe while lit. It's customary to leave the candlesticks in place until after *Shabbat* is over, so put them in a location that will work for 24 hours. It's nice to have them near the dining room so you can see them during the meal on Friday night.

Cover your head in preparation for reciting the blessing, if this is your custom. Light each candle with a match—don't use one candle to light the others. Slowly move your hands in a circular motion about 6 inches over the flames, as if you're bringing the candle's warm glow toward you and into the room. It's common to perform this gesture three times. When you've finished, place your hands over your eyes so you can't see the candles.

With your eyes covered, recite the blessing, either quietly to yourself or out loud:

> Praised are you, *Adonai,* Sovereign of the Universe, whose *mitzvot* add holiness to our lives, and who gave us the *mitzvah* to kindle *Shabbat* light.
>
> *Baruch ata Adonai Eloheinu, Melech Ha-Olam, asher kid'shanu b'mitzvotav, v'tzivanu le-hadlik ner shel Shabbat.*

With your eyes still covered, take a moment for personal reflection, and offer your own spontaneous words of prayer. Custom has it that women can request anything at all of God during these few sacred moments of private petition.

When you're ready, uncover your eyes, look at the glowing flames, and wish everyone around you *Shabbat Shalom* (peaceful Sabbath). It is now *Shabbat!* Give everyone celebrating with you a hug, kiss, or handshake, as appropriate!

There's a tradition that says as we welcome *Shabbat,* we are endowed with an additional "soul" that's with us only for the 24 hours of the Sabbath. This *neshama yeteira,* "extra soul," helps us live more fully, to enjoy *Shabbat* rest on a deeper level and bring us closer to God.

Blessings at the Table

The next step in welcoming *Shabbat* is a series of blessings recited at the table to sanctify the evening meal. This is one of the most special moments in the entire week, as we begin to celebrate as a family.

This meal traditionally takes place after sunset, after the Friday evening synagogue service. In the summer months, when the days are very long, it's not unusual for kids to fall asleep at the table! However, many families sometimes start well before the sun goes down so the kids can participate and still get to bed at a reasonable hour.

Family Blessings

If you're a parent, you can give each of your children a blessing on *Shabbat*. To do this, place your hands gently on top of your child's head and recite the appropriate blessing:

For girls:

> May God give you the blessings of Sarah, Rebecca, Rachel, and Leah.
>
> *Y'seemaykh Elohim k'Sarah, Rivkah, Rakhel v'Layah.*

For boys:

> May God give you the blessings of Ephraim and Menasseh.
>
> *Yesimcha Elohim ke-Ephrayi ve-keem'nasheh.*

For both boys and girls, continue with the priestly blessing:

> May *Adonai* bless you and guard you. May *Adonai* show you favor and be gracious to you. May *Adonai* show you kindness and grant you peace.
>
> *Yivarekhekha Adonai v'yishmerekha. Ya-air Adonai panav eylekha vee-khu-neka. Yisah Adonai panav eylekha v'yasem l'kha shalom.*

It's completely appropriate to follow the blessing with hugs and kisses and other displays of affection.

Next, some families sing a few traditional Hebrew songs. One is "*Shalom Aleichem*" ("Peace Unto You"), a song that welcomes the "angels of the Sabbath" to the table. Another, "*Eyshet Chayil*" ("Woman of Valor"), is adapted from Proverbs 31 and praises the skills of the woman who (presumably) prepared the Sabbath meal.

Wine and Bread

Following the family blessings, you're ready to begin the *Shabbat* meal. First, a special blessing is recited over a cup of wine. This blessing is called *Kiddush* (pronounced either *kee-DOOSH* or *KIH-dish*), and it begins with a passage from Genesis 1, describing God's creation of the Sabbath day.

Following *Kiddush,* you perform a ritual washing of the hands called *netilat yadayim*. In this ritual, you pass water over each hand back and forth a total of three times and then recite the hand-washing blessing noted in Chapter 9.

It's customary to refrain from speaking between the time you wash your hands and the blessing of the bread, although some people might sing or hum a tune to pass the time until everyone has finished washing their hands.

After everyone has washed, the host invites someone to say the blessing over the *challah* loaves, which is called *ha-motzi*. Lifting up the two loaves of *challah,* which symbolize the double portion of *mannah* God provided on *Shabbat* in the book of Exodus, you recite the blessing over bread:

> Praised are you, *Adonai* our God, Sovereign of the Universe, who brings forth bread from the earth.
>
> *Barukh Atah Adonai Eloheinu, Melech Ha-Olam, ha-motzee lekhem meen ha-aretz.*

You then take a bite of bread from the loaves, and the meal officially begins.

Spirituality Around the Sabbath Table

To say that food is an important element of *Shabbat* observance is really an understatement. For many Jews, the dining table is the very center of the *Shabbat* experience—even more important than what takes place at synagogue. *Shabbat* meals represent a time to celebrate with family, when no one is rushing off to take a phone call, head to the movies, or shop at the mall. It's a time to invite guests to your home and enjoy the richness of the day.

Whether you pull out all the stops and serve on your finest china or bring in a pizza for a more informal feel, taking the time to eat together with family and friends on *Shabbat* can be really grounding and a wonderful way to end a busy week.

Hospitality

Hakhnasat Orchim (*hakh-nah-SOT oor-KHIM*) is a *mitzvah* that means "hospitality." Welcoming guests into homes is an important value in Jewish culture. Hosting guests gives you the opportunity to provide the kindness of comfort to a visitor, which is a spiritual virtue in Jewish tradition.

Shabbat is a great time to invite guests to your home. While it's nice to invite guests in advance, it's also a special *mitzvah* to provide hospitality to a stranger or traveler. If you visit a synagogue for *Shabbat,* don't be surprised if you get invited to someone's home for a meal afterward! If you do get invited, don't be shy. You should go! Accepting the invitation is a great way for you to see how others observe *Shabbat* and learn about practices you can incorporate into your own. Plus, you give your host the opportunity to perform this important *mitzvah.*

MISC.

Three Meals

Three festive meals are eaten over the course of *Shabbat,* and each has its own unique atmosphere. Friday night is the most formal meal and includes a number of special rituals for welcoming *Shabbat* at home. Saturday afternoon lunch is the second meal. It's also a big meal but is a bit less formal than Friday evening's—and is usually followed by a nap. Saturday evening, there's a *seudah shleesheet,* or "third meal," that typically includes light fare like salads and fruit.

Words of the *Torah*

A tradition of the ancient rabbinic sages says that whenever three people eat together at a table, words of the *Torah* should be spoken. On *Shabbat,* it's customary for someone to share a *d'var Torah,* a short, informal teaching related to the biblical passage being read in synagogue that week.

Anyone can give a *d'var Torah*. At our house, we often ask our children to share something they might have learned from the *Torah* at school that week. It's also nice to invite guests to present a brief teaching—perhaps something they learned in synagogue that morning from the rabbi's sermon, or something they might have come up with on their own.

The point is that the Sabbath table should be infused with the spirit of *Torah*. Sometimes when we gather for meals on the Sabbath, it's hard not to revert to talking about matters related to work and worldly concerns. Reserving some time for studying even at the table can help preserve the atmosphere of the day.

Songs at the Table

The idea of the dinner table as a formal setting—where conversation is quiet and polite, and where children are seen but not heard—doesn't apply to a traditional *Shabbat* meal.

Because the table symbolizes the altar in the ancient Temple, Jewish festive meals are often accompanied by robust singing and praying. On *Shabbat*, in particular, it is customary to sing *z'mirot*, Hebrew songs that praise and thank God for the gift of *Shabbat*. You can find the text of traditional songs, usually with English translation and transliteration of the Hebrew, in small books called *bentchers* (from the Yiddish for "blessing") or *shironim* (from the Hebrew for "songbook").

Although it varies by community, in many homes, it's entirely appropriate to bang on the table to keep the beat as you sing. Children sometimes stay up way past their bedtimes and naptimes to participate in singing at the table. For them, it's the most enjoyable part of the day.

Torah Tip

To host a traditional *Shabbat* meal, you'll need two candles, two candlesticks, matches (for Friday night), wine or grape juice for *kiddush*, two loaves of *challah*, a napkin or cloth to cover the *challah*, *kipot* for anyone who wants to wear one, and *bentchers/shironim*. (You can make your own if you don't own any.) A traditional Ashkenazic meal often includes an appetizer of fish and salad, soup, *kugel* (a type of potato or noodle casserole), and roast chicken. But it's also okay to stay within your culinary comfort zone!

Singing at the table is a way of expressing the joyous nature of *Shabbat*. It helps draw out your time together at the table—after all, what else is there to do but spend time together?

The final song sung at any festive meal is the *birkat ha-mazon,* a lengthy series of blessings that follow a full meal. These blessings are often sung out loud to joyous melodies, and everyone at the table participates.

What Happens on Saturday?

After a restful night's sleep, the festivities continue on *Shabbat* morning. It is customary to have a very light breakfast before heading to synagogue for *shaharit* services, where the *Torah* is read and the rabbi delivers a sermon. If you live within walking distance of the synagogue, it's customary to walk because, traditionally, driving isn't permitted. However, rest assured that lots of people do drive to synagogue on Saturday, since not everyone lives close enough to walk. In more liberal congregations, driving is actually the norm.

After services, there might be a light snack at synagogue. If a special occasion is being celebrated, you might find a more formal lunch served for the congregation.

Returning home after synagogue, many families serve a large, festive meal, with some of the same blessings that were recited on Friday night. At *Shabbat* lunch, a special *kiddush* is recited over wine, and it's customary to say the *motzee* over two fresh loaves of *challah.* The *Shabbat* lunch menu might consist of leftovers from the Friday night meal or other dishes that have been kept warm overnight.

The meal concludes with still more singing, plus another round of the traditional *birkat ha-mazon* (Grace After Meals). After lunch, it's customary to take a nice, long nap; curl up with a book; or play a quiet game with the kids.

The Third Meal and *Havdalah*

As the sun wanes, it's time for yet another festive *Shabbat* meal. This one, known as *seudat shleesheet,* or "the third meal," is typically very light but still has a relaxed and festive atmosphere as we prepare to bring *Shabbat* to a close with the ritual of *havdalah.* It's been a long, restful *Shabbat,* but now it's time to transition back into weekday mode.

Havdalah is a special ceremony that helps us say good-bye to the Sabbath just after sundown on Saturday evening. *Havdalah,* which literally means "separation," is a way of saying good-bye to a guest you really enjoyed having around. When *Shabbat* departs, we need to transition back to "reality." After the spiritual high we experienced on *Shabbat, havdalah* appeals to all our senses to help console us as *Shabbat* drifts away, our "additional soul" departs, and we slip back into our weekday lives.

Havdalah uses wine, fragrant spices, and the warm flame of a multiwicked candle to ease us back into the week. It's customary to dim the lights and gather close as we recite the appropriate blessings. As we mark the end of the *Shabbat, havdalah* concludes with the following blessing:

> Praised are You, *Adonai* our God, Sovereign of
> the Universe, who has endowed all creation with
> distinctive qualities, distinguishing between sacred
> and secular time, between light and darkness,
> between the people Israel and others, between the
> seventh day and the six working days of the week.
> Praised are you, *Adonai,* who distinguishes between
> sacred and secular time.

Essential Takeaways

- The Sabbath is a day of complete rest celebrated every week from sundown on Friday evening through sunset Saturday night.
- Observing *Shabbat* is one of the 10 commandments and is among the most important holy days in Jewish tradition.
- Labor that transforms the natural world in any way is generally prohibited on *Shabbat,* including cooking, tearing, planting, or carrying things outside the home.
- Food plays an important role in the enjoyment of the Sabbath because the day is about nurturing both the body and the spirit.
- *Havdalah* is a ceremony to mark the conclusion of the Sabbath and includes blessings over wine, spices, and fire.

chapter 11

Days of Awe: The High Holy Days

The High Holy Days of *Rosh HaShanah* and *Yom Kippur* are two of the most sacred days in the Jewish calendar. They occur in the Hebrew month of *Tishrei* (*TISH-ray*) and are celebrated just 10 days apart. Each holiday is observed individually, and each has its own unique meaning. But taken together, these two central holy days are the centerpiece of a season devoted to intense introspection and emotional spiritual work. These are the *Yamim Noraim*—the Days of Awe.

Preparations for the Days of Awe actually begin a full month before *Rosh HaShanah,* the Jewish New Year's Day. The Hebrew month of *Elul* (*EH-lool*), which immediately precedes *Tishrei,* is dedicated to a process of personal repentance, called *teshuvah,* which prepares us to make the most of the holidays when they finally arrive.

Following the joyous festival of *Rosh HaShanah,* the season culminates with the solemn fast day of *Yom Kippur,* a day of personal and communal atonement. On *Yom Kippur,* we seek forgiveness for the ways in which we have fallen short during the past year, both as individuals and as a community. The process of *teshuvah* is one that aims to bring you closer to being the person you ultimately want to be.

A Spiritual Accounting

The *mahzor* (*makh-ZOOR*) is a special prayer book used only on the High Holy Days. It contains all the liturgy for *Rosh HaShanah* and *Yom Kippur,* which is quite extensive and differs substantially from the *siddur* used during the rest of the year.

The prayers in the *mahzor,* which were composed over many, many centuries, use the metaphor of a divine courtroom to communicate the solemnity of the season. Each year during this time, we appear in synagogue before God, the ultimate judge of our actions. We plead our own case and beg for forgiveness. This season encourages us to take stock of our lives and take responsibility for our actions over the past year. And it's a season in which we do our best to bring about necessary change in our lives.

Teshuvah is a Hebrew word meaning "repentance." It can also mean "turning," "returning," or even "answer" (as in responding to a question). The connection is simple: when we truly regret our transgressions and do *teshuvah,* we turn away from our negative behaviors and turn toward the divine presence. It's as if we're answering to the divine call to come closer to God.

Jewish tradition says we can seek forgiveness from God only for transgressions we've committed against God. If we've wronged individuals in our lives—family, friends, or co-workers—we must seek forgiveness from them directly. Part of preparing for the High Holy Days is taking time to repair the relationships in our own lives before we come to synagogue to heal our relationship with God.

The Call of the *Shofar*

The Hebrew month of *Elul* is dedicated to the work of preparing your soul for the experience of the High Holy Days. This month is the prelude to the Days of Awe.

Beginning on the first of the month, an ancient instrument called a *shofar* is sounded each morning in synagogue during the daily *minyan.* A *shofar* is crafted from an actual ram's horn, and it plays a very significant role in the synagogue rituals performed on *Rosh HaShanah.*

The daily blast of the *shofar* during the month of *Elul* is a piercing, primal sound that serves as a wake-up call. When we hear the familiar note of the *shofar,* we're reminded that the high holidays are approaching! It's time to start getting ready! Will you be prepared?

Elul as a Month of Preparation

If you had a real date to appear in a court of law, you probably wouldn't show up unprepared. You'd have a lawyer who would help you make your case, and between the two of you, you would have done the necessary background work to mount your best defense.

Well, when the High Holy Days come around, we want to be prepared spiritually. We want to stand before God's heavenly court and our community, having made the best possible effort at a thorough spiritual accounting.

Even if the dramatic metaphor of God as a sovereign judge doesn't move you, this season of deep reflection can be very powerful on a personal level. The high holidays are a time for being real—for facing up to our shortcomings and making a commitment to doing better next year. It's a time to let go of any illusions of perfectionism we might have about ourselves and take a hard look in the mirror.

If you have lingering bad feelings about something that happened between you and a friend or a family member, *Elul* is the time to approach that person and seek forgiveness and reconciliation, prior to the upcoming holidays. If you have a personal trait you really want to overcome, this is the time to start taking concrete steps toward change.

In our family, a night or so before the holidays begin, we all sit down and seek forgiveness for any wrongs we may have committed against one another. We invite siblings to apologize to one another and to accept one another's apologies. It's usually a time filled with tears and frowning faces, but getting things out on the table helps us all move into the high holiday season with a clear conscience.

Elul is also a time for studying the liturgy of the High Holy Days. Walking into services "cold" on the high holidays can be really intimidating because the prayers are so different from what we read all year long. It helps to take a little time to read through the *mahzor* or to read some of the many inspirational books out there on the spirituality of the season.

One of the most powerful prayers recited throughout the High Holy Days is a hymn called "*Avinu Malkeinu,*" or "Our Father, Our King." The prayer uses the traditional image of God as a parent as we offer our supplications:

> *Avinu Malkeinu,* have mercy on us, answer us, for our deeds are insufficient; deal with us charitably and lovingly, and redeem us.

> *Avinu Malkeinu, honaynu va'anaynu, kee ayn banu ma'aseem; assay eemanu tzedakah v'hesed, v'hoshee-aynu.*

Even if you don't connect to the idea of God as a literal father figure, you can still find profound meaning in this prayer. Try to locate that feeling deep inside yourself when you felt the unconditional love of a caregiver. Know that you can turn to God in this moment to bare your soul and beg for forgiveness, and you will be loved no matter how severe your transgressions.

The medieval Jewish mystics wrote that the Hebrew word *Elul* can be read as an acronym for *Ani L'Dodi V'Dodi Li,* a line from the biblical love poem Song of Songs that means "I am my beloved's and my beloved is mine." They understood the month of *Elul* as comparable to a courtship. Just as we can renew our love for a beloved, so we can return to God even after having strayed from the path of righteousness.

To make the High Holy Days more meaningful this year, make a list of the friends and acquaintances you've had a conflict with in the past year. Write each one a short note to express your feelings and get out any lingering negativity you might have about the situation. You don't have to send the letters, but they might inspire you to make a coffee date to clear the air.

Also consider going to synagogue for morning *minyan* at least one weekday during the month of *Elul* to hear the call of the *shofar* in person. If you can't get to a *minyan,* find a *shofar* blast online and play it every morning. It's not the same as hearing it live, but it can still work!

You could also jot down a list of your immediate goals. Where do you see yourself a year from now? Figure out what it's going to take for you to achieve those goals, or even just one of them. Do you have to make any big changes to actualize your vision for yourself?

Jewish Ideas About Sin and Repentance

Judaism does not believe in the concept of original sin. According to Jewish tradition, human beings are born essentially good with the power to make choices.

Sometimes the choices we make bring us closer to God, as in when we choose to follow the *Torah's mitzvot.* Sometimes, however, our choices can push us farther away from God. Judaism understands that no human being is perfect—everyone makes choices that aren't always the most virtuous. This is part of being human, and it's important to accept this reality.

Free will is given to every human being. If we wish to incline ourselves toward goodness and the path of righteousness, we are free to do so; and if we wish to incline ourselves toward evil, we are also free to do that. We learn in the *Torah* (Genesis 3:22) that the human species, with its awareness of good and evil, is unique among earth's creatures. Of our own accord, with our intelligence and understanding, we can distinguish between good and evil, doing as we choose. Nothing holds us back from making the choice. The power is in our hands.

—Maimonides, *Mishneh Torah, Hilkot T'shuvah*

No matter how great the transgression, forgiveness is possible. The daily liturgy includes a simple prayer for forgiveness that is recited as part of the weekday *Amidah*. Each day, we have an opportunity to seek God's forgiveness for our transgressions.

Judaism does not require any intermediary, like a priest or pastor, to absolve us of our transgressions. We pray directly to God for forgiveness and hope that our prayer is genuine and meaningful enough of an experience that it brings about the desired change in us.

The High Holy Days are a time when our entire focus turns toward the process of repentance. Instead of just one prayer in the *Amidah*, the liturgy includes pages and pages of confessional prayers and petitions we can use to seek forgiveness and ask God for the strength to bring real change and real growth to our lives.

Rosh HaShanah: The Jewish New Year

Rosh HaShanah literally means the "Head of the Year." This festival marks the day the entire world was born, for before God created the universe, time itself did not exist. *Rosh HaShanah* is thus the "birthday of the world." It's a time for reflection, for joyful celebration, and for making resolutions toward change. The festival is traditionally celebrated for two full days, although some liberal communities celebrate only one day.

Rosh HaShanah is also known as *Yom ha-Zikaron,* or the Day of Remembrance, because on it, we ask God to remember us. We acknowledge that, as finite, mortal human beings, we don't at all compare to the grandeur of the Divine. Nonetheless, on this day, we ask that God consider our prayers and bless us with life for the coming year. According to Jewish tradition, God inscribes our fate for the year ahead on *Rosh HaShanah* and seals that fate on *Yom Kippur,* 10 days later.

Special Prayers for *Rosh HaShanah*

In synagogue, the themes of remembrance and life are very prominent in the *Rosh HaShanah* liturgy. We pray to be inscribed in God's *Sefer ha-Chayim,* or "Book of Life," for a new year filled with health and happiness. This idea punctuates the liturgy in various places, but it's most dramatically pronounced in the *Amidah,* the central prayer in each service over the course of *Rosh HaShanah.*

In each *Amidah,* we add the following section to the introductory blessings:

> Remember us for life;
> Sovereign who delights in life;
> And inscribe us in the Book of Life
> For your sake, God of Life.
>
> *Zokhraynu l'hayim;*
> *Melech hafetz b'hayim;*
> *V'kotvaynu b'sefer ha-hayim*
> *L'ma-ancha, Elohim hayim.*

At the conclusion of the *Amidah,* we also add:

> May we and the entire House of Israel be called to
> mind and inscribed for life, blessing, sustenance, and
> peace in the Book of Life.
>
> *B'sayfer hayim berakha v'shalom, u'farnasah tovah.*
> *Nizakher v'nikatayv, l'fahnekha.*

Sandwiched in between the beginning and the end of the *Amidah* are some of the most special prayers in the high holiday liturgy. After the introductory blessings of the *Amidah,* the ark is opened and we recite the *U'netaneh tokef,* a prayer that affirms the sacred power of the day. Here are a few excerpts to give you a sense of its majestic tone:

> Let us speak of the sacred power of this day—
> profound and awe-inspiring. On it, Your sovereignty
> is celebrated, and your throne, from which You rule
> in truth, is established with love. Truly, You are Judge
> and Prosecutor, Expert and Witness, completing the
> indictment, bringing the case and enumerating the
> counts. You recall all that is forgotten, and will pen
> the book of remembrance, which speaks for itself,
> for our own hands have signed the page. The great
> *shofar* will be sounded and the still small voice will
> be heard … on *Rosh HaShanah* it is written, and on
> the Fast of the Day of Atonement, it is sealed.
>
> How many will pass on, and how many will be born;
> Who will live and who will die;
> Who will live a long life and who will come to an
>   untimely end …
> But repentance, prayer, and charity have the power
>   to transform the harshness of our destiny.

This last line is one of the most significant statements in Jewish liturgy. The quality of our *teshuvah,* the intensity of our prayer, and the depth of our generosity can help make up for our transgressions and soften God's decree on this day. This concept really gets to the heart of Jewish theology. Forgiveness is always available to us, and change is always possible when we express our genuine desire to become closer to God through prayer and good deeds.

This motif continues in three special sections added to the *Musaf Amidah*. These prayers, which are completely unique to *Rosh HaShanah,* are devoted to three basic themes: God's sovereignty, God's capacity to remember us, and the power of the *shofar* to awaken our hearts and souls.

While reciting the prayers that celebrate God's sovereignty, the prayer leader makes a full prostration before the ark. The rabbi or cantor kneels all the way to the floor and then stretches out so he or she is lying completely face down as the prayers are sung.

I find this gesture of submission to be a very powerful and moving affirmation of God's sovereignty in the world. Usually, we hold our leaders up high on a pedestal and look up to them. In this prayer, the leader puts aside her or his appearance of power and, with humility, acknowledges that God is the supreme power in the universe.

The *Shofar* Service

Another highlight of *Rosh HaShanah* services is the ritual blowing of the *shofar*. On the morning of the festival, after the *Torah* has been read, the *shofar* is blown as an announcement that the New Year is upon us. The sound of the *shofar* today is the same as it was in antiquity. Its blast gives us just a small glimpse of what worship in the ancient Temple might have sounded like, in part.

Sounding the *Shofar*

If *Rosh HaShanah* falls on *Shabbat,* the *shofar* is not sounded. However, since *Rosh HaShanah* is usually celebrated for two days, you can still hear the *shofar* on the second day of the holiday.

The *shofar* is sounded according to a specific pattern of notes, alternating short, staccato blasts with longer, more soulful ones. It's customary for the prayer leader to call out the pattern and for the *shofar* blower to blow according to that pattern. The final note in the series of *shofar* blasts is held as long as the person blowing can sustain his or her breath.

Although the *Torah* commands us to blow the *shofar,* it became a rabbinic custom that everyone is required to hear the *shofar.* Listening to its piercing sound, our hearts and souls are awakened to repentance.

Tashlikh: Casting Away Our Sins

Another unique *Rosh HaShanah* practice is the symbolic casting away of our sins through the ritual of *tashlikh* (*TASH-leekh;* literally, "sending away"). *Tashlikh* takes place on the first day of *Rosh HaShanah,* or if the first day is *Shabbat,* it's performed on the second day.

The ritual is performed near a body of water, like a river, stream, or lake. It's the custom to bring small crusts of bread and throw them into the water as a symbolic "casting off" of our sins. A collection of prayers that focus on forgiveness is recited both before and after bread is thrown into the water.

Many meanings are attached to *tashlikh.* Some say that just as the bread we throw will nourish the fish in the lake, so our transgressions should ultimately turn us toward some good. In some communities, *tashlikh* is a time when Jews from different communities gather near a local body of water to perform the rite. In this case, the water, in receiving our sins, symbolically unites differences across the Jewish community.

Symbolic Foods

Rosh HaShanah wouldn't be the same without certain symbolic foods that are essential to the celebration of this holiday. By eating foods that are sweet, we symbolize our hopes for a sweet new year. The most common symbol of *Rosh HaShanah* sweetness is an apple dipped in honey. On *Rosh HaShanah* eve, we dip a small piece of apple in honey and recite the following blessing:

> May it be your will, Our God, and God of our
> ancestors, that we be renewed for a good and sweet
> New Year.
>
> *Y'hee ratzon mee-l'fanekha, Adonai Eloheinu v'elohey
> avoteinu she'tichadeish aleinu shanah tovah um'tukah.*

We also use food to inaugurate the New Year by trying fruits or foods that have recently come into season. There's even a special blessing to recite when it's the first time we've tasted these foods this year. Some families also include a whole fish, head and all, on the *Rosh HaShanah* table to symbolize the "head" of the year.

It's also customary to eat loaves of *challah* that are braided in a circular pattern. The round loaves symbolize the circle of life. Some people like to put raisins in the *challah* during this season as another symbol of sweetness. And if that's not sweet enough, during the entire High Holy Day season, you can dip the *challah* into honey before reciting the blessing over the bread at each holiday meal.

MISC.

High Holiday Greetings

Here are some customary greetings for the high holiday season: *L'Shanah Tova* (*Le'shah-NAH to-VAH*), which means "for a good year"; *L'Shanah Tovah u'Metukah* (*Le'shah-NAH to-VAH oo-meh-too-KAH*), or "for a good and sweet year"; *L'Shanah Tovah Tikateyvu* (*Le'shah-NAH to-VAH tih-kah-TAY-voo*), or "May you be inscribed for a good year"; and *G'mar Hatimah Tovah* (*ge-MAHR hah-tee-MAH to-VAH*), which means "May your fate be sealed in the Book of Life this year."

Festive meals on *Rosh HaShanah* are similar to meals on *Shabbat,* in that they're abundant and characterized by a joyous mood. Candles are lit on the eve of each night of the festival, and family often travels far and wide to be together during this special time.

Yom Kippur

Yom Kippur, the Day of Atonement, is the holiest day in the entire Jewish calendar. All the introspection and hard, spiritual work you've done during the Days of Awe culminate in this one, solemn day of fasting and prayer. Many Jews wear white on *Yom Kippur* to symbolize purity and renewal. Even Jews who don't practice Judaism all year round often observe *Yom Kippur* in some regard.

Yom Kippur is known as the Sabbath of Sabbaths—the ultimate *Shabbat*. It's a day of complete rest, but it's not celebrated with joyful feasting like a regular *Shabbat*. By contrast, *Yom Kippur* is observed with fasting and abstinence from physical pleasures for a full 25 hours.

Why fast on *Yom Kippur?* The *Torah* instructs that the Day of Atonement shall be a time for us to "afflict our souls." (Numbers 29:7) The ancient rabbis interpreted this command to prohibit eating and drinking, bathing, and intimate physical contact with one's spouse. It's also customary to refrain from certain luxuries, like wearing cosmetics, using perfumes and creams, and wearing leather shoes.

Dressing in white and depriving ourselves of physical pleasures on *Yom Kippur* are practices that, in the ancient rabbis' imagination, symbolize death. For 25 hours, in an effort to go as deep as possible into the process of *teshuvah,* we imagine that this is our very last day on Earth—our last day to acknowledge our shortcomings and become the person we truly want to be. The discipline of fasting and physical deprivation is meant to help us get there.

Although it's a solemn and serious day, there's also a joyful element to *Yom Kippur*. The liturgy for the holiday is filled with images of God as merciful and compassionate. God's steadfast love for humanity overrides divine judgment, and this is cause for joyous celebration. Legend has it that on *Yom Kippur,* the gates of heaven are wide open, ready to accept our prayer offerings.

This intense day of prayer and fasting is your last chance to get real, to search your soul, and to make amends. The good news is, of course, that our lives are not over on this day. At the conclusion of *Yom Kippur,* as the heavenly gates close for another year, we move back into our ordinary lives. As we eat, drink, and resume physical enjoyment, hopefully we are spiritually and emotionally transformed for the better.

Kol Nidre

Yom Kippur services begin in the evening with a special ceremony called *Kol Nidre (kohl need-RAY)*. The service begins at synagogue before sunset. It's customary to eat a substantial meal before arriving, since this service marks the start of the 25-hour fast.

Kol Nidre means "all our vows." Its liturgy consists of a very ancient, legalistic formula that negates any personal vows we might make to God during the coming year. The idea is that we won't be held accountable in the event that we don't fulfill our promises to God. The prayers are recited before an open ark in the sanctuary. Often three individuals stand before the congregation, each holding a *Torah* scroll. These three individuals are symbolic of a *beit din,* a Jewish court of law. We then say:

> By the authority of the court on high and by the
> authority of this court below, with divine consent
> and with the consent of this congregation, we
> grant permission to pray with those who have
> transgressed.

This statement affirms our coming together as a community in order to make atonement for our transgressions together, as a community. The central liturgy of *Kol Nidre* is then recited three times:

> All vows, renunciations, bans, oaths, formulas of
> obligations, pledges, and promises that we vow
> or promise to ourselves and to God from this
> *Yom Kippur* to the next—may it approach us for
> good—we hereby retract. May they all be undone,
> repealed, canceled, voided, annulled, and regarded
> as neither valid nor binding. Our vows shall not
> be considered vows, our renunciations shall not be
> considered renunciations, and our promises shall not
> be considered promises.

Chanting a legal release in Aramaic may seem like a strange way to start the most sacred holy day in the Jewish year. But *Kol Nidre* has deep significance in Jewish history, and many people find its haunting melody and ancient words very moving and inspiring. The mood that's established at *Kol Nidre* sets the tone for the entire 25 hours to come. While we're still engaged in personal reflection and spiritual accounting, on *Yom Kippur,* we offer collective confessions on behalf of the entire community.

During the Inquisition, when many Jews were forced to convert to Christianity, this prayer was especially powerful. It released even those Jews who had renounced Judaism to remain part of the Jewish community, if only in secret.

Confessional Prayers

Unlike other Jewish holidays, *Yom Kippur* is observed with five distinct prayer services over the course of the day, instead of four. The evening *ma'ariv* service begins with *Kol Nidre* at sunset the night before. In the morning, the traditional *shaharit* and *musaf* services take place on every *Shabbat* and holiday. In the afternoon, there's a *mincha* service, during which the biblical Book of Jonah is read. And in the evening, another *ma'ariv* service brings the day to its close. But on *Yom Kippur,* we add one additional service, called *Neilah* (*neh-ee-LAH*), which means "closing the gates."

The distinguishing feature of each one of these services on *Yom Kippur* is the addition of extensive confessional prayers called *selichot* (*slee-KHOAT*). We appeal to God's capacity for mercy and forgiveness through prayers that praise God's compassion:

> *Adonai, Adonai,* God, merciful and compassionate,
> patient, abounding in love and faithfulness, assuring
> love for thousands of generations, forgiving iniquity,
> transgression and sin, and granting pardon.
> (Exodus 34:6)

We then recite a litany of sins, in the collective "we" form. Some Jews make a fist and gently strike their heart as a gesture of repentance while naming each transgression. If you don't like the idea of beating your breast out of regret, you can also think of it as a gentle knocking on the door to your heart, coaxing it to open in genuine prayer.

We first recite the confessions silently, then together, out loud, as a community:

> We abuse, we betray, we are cruel, we destroy, we
> embitter, we falsify, we gossip, we hate, we insult,
> we jeer, we kill, we lie, we mock, we neglect, we
> oppress, we pervert, we quarrel, we rebel, we steal,
> we transgress, we are unkind, we are violent, we are
> wicked, we are extremists, we yearn to do evil, we are
> zealous for bad causes.

This is one of several lists of sins included in the *Yom Kippur* prayers. Each list is composed as an alphabetical acrostic—an A-to-Z litany of transgressions against God.

When I first started to attend *Yom Kippur* services in college, I thought the idea was to go through the long list of transgressions and choose the sins I had personally committed. Why should I repent for an act I'm not guilty of? I came to learn that while the confessional prayer is deeply personal, it's not just about me.

We confess our sins collectively because we are all responsible for each other. On *Yom Kippur,* we atone for our sins as a community and on behalf of humanity as a whole. As we conclude the longest list of transgressions, we pray for collective forgiveness:

> For all these sins, forgiving God, forgive us, pardon
> us, grant us atonement.

Yizkor: The Memorial Prayer

Since *Yom Kippur* causes us to reflect on our own mortality, it's a fitting time to remember those loved ones we've lost. On *Yom Kippur* morning, we recite a brief memorial service. Sometimes the service includes time for meditation or guided visualization to help you connect to the memories of those who have passed on.

If your parents are still living, some authorities believe it's proper to leave the room during *Yizkor,* since the service includes prayers for parents who have died. But in some communities, it's customary for everyone to stay and offer prayers for friends, distant relatives, or even soldiers and martyrs who gave their lives for the Jewish people.

When you recite *Yizkor,* you add the specific names of the loved ones you're remembering to this standard prayer:

> May God remember the soul of my loved ones who have gone to their eternal home. In loving testimony to their lives, I pledge charity to help perpetuate the ideals important to them. Through such deeds, and through prayer and remembrance, may their souls be bound up in the bond of life. May I prove myself worthy of the many gifts with which they blessed me. May these moments of meditation strengthen the ties that link me to their memory. May they rest in peace forever in God's presence. Amen.

Yizkor concludes with the Mourner's *Kaddish* and recitation of Psalm 23.

Yom Kippur is not your only opportunity to recite *Yizkor.* This service is also included in holiday services during Passover and *Shavuot.*

Essential Takeaways

- The Days of Awe are a time of personal transformation.
- Starting a full month before *Rosh HaShanah*, the blast of the *shofar* calls us to begin the process of *teshuvah*, or repentance.
- *Teshuvah* requires that we assess where we are spiritually so we can move into the High Holy Days with a better idea of the person we want to become.
- Prayer services on *Rosh HaShanah* and *Yom Kippur* are both joyful and solemn. The liturgy takes us on an emotional and spiritual journey that forces us to acknowledge our limitations but also see our true potential for change.

chapter 12

Prayers for Jewish Festivals

Celebrating freedom on Passover

Experiencing revelation on *Shavuot*

Sukkot and the joy of simplicity

Why *Hanukkah* is not the Jewish Christmas

The Jewish calendar has a distinctive rhythm. Each season is defined by unique celebrations that help us move through the passage of time in a Jewish way. Jewish holidays link key moments in the history of the Jewish people to particular seasons of the year. The themes and motifs central to these historical moments translate into spiritual lessons that help us grow from year to year.

In ancient times, three of Judaism's seasonal festivals (Passover, *Shavuot,* and *Sukkot*) were directly linked to the agricultural cycle of the year and were celebrated with a seasonal rite of pilgrimage to the Temple in Jerusalem. Today these ancient Temple rituals have been transformed into practices we can perform both at home and in the synagogue.

In this chapter, I take you through some of the most important festivals in the Jewish calendar. I show you the basic themes of each holiday and help you find meaning in them throughout the year.

Three Pilgrimage Festivals

Passover, *Shavuot,* and *Sukkot* are known as the *shalosh regalim,* the "three feet," because they were once celebrated as pilgrimage festivals. Worshippers would journey on foot to the ancient Temple from far-off places in the Jewish diaspora. These festivals have a strong link to the cycle of the agricultural year. In fact, it's entirely possible that these holidays actually started out as agricultural festivals that later took on deeper meanings related specifically to Judaism and Jewish history.

Passover takes place during the spring and celebrates the spring themes of rebirth and renewal. *Shavuot* comes in early summer and celebrates the ancient barley harvest and the first fruits of spring planting. *Sukkot* arrives in early fall and draws on the theme of fall harvest and the blessing of four specific species of plants that grow in the land of Israel.

Although we don't practice sacrifice or pilgrimage today, these festivals help us appreciate the sacred uniqueness of each passing season and connect in a Jewish way to the rhythm of the natural world.

A beautiful collection of psalms is added to the daily liturgy on each of the three pilgrimage festivals. This collection of six psalms, composed in the time of King David, is called *Hallel,* which means "praise" in Hebrew. The recitation of *Hallel* is a high point of synagogue services during these three festivals. The melodies of *Hallel* are upbeat and joyful, sung with a "call and response" type of arrangement between the prayer leader and the congregation.

In my family, we often rush to synagogue to be sure we make it there in time to participate in *Hallel,* which is recited while standing, right after the *Amidah* in the *Shaharit* service. The beautiful Hebrew words capture the spirit of the festival as we celebrate God's wondrous powers and supreme goodness. Although many of the rituals for the three pilgrimage festivals are celebrated at home, the inclusion of *Hallel* in services is a great motivation to attend synagogue.

Here are a few of my favorite verses from *Hallel:*

> Praise *Adonai,* for God is good; God's love endures forever.
>
> Let the House of Israel declare: God's love endures forever. Let the House of Aaron declare: God's love endures forever. Let those who revere *Adonai* declare: God's love endures forever. In my distress I called to *Adonai;* God answered by setting me free ....
>
> Open for me the gates of triumph, that I may enter to praise *Adonai.* This is the gate of *Adonai,* the righteous shall enter therein. (from Psalm 118; *Siddur Sim Shalom*)

Passover

What does it mean to be truly free? This is the central question of Passover, an eight-day festival known also as the "time of our liberation" (*z'man heruteinu; z'MAHN hay-roo-TAY-nu*). As spring arrives and we experience the reawakening of the natural world after a long, dormant winter, we turn our attention to celebrating the season of liberation.

> In every generation it is incumbent upon us to see ourselves as one who personally went out from Egypt. As scripture says, "You shall tell your child on that day: 'It is because of what God did for me when I went out of Egypt.' (Exodus 13:8)" (from the Passover *Haggadah*)

One of the reasons I think Passover is such a popular holiday among Jews today is that its central message resonates so well with American democratic values. The biblical story of the Israelites' liberation from Egyptian bondage is the focal point of Passover, but it's a story that has universal relevance.

By telling this story from generation to generation, Jewish tradition celebrates God as liberator and champion of social justice. In fact, God's act of redemption during the time of the Exodus is a defining characteristic of God's relationship with the Israelites. The very first thing God reveals at Mt. Sinai is this:

> I am *Adonai,* Your God, Who brought you out of the
> land of Egypt.

The festival of Passover is an opportunity to consider what that really means.

Springtime and Renewal

Passover, coming as it does at the start of the springtime planting season, represents a second New Year's festival in the Jewish calendar. On the first day of Passover, a special prayer for dew is added to the *Musaf Amidah.* It reflects the idea that ample dew in its proper season is a blessing from God:

> Our God and God of our ancestors,
> Dew, precious dew, unto Your land forlorn,
> Pour out our blessing in Your exultation.
> To strengthen us with ample wine and corn,
> And give Your chosen city safe foundation in dew.

This special prayer is recited only once a year, chanted to a beautiful melody reserved only for the first day of Passover. Praying that the land will be wet with springtime dew reminds us of Passover's seasonal roots.

While *Rosh HaShanah,* the actual Jewish New Year, falls in the seventh month of the Hebrew calendar, Passover falls in the month of Nissan, which is actually the first month of the year. Passover isn't really a time for soul-searching or major resolutions, but it is a time for clearing away the old and making way for the new.

One of the basic customs of the Passover holiday is abstention from leavened bread for the entire eight days of the festival. This practice is linked to the story of the Exodus from Egypt. Because the Israelites had to flee in a hurry, there was no time to allow their bread to rise. As a result, today we eat the Passover meal with *matzah* (unleavened bread).

During Passover, we cleanse our homes of *chametz* (*kha-MAYTS*), the Hebrew term for all forms of leaven or leavened products. We clean every room thoroughly, making sure we remove crumbs out of every corner— including that cookie someone left in a coat pocket last fall.

We also clean out the cupboards and toss anything that's been there more than a year. The same goes for the fridge. Take old papers and magazines to the recycling center. And while you're at it, consider giving away all those old clothes piled up in the attic—someone in need could really use them.

MISC.

Spring Cleaning

The detailed cleaning we do in preparation for Passover is healthy for your home, but it's also healthy for your mind and your spirit. You'll be surprised at how a thorough spring cleaning can help you feel lighter, happier, and more open to spiritual renewal.

The room that gets the most attention at Passover time is the kitchen. Traditional Jews use a completely different set of dishes, pots and pans, and silverware during Passover so they don't eat with utensils that have ever made contact with *chametz.* A home that's "kosher for Passover"—meaning free of all *chametz*—might even cover the countertops with aluminum foil or plexiglass for the entire eight days.

So how does all this connect with the idea of freedom? From what I've written so far, you'd think preparing for Passover involves as much labor as the Israelites endured under Egyptian slavery! Can there really be a spiritual side to all these detailed preparations?

Indeed, all of Passover's seemingly mundane practices have deep, symbolic meanings. On a practical level, abstaining from bread and other forms of *chametz* challenges us to follow a more simplified diet. This means sticking to the basics, like fresh fruits, vegetables, and proteins, and avoiding pastas, crackers, and other processed foods that contain *chametz*.

Symbolically, food restrictions during the festival can be understood as a kind of spiritual discipline. Leaven is a symbol of arrogance. We purge our homes and our bodies of all the yeasty, leavened foods that "puff us up" all year long. The simplicity of the Passover diet and the humble nature of *matzah* represent the qualities of modesty and humility we want to embody.

The *Seder*

The first two nights of Passover are celebrated with a special meal called a *seder*. The *seder* is a very ancient ritual—we know that the *haggadah*, which serves as the script for the ritual, dates to early rabbinic times and has been embellished and modified over the centuries.

Definition

Seder literally means "order." It's a ritual meal that uses symbolic foods and a set script to remind us of the story of God's liberation of the Jews from Egyptian slavery. The text of the *seder* ritual is included in a book called the *haggadah*. Today many families adapt the model of the *seder* into a festive meal that celebrates other types of social freedoms, such as feminism, gay rights, and the struggle for the civil rights of African Americans.

The *seder* is an interactive ritual, driven by the questions of the youngest children present. Although the questions are scripted, they're meant to generate discussion and learning at the *seder* table. Children are an integral part of the *seder*. According to tradition, the youngest child at the table begins the whole discussion by asking the "Four Questions."

The Four Questions begin with the most basic question of all: "Why is this night different from all other nights?" In response, the adults begin to tell the story of the Israelites' exodus from Egypt. Through the story, everyone at the table relives this important biblical event and reflects on its significance to the present day. With four symbolic cups of wine, God's role as liberator is blessed and celebrated.

The *seder* plate is used to display the symbolic foods that are part of the *seder* ritual.

Passover is a perfect example of the emphasis Judaism places on educating the next generation. The *seder* table is festive and fun, usually set with fine china and delicious food. But it's also a child-friendly atmosphere. Many families use puppets and games to hold the children's interest as the ritual proceeds through the story.

The *seder* is also a time to practice hospitality. It's a *mitzvah* to invite guests to the *seder* table. In fact, there's one moment in the *seder* ritual when we symbolically invite all who are poor and hungry to come and share in our "bread of affliction" (*matzah*):

> This is the bread of poverty that our ancestors ate
> in the land of Egypt. Let all who are hungry come
> and eat. Let all who are in need come and share this
> Passover meal.

Passover is also a time to give charity—either gifts of food or financial contributions that might help the needy in other ways.

Shavuot

Fifty days after we commemorate the Exodus from Egypt at Passover, we celebrate *Shavuot* (*shah-voo-OAT*), a pilgrimage festival that celebrates the revelation of the *Torah* at Mount Sinai. The observances practiced on *Shavuot* emphasize a love of *Torah* and an affirmation of the importance of study at all ages.

Shavuot is celebrated with joyful synagogue services, which include *Hallel* and a reading of the biblical Book of Ruth, set during a harvest time. While the festival marks the experience of revelation back in biblical times, it also celebrates our ongoing engagement with *Torah*. In many communities, *Shavuot* is a time for celebrating milestones in our children's religious education.

In some communities, *Shavuot* includes a ceremony called "confirmation," in which a student who has continued her or his education for a number of years past the *bat/bar mitzvah* receives public honors. Confirmation is a bit like "graduation" from religious school.

But *Shavuot* isn't just for kids. It's also a time to affirm adult commitment to Jewish education. Medieval Jewish mystics developed the custom of staying up all night to study the *Torah* in a ritual called a *Tikkun Leyl Shavuot.* Today many synagogues organize lecturers and study sessions that last all night long (or close to it).

If you haven't pulled "an all-nighter" since you were in school, challenge yourself to attend a *Tikkun* sometime! It's truly a special experience to spend the night learning *Torah* and greet the dawn with the morning prayers at sunrise.

In terms of its agricultural roots, *Shavuot* celebrates the culmination of the grain harvest. In antiquity, the grain harvest lasted a period of seven weeks and began during the festival of Passover. *Shavuot* was celebrated with a temple ritual called *bikkurim,* which was an offering of the first fruits of the fields. In Temple times, the first fruits were brought from seven species named in Deuteronomy: wheat, barley, grapes, figs, pomegranates, olives, and dates.

MISC.

Between Passover and *Shavuot*

The period of seven weeks between Passover from *Shavuot* is called the *Omer. Omer* literally means "barley sheaf" and is named for the barley harvest. Beginning on the second night of Passover, we mark each day of the seven weeks as a "countdown" both to the end of the grain harvest and to the revelation of the *Torah* on *Shavuot.* When we anticipate a special event in our personal lives, we count the days until it's here. During the *Omer,* we eagerly mark the passage of time between the redemption celebrated on Passover and our experience of receiving the *Torah* at Sinai.

Although the origins of the practice aren't clear, it's become customary among some Jews to eat dairy products during *Shavuot.* The most convincing explanation I've heard is that the practice is based on a text from the biblical book Song of Songs, in which the *Torah* is metaphorically compared to milk. A typical holiday meal might include cheese blintzes, pasta, or perogies. Of course, cheesecake is the traditional dessert of choice!

Unfortunately, because *Shavuot* falls during the summer months, it's one of the least-observed Jewish festivals in the mainstream Jewish community. However, according to Jewish tradition, it's just as important a festival as Passover and *Sukkot!* The essence of *Shavuot* is to re-experience the wonder of revelation. Through the study of *Torah,* we reaffirm our acceptance of God's commandments on this very special festival.

Sukkot: The Time of Our Joy

Sukkot (*soo-COAT*), the Feast of Booths, is the third of the pilgrimage festivals. *Sukkot* is an autumn, harvest-themed holiday that, in a nutshell, celebrates the very important Jewish value of hospitality. The name *Sukkot* refers to temporary booths or dwellings we build outside our homes in the days just prior to the festival.

The celebration of Sukkot has its roots in the Bible:

> On the fifteenth day of the seventh month is the
> Festival of *Sukkot,* seven days for *Adonai* …. You will
> dwell in booths for seven days; all natives of Israel
> shall dwell in booths. (Leviticus 23:34–42)

Sukkot arrives just five days after *Yom Kippur,* on the fifteenth of the month of *Tishrei. Sukkot* is a breath of fresh air after the intensity of the *yamim noraim.* One of the reasons I look forward to *Sukkot* each year is that it's celebrated partly outdoors. After spending so much time inside synagogue during the High Holy Days, *Sukkot* brings us the opportunity to tap into Jewish spirituality in a way that's literally "outside the box."

Sukkot is also known in rabbinic sources as *z'man simchateinu,* the "time of our joy." Like Passover and *Shavuot,* it commemorates a biblical episode central to the history of the Jewish people. During *Sukkot,* we remember the Israelites' 40 years of wandering in the desert following the Exodus from Egypt.

You're probably thinking, *What's so joyous about wandering in the desert for 40 years?* Well, *Sukkot* is a holiday that remembers the fragility of existence during those long years of wandering, but at the same time, celebrates with great joy the protection God provided during that turbulent period.

Like the other pilgrimage festivals, *Sukkot* also is linked to the fall harvest and has a number of symbols that draw our attention to nature.

Building a *Sukkah*

One of the main observances of *Sukkot* is the construction of a temporary dwelling called a *sukkah*. A *sukkah* must have a minimum of three walls and be sturdy enough to withstand a strong wind. However, its roof, which must be made of natural materials like bamboo stalks or leafy tree branches, should provide only minimal protection. According to rabbinic custom, it should be constructed in a way that it keeps out a light rain but still provides a view of the stars.

The *sukkah* is a simple structure with a minimum of three walls and
a roof that provides modest protection from the elements.
(Courtesy of Marian Frankston)

Decorating the *sukkah* is a time to get creative.
(Courtesy of Marian Frankston)

I think the *sukkah* can be read as a powerful symbol of Judaism. Like the *sukkah*, Jewish tradition provides us with a framework of protection and shelter. But at the same time, this structure doesn't blind us to the larger world.

People who live in warm climates often choose to sleep and eat in the *sukkah* for the entire seven-day festival. Where sleeping out isn't practical, it's customary just to eat all your meals in the *sukkah* and then go back inside for the night.

MISC.

Sukkah Origins

Some biblical scholars think the practice of building a *sukkah* actually derived from the temporary field dwellings farm laborers lived in during the peak harvest season.

Hospitality

You've built a beautiful *sukkah* in your backyard. Now what? Interestingly enough, the central *mitzvah* of *Sukkot* is actually not to build a *sukkah*, but to sit in one. So here's where the fun begins.

Sukkot is a wonderful time to invite guests to your home. Even if you don't usually entertain, having friends over for an informal meal or even just dessert in the *sukkah* can be a lot of fun. And because the *sukkah* is, by definition, a modest dwelling place, you don't have to feel bad about not having that formal dining room!

One way to liven up your *sukkah* is to decorate it. This is a time to get creative, so choose a theme or a color scheme and go for it! Faux fall leaves, plastic fruit, and even tiny "Christmas" lights (when appropriate for outdoor use) can add beauty and warmth to your *sukkah* for a relatively small investment. Kids love to take part in decorating the *sukkah*. When mine make something really special, I laminate it so it can be used year after year.

In neighborhoods where many families build a *sukkah*, it's really special to "hop" from *sukkah* to *sukkah* to check out the different decorations and styles. Where I live, the Jewish community organizes a formal "*sukkah* hop" for children during one day of the holiday. The kids are given a list of homes in the area where they can stop in, have a bite to eat in the *sukkah*, and recite a special blessing.

Torah Tip

Use *Sukkot* as an opportunity to reflect on your openness to God's presence into your home. How do you open yourself to receiving the divine presence? In what ways do you block God from entering your home? *Sukkot* is a great time to consider these questions. When we build a *sukkah*, we certainly want it to be filled with guests. But we also want it to be filled with the holiness of the divine spirit.

While it's great to welcome friends and family into the *sukkah*, it's a kabbalistic tradition to welcome mystical guests as well. In a ritual known as welcoming the *Ushpizin* (*oosh-pee-ZEEN*, which means "guests" in Aramaic), seven biblical figures, one for each day of the holiday, are invited to share in the festivities.

Each figure is one of the founding fathers of the Jewish people, known as the "Seven Shepherds of Israel"—Abraham, Isaac, Jacob, Moses, Aaron, Joseph, and David—and each one represents a different virtue:

- Abraham represents love and kindness.

- Isaac represents restraint and personal strength.

- Jacob represents beauty and truth.

- Moses represents eternality and dominance through the *Torah*.

- Aaron represents empathy and receptivity to divine splendor.

- Joseph represents holiness and the spiritual foundation.

- David represents the establishment of the kingdom of heaven on Earth.

In recent years, it's also become a custom in some communities to welcome *Ushpizot*, the biblical matriarchs, into our *Sukkot*. There are different traditions about which seven women are invited, but the most common list includes the biblical matriarchs, Sarah, Rebecca, Rachel, and Leah, plus other celebrated biblical women like Esther, Ruth, Hannah, Deborah, and Miriam.

Finally, *Sukkot*, which is also called the "Feast of Tabernacles," is also a time when we welcome the divine presence into our midst. Just as the biblical tabernacle was a dwelling place for God, at *Sukkot*, we welcome the divine presence into our *sukkah* at every meal.

Four Species: The *Lulav* and *Etrog*

Another important ritual unique to *Sukkot* is the practice of waving four species of plants named in the *Torah* in four directions:

> And you shall take for yourselves on the first day, the fruit of the beautiful citron tree, tightly bound branches of date palms, the branch of the braided myrtle tree and willows of the brook, and you shall rejoice before *Adonai* your God for seven days. (Leviticus 23:40)

The green leaves are bundled together to form a *lulav* (*LOO-lav*, which is the Hebrew name for the palm branch) and then joined with the fruit of the citron tree, which is called an *etrog* (*EH-troag*). The ritual involves holding all four species together, reciting a special blessing, and shaking the branches together with the *etrog* in all four directions: in front, behind, above, and below.

The four species that make up the *lulav* and *etrog* are the palm branch, the willow, myrtle, and citron.

Bringing together the four species is a symbol of the unity of the Jewish people. Although there are many different kinds of Jews, this ritual reminds us that we are all one people.

Lulav and *Etrog*

MISC.

The practice of waving the *lulav* originated in ancient times and was part of the celebration of *Sukkot* in the Jerusalem Temple. As Jews spread out into the diaspora and lived far from lands where these plants grew, acquiring a *lulav* and *etrog* wasn't so simple. Sometimes entire communities had to share one set! Even today, a high-quality *lulav* and *etrog* can cost more than $50.

The ceremony of waving the four species can be done in synagogue or at home but is not performed on *Shabbat*. In synagogue, during the recitation of *Hallel*, special prayers for salvation, called *hoshannot*, are recited as all the congregants in attendance process around the sanctuary in a circle. On the last day of *Sukkot*, which is also called *hoshannah rabbah*, congregants process around the room seven times and then beat the willow branch on the ground until all its leaves have fallen off.

During the festival, worshippers process around the sanctuary carrying the *lulav* and *etrog* along with the *Torah*.
(Photo by Boris Diakovsky/Shutterstock.com)

The *hoshannot* are prayers that petition God for protection and favor. On *hoshannah rabbah,* the focus turns to prayers for rain. Each of the four species comes from plants that require a great deal of water to grow. So it's possible that this ritual, which takes place just at the onset of the rainy season in the land of Israel, was in part a prayer of hope for ample rain that would yield abundant crops.

You can see what I mean in this excerpt from the *hoshannot:*

> Save humanity and the animal kingdom, flesh, spirit, and soul; renew the earth and bless its produce. Send rain to nurture greenery; let cool waters flow. Sustain the world, our earth, suspended in space. Help us now!

Just as Passover includes a special prayer for dew in its proper season, during *Sukkot,* we recite a special prayer for rain—one that's recited only once a year. This prayer, called *geshem* (rain), includes a liturgical poem that links the biblical patriarchs Abraham, Isaac, Jacob, Moses, and Aaron with water. The poem concludes by saying:

> You are *Adonai,* who causes the wind to blow and the rain to fall.

Shemini Atzeret and Simchat Torah

The very last days of the *Sukkot* festival are actually two distinct holidays that finish out the festival season with a bang. *Shemini Atzeret* literally means the "eighth day of assembly." It's an extra day of rejoicing, meant to help the fun last just a little longer. If you've ever hosted a party that went by all too quickly, you can understand what *Shemini Atzeret* is all about— it's as if we don't want to let go of all the spiritual energy we've been able to experience throughout the *Sukkot* holiday.

The festivities finally culminate in the joyous celebration called *Simchat Torah,* which means "rejoicing in the *Torah.*" On this day, we complete the annual cycle of reading the *Torah* by reading the final verses in Deuteronomy 34 and then starting all over again with Genesis 1. This practice is a gesture to show that the process of reading the *Torah* is a cycle that never ends.

Simchat Torah celebrations often include festive dancing in the synagogue that extends into the streets. It's customary to take turns dancing with a *Torah* scroll as an expression of joy and love for these holy scriptures.

Simchat Torah celebrations are usually very family friendly because kids love to join in the dancing as the adults go wild. In my synagogue, the rabbi usually unrolls an entire *Torah* scroll, asking volunteers to hold up the parchment as the scroll stretches around the entire room. For me, this ritual is a high point of the year. I love to see the amazing calligraphy of an entire *Torah* scroll all at once!

Hanukkah: The Time for Miracles

Winter is the darkest time of the year. Our days end so early, and for those who live in colder climates, it's easy to spend a lot of time indoors. *Hanukkah* is a midwinter festival that lasts for eight days and comes to celebrate the miracle of light just when we need it the most.

Hanukkah literally means "dedication" and is named for the rededication of the Temple in Jerusalem, following the military victory of the Maccabees that took place back in the second century B.C.E.

Unlike the Days of Awe and the three pilgrimage festivals, *Hanukkah* is not biblical in origin. In fact, it seems that *Hanukkah* actually developed over time as a way for Jews throughout the diaspora to celebrate the Temple's rededication.

For most of its history, *Hanukkah* has been celebrated as a minor festival. There's no prohibition against work during *Hanukkah,* so synagogue services during the eight days are brief and take place early in the morning before folks head off to work.

In America, *Hanukkah* has become popular largely because of Christmas. But it's really important to understand that *Hanukkah* is not nearly as significant in the Jewish calendar as Christmas is in the Christian calendar. In fact, *Hanukkah* sometimes falls weeks before Christmas!

But just because *Hanukkah* is a relatively minor holiday doesn't mean it doesn't play an important spiritual role in Jewish life today. *Hanukkah* is a celebration of miracles—those moments when the impossible becomes a reality.

Lighting the *menorah* on *Hanukkah* is a special time for family.

The practice of lighting the *Hanukkah* candles in the *menorah* each night with friends and family is a way of bringing warmth into our homes to sustain us during those dark, cold winter nights. We celebrate at home by spinning the *dreidel,* exchanging gifts, and eating customary foods like potato pancakes and jelly donuts.

A **menorah** is a lamp stand that was used in the ancient Temple to kindle lights during festivals. A standard *menorah,* used throughout the year, had seven branches—three on each side and one in the center. The nine-branched candelabrum used during the festival of *Hanukkah* is technically called a *Hanukkiyah,* although many people also call it a *menorah.* A **dreidel,** also called a *s'vivon* in Hebrew, is a four-sided top. The Hebrew letters on each side are an acronym for the phrase "A Great Miracle Happened There." Playing *dreidel* is one of the highlights of *Hanukkah* for children. Each letter has a different value. You spin it, and the letter that's on top when it falls tells you whether you gain or lose *gelt,* the gold coins that usually have chocolate inside!

Remembering the heroic pride of the Maccabees inspires us to rededicate ourselves to our traditions and our beliefs. *Hanukkah* is also a time to celebrate miracles—both the big ones that take place once in a generation and the small ones that occur every day—as we recite a special blessing just for *Hanukkah:*

> Praised are You, *Adonai* our God, Sovereign of
> the Universe, who accomplishes miracles for our
> ancestors in ancient days, and in our time.
>
> *Barukh Atah Adonai Eloheinu, Melech Ha-Olam,*
> *sheh-asah neeseem l'avoteinu ba-yameem ha-heim*
> *u'va-z'man ha-zeh.*

Just as light comforts us in times of darkness, miracles have the capacity to brighten our world, even when we have come close to giving up all hope. Although small gifts are exchanged during the festival, the main themes of this holiday celebrate light, hope, and the historic dedication of the Jewish people to maintain our traditions.

Purim

The festival of *Purim* is a joyous holiday that comes on the cusp between winter's end and spring's beginning in the Hebrew month of *Adar. Purim* commemorates events described in the biblical Book of Esther, a heroic story of Jewish survival set in ancient Persia. Through her cunning and bravery, Queen Esther saved the Jewish people from destruction at the hands of the evil villain Haman.

In the story, Esther becomes the wife of the Persian king Ahasuerus after his first wife, Queen Vashti, is banished for insubordination. Esther assumes this honored role but hides her Jewish identity from the king.

When Haman, the king's top adviser, hatches a plan to murder all the Jews in the kingdom, Esther reveals her identity and saves her people. In a dramatic twist of plot, Haman and his 10 sons are hanged on the very gallows that had been constructed at Haman's command, originally intended for the Jews.

Purim is celebrated in a carnival-like atmosphere, with festive food, drink, and dancing. Just as Esther disguised her identity, on *Purim*, it's customary for children to wear costumes, often dressing up like the characters in the *Purim* story.

The playful spirit of *Purim* celebrates the reversals and twists of fate that typify the story. Rabbinic tradition actually holds that one should drink on *Purim* until you can't tell the difference between evil Haman and the heroic King Ahasuerus!

The Book of Esther is chanted aloud from a small scroll called a *megillah*. During the reading, the practice is to make lots of noise whenever Haman's name is read. The idea is to blot out his name by drowning it out with boos, jeers, and the sound of noisemakers called *groggers*. At *megillah* readings, things get loud!

Another *Purim* tradition is to give gifts of food to friends and family. Small packages of *shalakh manot* (*SHA-lakh MAH-note*), containing fruits, nuts, and candy, are delivered throughout the community. It's also customary to include *hamantashen,* a three-pointed cookie filled with fruit or poppy seeds, that's a symbol of the hat Haman wore.

Essential Takeaways

- The three festivals of Passover, *Shavuot,* and *Sukkot* are known as the *shalosh regalim,* or "three feet," because in ancient times, it was the custom to make a pilgrimage to the Jerusalem Temple.

- Passover is a spring festival that celebrates freedom and renewal through the story of the Jews' exodus from Egyptian bondage.

- *Shavuot* celebrates the revelation of the *Torah* at Mount Sinai, along with the first fruits of the spring harvest.

- *Sukkot* is celebrated by dwelling in a *sukkah,* a temporary booth that reminds us of the *mitzvot* of hospitality and humility.

- *Hanukkah* and *Purim* are festivals that entered Jewish tradition after the biblical period and don't carry any restrictions against work.

chapter 13

Prayers for Family Milestones

A blessing for every special occasion

Rituals for welcoming new life

Coming of age in the Jewish community

Blessings for marriage

Every culture celebrates rites of passage—those special events that mark the transition from one stage of life to the next. In American culture, ritual gatherings like graduations and baby showers celebrate important changes and accomplishments and help us feel connected to our families and our communities.

An essential aspect of Jewish tradition is the celebration of sacred, special moments through prayer and ritual. Throughout its long history, Jewish culture has developed many unique customs to mark important moments in the human lifecycle. Lots of these traditions are ancient, while some are relatively new. And because there's tremendous variation in Jewish practice, it can be quite challenging to make sense of all the details.

In the next two chapters, I explore the role prayer plays in lifecycle customs. Jewish prayer is like a spiritual compass that guides us through the course of our days, our weeks, and our years. And prayer is also there to help us cherish those unique moments in our lives that may be both joyous and mournful but are nonetheless sacred.

Celebrating the Present

From time to time in our lives, we experience moments we want to remember forever. Maybe it was the first time you held your child, the day you signed your first mortgage, or your first time winning a swim meet. The feelings of overwhelming joy, gratitude, satisfaction, pride, or even fear come in a fleeting rush, and before we know it, the moment is gone.

Experiences like these stop us in our tracks, but they are fleeting. It's so important to understand these moments in time as spiritual opportunities. When we pause to acknowledge them, we allow ourselves to feel our full range of emotions—to be fully and consciously in the present.

Judaism has a special blessing to mark these sacred moments in time. The *shehecheyanu* blessing is a short prayer that thanks God for enabling us to reach a particular moment in time. It's an expression of gratitude that helps us be fully "there" in a given moment and allows us to savor the experience a little longer.

When we want to express our gratitude for a particular experience, or acknowledge a "first," we say:

> Praised are You, *Adonai* our God, Sovereign of the Universe, who gives us life, sustains us, and has enabled us to arrive at this moment.

> *Barukh atah Adonai Eloheinu, Melech Ha-Olam, sheh-heh-khayanu v'kee-manu, v'heegeeyanu laz'man ha-zeh.*

I find that when I use this blessing to acknowledge a sacred or secular moment, it helps add an important spiritual dimension to my sense of accomplishment. *Shehecheyanu* can be used to sanctify Jewish "firsts," like your first time leading a *minyan* or reading from the *Torah*. But it can also be used for more mundane activities, like wearing a new garment, tasting a new food, or casting your first ballot.

There are many ways to use the *shehecheyanu* prayer to mark special occasions in your children's lives. Think of it as an opportunity to connect your Jewish values to any milestone or accomplishment, no matter how trivial. Not too long ago, my oldest daughter bought her first pair of "grown-up shoes" from the ladies' section. She was so excited, we stopped for a minute in the shoe store and recited the blessing together!

However you use it, this versatile blessing really comes in handy when you want to mark time in a way that acknowledges your Jewish spirituality.

Celebrating New Life

As we've seen, Judaism is a religious tradition that wholeheartedly affirms life. So many Jewish teachings emphasize the importance of transmitting our heritage from generation to generation. In fact, the very first command God presented to Adam and Eve when they were created was to "be fruitful and multiply"! (Genesis 1:28) So in a nutshell, having a baby is a big deal in Jewish culture.

The timing and type of celebration for a new Jewish baby depends on the sex of the child. Traditionally, baby boys are celebrated with a formal, communal ceremony known as a *bris* or *brit milah,* while baby girls are welcomed with different rituals, sometimes known as a *simchat bat* (*bat* rhymes with "hot") or "baby naming." Whereas the *bris* is an ancient rite celebrated on the eighth day of life, ceremonies for girls are much newer, take many different forms, and do not take place at a fixed time.

With every child, the world begins anew.

—Ancient Hebrew saying

In this section, I discuss the essential differences between these celebrations and help you understand the meaning behind them. But first, I think it's important to begin with what these ceremonies have in common.

Celebrations for both boys and girls are opportunities to gather with friends and relatives and rejoice in the awesome potential of a new life. These celebrations emphasize three key themes: Jewish peoplehood, divine covenant, and the bestowing of a Jewish name. Understanding these themes is essential to understanding what it means to celebrate new life in the Jewish community and why these practices continue to feel relevant today.

Jewish Peoplehood

Although there's tremendous cultural and religious diversity among Jews, we consider ourselves to be one "people." The Hebrew term for this concept is *k'lal yisrael,* which means "community of Israel," or *am yisrael,* which means "people of Israel."

An individual joins the Jewish people either through birth or through a process of formal conversion. When a child is born, she or he is welcomed into the Jewish people with prayers and rituals that celebrate and rejoice in this sense of belonging.

Divine Covenant

In religious terms, the Jewish people are a sacred community as well, engaged in an everlasting covenant with God. As discussed in Part 1, this idea of a divine covenant between God and the Jewish people has its roots in the Hebrew Bible. Ceremonies like *brit milah* and *simchat bat* are formal rites for welcoming babies into the eternal covenant between God and the Jewish people.

A Jewish Name

In Jewish culture, names are an important link to the past. Babies are sometimes named after biblical figures, carrying with them the rich stories and legends associated with those names. Ashkenazic Jews often give their children names of deceased relatives, extending the legacy of their loved ones into the future. Sephardic Jews, on the other hand, sometimes name their children after living relatives, according to a specific pattern of descent. Ceremonies welcoming a new baby into the community almost always include an announcement of the baby's Hebrew name.

This name will be used to celebrate important religious milestones in the child's life. When the child comes of age, he will be called to the *Torah* with his Hebrew name. When he marries, his Hebrew name will appear on the marriage contract. When he dies, his Hebrew name will appear on his tombstone. And perhaps some future relative will name a child after him.

Torah Tip

A Hebrew name uses a specific formula combining the child's name with the name of the father and/or the mother. For example: *Sarah bat Yosef* means "Sarah, daughter of Joseph." *Sarah bat Yosef v'Rachel* means "Sarah, daughter of Joseph and Rachel." *Yitzchak ben Avraham*, means "Isaac, son of Abraham." And *Yitzchak ben Avraham v'Rivka* means "Isaac, son of Abraham and Rebecca."

Brit Milah: Circumcision

A *bris* is an ancient Jewish practice that means "Covenant of Circumcision" and dates to the biblical story of Abraham. Abraham is commanded by God to circumcise himself and his son Isaac as a physical sign of their covenant with God. In exchange for Abraham's loyalty, God promises that he will be the progenitor of a great nation. In this respect, even in ancient times, circumcision was a ritual that was symbolically linked to fertility and kinship.

A *bris* typically takes place on the eighth day of a child's life, as prescribed in the *Torah*. A *bris* can take place on any day of the week, including the Sabbath, and can be postponed past the eighth day if the baby isn't deemed well enough to endure the procedure. Sometimes a hint of jaundice can be enough to postpone the *bris* for a week or two.

A *bris* can be performed anywhere. Many traditional Jews celebrate the *bris* during the early morning hours at synagogue, following morning prayers. When the eighth day falls on a weekend, many families are able to hold larger celebrations in their homes, at Jewish community centers, or even at restaurants or catering halls.

> **wisdom of the sages**
>
> You shall circumcise the flesh of your foreskin, and that shall be the sign of the covenant between Me and You. Throughout the generations, every male among you shall be circumcised at the age of eight days.
>
> —Genesis 17:11–12

It's customary to hold a joyous feast or *seudat mitzvah* (a meal to celebrate the completion of a sacred duty) following the *brit milah* ceremony. So wherever the event takes place, there's sure to be great food!

The *Mohel*

It may seem strange to you that a surgical procedure like circumcision, which in American culture is performed in a hospital by a licensed physician, could be the centerpiece of a religious ritual, performed in full view of family and friends. Whether it takes place in the hospital or in the synagogue, circumcision is the surgical removal of the foreskin from the newborn's penis.

In many cities, Jews who choose to have a religious circumcision must make a point of refusing circumcision in the hospital, where they're ordinarily done in the first 1 or 2 days of a baby's life. In America, hospital circumcisions are routine, but they don't fulfill the religious obligation to circumcise one's child.

A *brit milah* must be performed by a specialist known as a *Mohel* (rhymes with *oil*). A *Mohel* is trained in Jewish law to perform both the covenantal prayers (*brit*) and the circumcision procedure (*milah*).

Sometimes a *Mohel* is also ordained as a rabbi or a cantor, but this isn't necessarily the case. Many Jewish pediatricians, who are trained to perform the surgical aspects of circumcision, pursue Judaic training to become a *Mohel*. While a *Mohel* is traditionally a male figure, it's increasingly common in the liberal denominations of Judaism to encounter women in this role. A *Mohelet* is the term used to describe a woman trained to perform *brit milah*.

A Family Affair

The *Mohel* takes a lead role in a *bris*. As a "master of ceremonies," of sorts, the *Mohel* explains the rituals to the guests, recites the required prayers, and announces the baby's Hebrew name. A *bris* is an occasion to honor grandparents, relatives, and close friends with a role in the ceremony, so many couples choose to pass the baby from one relative to the next as he makes his "entrance" at the ceremony.

A special individual is designated as the *sandek,* the person who holds the baby during the ceremony. This honor often goes to a particular grandparent or close friend.

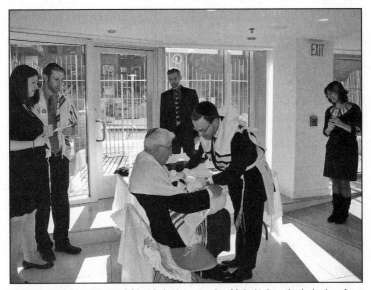

Parents, grandparents, and friends look on as the *Mohel* takes the baby boy from the *sandek* to begin the circumcision procedure.

The parents of the baby usually speak for a few minutes about how they chose the baby's name. One of the guests might present a short sermon related to the section of the *Torah* that's read in the synagogue that particular week.

At every *bris* I've attended, the mother of the newborn remains somewhat removed from the festivities, but this practice isn't prescribed by law or tradition. A *bris* can be hard on a new mother. Think about it—your brand-new baby is about to have surgery! And not only that, you're in the early stages of recovering from childbirth, suffering from sleep deprivation with hormones that are all out of whack. What's more, you have to host a party for 50 of your closest friends and relatives! It's a nice gesture to give a little TLC to the new mom at her son's *bris.* Be sure she's getting something to eat and has lots of water to drink. Helping out with cleanup can also be a big help for the family.

Liturgy

The majority of a traditional *bris* takes place in Hebrew. In most cir-cumstances, the *Mohel* translates and interprets the various blessings so all present can understand what's happening. I've included here some of the basic prayers recited at a *bris* so you can see how the concepts of covenant and peoplehood, God and *Torah,* are emphasized on this special occasion.

When a *bris* begins, the baby is ushered into the room with joyous anticipation as those present shout, *"Baruch ha-ba!"* (Welcome!) The newborn is sometimes passed among relatives (*kvatterin*) and for a moment is placed in a special seat called "Elijah's throne."

Elijah was a prophet of ancient Israel who is associated with rites of transition (like the conclusion of the Sabbath or the Passover *seder*) in Jewish folklore. The baby is then passed to the baby's father and then to the *sandek,* and prepared for circumcision. Once he is ready, the following blessing is recited (usually in Hebrew):

> Praised are You, *Adonai* our God, Sovereign of the
> Universe, who sanctifies us with commandments and
> commands us regarding circumcision.

Barukh atah Adonai Eloheinu, Melech ha-Olam,
ahser kid'shanu b'mitzvotav, v'tzeevanu al ha-meelah.

As the *Mohel* proceeds with the removal of the baby's foreskin, the father recites (usually in Hebrew):

Praised are You, *Adonai* our God, Sovereign of the Universe, who has sanctified us with commandments and commanded us to enter him into the Covenant of Abraham our father.

Barukh atah Adonai Eloheinu, Melech Ha-Olam,
ahser kid'shanu b'mitzvotav, v'tzeevanu l'hakhneeso
bi'vreeto shel Avraham aveenu.

Everyone present then responds:

Just as he has entered into the Covenant, so may he enter into *Torah,* into marriage, and into good deeds.

K'shem sheh-nikhneys la-breet, ken yi-kaness l'Torah,
u-'huppah, u-l'ma'aseem toveem.

After the circumcision is completed (if done well, this takes about 20 to 30 seconds), the *Mohel* recites over a cup of wine:

Blessed are You, *Adonai* our God, Sovereign of the Universe, who creates the fruit of the vine.

Blessed are You, *Adonai* our God, Sovereign of the Universe, who sanctified the beloved one from the womb, set His statute in his flesh, and sealed his descendants with the sign of the holy Covenant. Therefore, as a reward of this (circumcision), the living God, our Portion, our Rock, has ordained that the beloved of our flesh be saved from the abyss, for the sake of the Covenant which has been set in our flesh. Blessed are You Lord, who makes the Covenant.

Following this blessing, the child's name is announced, and the *Mohel* recites the following blessing:

> May the One who blessed our fathers, Abraham, Isaac and Jacob, Moses and Aaron, David and Solomon, bless this tender infant _____ (*name*) the son of _____ (*name*) because _____ (*name*) the son of _____ (*name*) pledged charity for his sake. In this merit, may the Blessed Holy One hasten to send a complete recovery to all his two hundred forty-eight bodily parts and three hundred sixty-five veins, and raise him to *Torah,* to marriage, and to good deeds; and let us say, Amen.

One of the most beautiful aspects of a *bris* ceremony is the way past, present, and future intersect in this ritual. On the one hand, the ceremony is about embracing a connection with the past through our ancestors. On the other hand, the ceremony is about the present, in that it welcomes a new life into the world and acknowledges this special time in the lives of his parents and extended family. And still, the ritual looks toward the future in imagining the life this child will go on to lead—a life filled with *Torah,* marriage, and good deeds.

MISC.

Happy Birthday!

When a Jewish child is born, she has two birthdays! One birthday is based on the secular calendar (such as August 30, 2001). This is the date that appears on birth certificates and other forms of secular documentation. Her other birthday is based on the Hebrew calendar, which is a lunar calendar based on a 28-day month. Because this calendar is a lunar calendar, it makes a difference whether a baby is born before or after sunset. A baby born on August 30, 2001, before sunset, has a Hebrew birthday of Elul 10, while a baby born after sunset on that same day has a Hebrew birthday of Elul 11. Hebrew birthdays are important for determining when a child becomes eligible to become a *bar/bat mitzvah.*

Rituals for Welcoming Baby Girls

Until relatively recently, there were no formal, community-wide celebrations like a *brit milah* for welcoming a Jewish daughter into the covenant of the Jewish people.

Traditional practice was that the father of the newborn would attend the first synagogue service of the week where the *Torah* was read and receive the honor of being called up to the *Torah*. As part of this honor, he would announce the baby girl's name publicly for the first time. Typically, the mother didn't participate at all in this ceremony, because she was still recovering from childbirth, perhaps even still in the hospital.

Why the disparity between welcoming baby boys and girls? One way of understanding it is that a baby girl's inclusion in the sacred covenant of the Jewish people was simply assumed. With no physical transition to mark the covenant on a baby girl's body, the joy of bringing home a baby girl was celebrated simply and privately.

But because the commandment of circumcision places so much attention on the formal ceremony to welcome boys into the covenant, the lack of a ceremony for girls does not sit well with contemporary, egalitarian values. It's hard not to imagine that classical Judaism simply values baby boys more than baby girls.

In response to these concerns, parents in recent years have searched for ways to welcome their Jewish baby boys and baby girls with similar fanfare. This desire for gender equality has been the source of some very creative new ceremonies for celebrating Jewish daughters.

You might be invited to a *simchat bat,* a *brit bat,* a *zeved ha-bat,* or simply a "baby naming." The event might take place in the synagogue, at home, in a catering hall, or in a community center. I've even participated in a *simchat bat* that took place outdoors in a park where trees were planted in the child's honor. It might take place on the eighth day of the baby's life, or it might be planned when the baby is 3 months old and her parents have had more time to adjust to their new addition.

Like the *bris,* ceremonies for daughters emphasize the themes of Jewish peoplehood, covenant, and naming. Like the *bris,* they also weave together a concern for past, present, and future; involve the participation of close family and friends; and incorporate symbols like bread, wine, and *Torah.* Sometimes a member of the Jewish clergy officiates, and sometimes the parents themselves take the lead in organizing and facilitating the event.

Adoption

When a Jewish family adopts a child, a number of creative ceremonies are held to welcome this child into Jewish people. This is a prayer I find particularly moving:

Prayer for an Adopted Child

by Rabbi Sandy Eisenberg Sasso

Adonai is mindful of us, will bless us; will bless the house of Israel; will bless the house of Aaron; will bless those who revere *Adonai,* the little ones and the big ones together. (after Psalms 115:12–13)

We have been blessed with the precious gift of this child. After so much waiting and wishing, we are filled with wonder and gratitude as we call you our daughter/son. Our daughter/son, our child, you have grown to life apart from us. But now we hold you close to our hearts and cradle you in our arms with our love. We welcome you into the circle of our family and embrace you with the beauty of a rich tradition.

We pledge ourselves to the creation of a Jewish home and to a life of compassion for others, hoping that you will grow to cherish and emulate these ideals.

God of new beginnings, teach us to be mother and
father, worthy of this sacred trust of life. May our
daughter/son grow in health. May she/he be strong
in mind and kind in heart, a lover of *Torah*, a seeker
of peace. Bless all of us together beneath your shelter
of *shalom* (peace), and grant our new family, always,
the harmony and love we feel today.

An adopted child can be converted to Judaism. The process involves
immersion of the child in the *mikvah*, or ritual bath, and a conversion
ceremony in which the parents promise to raise the child as a Jew.

Coming of Age

What does it mean to "come of age"? In American culture, we don't really
have any formal rites of passage to mark a child's transition to adulthood.
The bestowing of drivers' licenses and sweet 16 celebrations are probably as
close as we come to acknowledging the new privileges and freedoms that
come along with physical and emotional maturity.

In Jewish tradition, when a child reaches the age at which he or she is
responsible for observing the *mitzvot*, the child becomes a *bar* (or *bat*)
mitzvah, literally a "son" or "daughter" of the commandments (*mitzvot*).

In traditional circles, girls become a *bat mitzvah* at the age of 12, and boys
become a *bar mitzvah* at the age of 13. The age difference has to do with
the fact that, in general, girls reach physical maturity earlier than boys
do. However, some egalitarian communities celebrate a child's *bar* or *bat*
mitzvah at the age of 13, regardless of the child's gender, out of a desire to
reflect gender equality.

It's not necessary to "have" a *bar* or *bat mitzvah* ceremony in order to
become a *bar* or *bat mitzvah*. Simply by reaching the age of maturity,
a young man or woman becomes obligated to observe the *Torah*'s
commandments. However, the custom of celebrating the *bar* or *bat mitzvah*
as a rite of passage is one that has grown tremendously popular in recent
times.

Preparation for Becoming a *Bar* or *Bat Mitzvah*

Study is a major part of the preparation for the passage into Jewish adulthood. The ceremony is typically the culmination of many years of study, through which the child gains a foundation in Jewish history, Hebrew language, and prayer.

A child may learn how to chant from the *Torah* scroll and to sing a section from the Prophets called a *haftarah*. The child might also lead services and prepare a short teaching called a *d'var Torah,* a speech that explores the relevance of the weekly *Torah* portion to his or her life.

Because becoming a *bar* or *bat mitzvah* is about taking on more personal responsibility as a Jewish adult, many children prepare for this event by pursuing a social justice project as well. This *mitzvah* project might involve work with a particular charity or nonprofit organization. The idea is that the child should take ownership of the *Torah's* injunction to practice good deeds.

An irony of the *bar/bat mitzvah* as a rite of passage is that, although children become a Jewish "adult" at 12 or 13 according to Jewish law, they're still far away from becoming an adult in secular culture. It may seem silly to talk about treating a young adolescent as an adult. However, in Jewish tradition, it's at this time that kids begin to take responsibility for their own Judaism. They begin to take ownership of their beliefs and their values, so they might spend some time studying key areas of Jewish thought or Jewish approaches to ethical questions.

Some children preparing for this rite of passage might begin to compile a family history to build awareness of their place in the chain of Jewish tradition. This is a great way to involve the extended family in the process of a child's journey to maturity.

The *Bar/Bat Mitzvah* Ceremony

Since the origin of this ceremony in the middle ages, a Jewish boy became a *bar mitzvah* with very little pomp and circumstance. On his thirteenth birthday, he would be called up to the *Torah* by his Hebrew name and receive an *aliyah,* the honor of blessing the *Torah.* After that, he might receive some words of congratulations, but that's about it.

Today *bar* and *bat mitzvah* celebrations have become much more extensive and elaborate. In many communities, the celebratory party following synagogue services has become more meaningful to the family than the ceremony itself. Fortunately, this trend is reversing itself, as families look to this milestone as an opportunity to instill a meaningful sense of Jewish identity in their children.

Today this rite of passage takes many different forms. The most common approach is a ceremony that takes place in synagogue during the *Shabbat* morning service, where the *bar* or *bat mitzvah* marks his or her transition to Jewish adulthood by taking on responsibility for various parts of the synagogue service.

With increased responsibility also comes additional privileges in the realm of Jewish ritual. Once a boy reaches the age of *bar mitzvah,* he is counted as part of the *minyan.* In egalitarian congregations, this is true for girls as well. Many celebrants wear a *tallit* for the first time at their *bar* or *bat mitzvah* and put on *tefillin* for the first time during weekday services.

But sometimes families choose to have a different kind of ceremony. The truth is, there are many creative ways to mark this transition, and not every kid finds the traditionalism of a *Shabbat* morning service to be meaningful. A popular option nowadays is to have a Saturday evening *havdalah* service, where the symbols of *havdalah* are used to mark the child's transition into adulthood.

The *bar mitvah* boy takes hold of the *Torah* in celebration of this special occasion.
(Photo by Maksim Dubinsky/Shutterstock.com)

A *bar* or *bat mitzvah* can also take place during the week on a Monday or Thursday morning when the *Torah* is read. Such a celebration is naturally much less formal, and this might suit the needs of a child who is less comfortable with the "performance" aspect of the ritual.

It's also possible to celebrate a *bar* or *bat mitzvah* without having a formal service. In Secular Humanistic Judaism, the custom is for the child to do an extensive research project and family history, which is then presented to family and friends at a very different kind of ceremony. In this case, the child expresses her Jewish coming of age by engaging with Jewish beliefs, culture, and traditions on a more intellectual level.

Adult *Bar* and *Bat Mitzvah*

While the vision of a *bar mitzvah* boy calls to mind a nervous 13-year-old, a growing trend these days is the adult *b'nai mitzvah* ceremony.

There are many reasons why a Jewish adult might not have had the opportunity to celebrate or train for a traditional *bar/bat mitzvah*. Until relatively recently, women didn't have public ceremonies to celebrate their coming of age in the Jewish ritual sphere. So many older women who grew up before having a *bat mitzvah* was the norm are eager to affirm their commitment to Jewish ritual life through this tradition.

Jews who were raised in secular families also might not have had the opportunity to attend religious school and celebrate this rite of passage. And those Jews who are Jews by choice might also not have had the opportunity to declare and celebrate publicly their commitment to the *Torah*.

To meet these needs, many synagogues have established adult *bar* and *bat mitzvah* educational programs. They usually involve a 1- or 2-year part-time course of study that culminates in a formal *bar* or *bat mitzvah* ceremony for the class. The ceremony usually takes place in synagogue on *Shabbat*. The celebrant takes on a leadership role in the service, perhaps chanting from the *Torah* or the Prophets and leading some of the prayers.

These ceremonies can be so moving for many reasons. For one, it takes a lot of guts to go back to school to follow a course of study designed for a 12-year-old! At the same time, it's very inspiring to celebrate with a group of people demonstrating their willingness to learn and grow in their commitment to Judaism.

Blessings for Marriage

Few rituals are more beautiful than a Jewish wedding ceremony. As we've seen, Judaism values home, family, and the teaching of traditions to the next generation. It should come as no surprise, then, that marriage is a highly valued institution in Jewish tradition. In fact, it's more than valued—it's considered holy. When two individuals come together to build a Jewish home, their commitment is to continue the divine work of creation.

A Jewish wedding actually combines two ceremonies that were once separate rituals. The first is called *kiddushin,* which means "sanctification." *Kiddushin* stems from the word *kadosh,* which, as we've seen, means "holy." In the context of a Jewish wedding, *kiddushin* refers to the sacred bond established between two individuals. Partners become holy to one another, joining together for the sacred purpose of creating a Jewish home and family.

The second ceremony, called *Nisuin,* includes seven special blessings for marriage that are recited for the couple.

Huppah: The Marriage Canopy

A Jewish couple is married underneath a wedding canopy called a *huppah* (*khoo-PAH*). A traditional *huppah* is a simple structure of four poles with a square piece of fabric over the top. Many couples use a *tallit* or other family heirloom to make their *huppah.* Sometimes a florist or catering hall will construct a more ornate *huppah* using columns, flowers, candles, or tulle. But regardless of its style, the *huppah* is the central symbol in a Jewish wedding.

The *huppah* symbolizes the home the couple will build together. It provides shelter above but is open on all four sides to reflect the value of hospitality and openness to the community. Under the *huppah,* the couple is surrounded by close family and loved ones who, by their presence, pledge to support them in their life together. It's customary to have close friends or relatives hold up the *huppah* poles during the ceremony, also as a symbolic gesture of support.

The couple processes to the *huppah* escorted by family and friends. In traditional ceremonies, the bride circles the groom seven times as a symbol of her devotion to him. In more egalitarian settings, the bride and groom take turns circling one another or skip this part of the ceremony altogether.

The rabbis inspect the ring as the couple stands under the *huppah.*
(Photo by Kyle Bergner, courtesy of Marian Frankston)

Once the couple and their attendants are underneath the *huppah,* the formal ceremony begins with a prayer of welcome to all those present. The officiant, who could be a rabbi or a cantor, recites:

> Blessed are those who have come in the name of God;
> May you receive blessing from this house of God.
> May the one who is sovereign over all,
> Who is blessed above all;
> Who is greatest of all;
> Shall bless the Bride and the Groom.

Invoking God at the very start of the ceremony sets the tone for the wedding as a sacred and holy ritual. Wine is blessed under the *huppah*, and since many couples have the custom of fasting on their wedding day, this might be the first nourishment they've had all day!

Clean Slates

In traditional communities, the wedding day is likened to a personal *Yom Kippur*. The Day of Atonement is the holiest day in the Jewish calendar, when we fast, pray, and do a thorough spiritual accounting of our past actions. At the end of *Yom Kippur,* our slate is wiped clean, and we begin the year anew with a clear conscience. On the wedding day, it's customary to fast and recite special prayers throughout the day and ask for forgiveness for any transgressions of youth that may be haunting us. This way, we enter into the holy state of marriage with a pure soul, ready to begin a new life together.

Kiddushin: Sanctification

In a traditional Jewish wedding, the bride is sanctified to the groom in the act of *kiddushin*. The groom places a simple gold band on the bride's finger and says:

> Behold, you are consecrated to me with this ring,
> according to the laws of Moses and the people Israel.
>
> *Harei at m'kudeshet li, b'taba'at zo, k-dat Moshe
> u-b'nei Yisrael.*

In some communities, the bride responds with a verse from the Song of Songs:

> I am my beloved's and my beloved is mine.
>
> *Ani l'Dodi v'Dodi Li.*

According to Orthodox practice, the bride does not reciprocate by presenting the groom with a ring. For this reason, you won't see very traditional Jewish men wearing a wedding ring.

However, in the more liberal denominations, it's common for both bride and groom to present one another with rings, using the traditional formula.

Ketubah: The Marriage Writ

Next, the officiant under the *huppah* reads the marriage contract, which would have been prepared and signed by witnesses prior to the *huppah* ceremony. A Jewish writ of marriage is called a *ketubah* (*keh-TOO-bah;* plural, *ketubot, keh-too-BOAT*). This ancient document was developed in early rabbinic times to protect the rights of a woman in marriage.

Prior to the wedding, witnesses sign the *ketubah* in a festive ceremony.
(Photo by Kyle Bergner, courtesy of Marian Frankston)

Today there are many different variations in *ketubot,* both in terms of artistic style and with respect to the nature of the contractual language written in it. There are *ketubot* for every religious denomination, for intermarriages, same-sex marriages, and even non-Jewish marriages.

If you have a particularly beautiful *ketubah,* it's customary to frame it and hang it in the home.

Sheva Berakhot: Seven Wedding Blessings

In the next part of the ceremony, seven special blessings are recited for the couple. These seven blessings, called the *sheva berakhot* in Hebrew, emphasize God's role as creator of humanity and compare the new couple to Adam and Eve in the Garden of Eden. These blessings can be recited by family and friends or by the rabbi or cantor officiating.

> Praised are you *Adonai,* Our God, Sovereign of the Universe, who created everything for your Glory.

> Praised are you *Adonai,* Our God, Sovereign of the Universe, creator of humanity.

> Praised are you *Adonai,* Our God, Sovereign of the Universe, who created human beings in your image, in the pattern. Praised are you, *Adonai,* creator of humanity.

> Let the barren city be jubilantly happy and joyful at her joyous reunion with her children. Praised are you, who makes Zion rejoice with her children.

> Let the loving couple be very happy just as you made your creation happy in the Garden of Eden long ago. Praised are you *Adonai,* who makes the bridegroom and the bride happy.

> Praised are you *Adonai,* Our God, Sovereign of the Universe, who created joy and celebration, bridegroom and bride, rejoicing, jubilation, pleasure and delight, love and brotherhood, peace and friendship. May there soon be heard, *Adonai* our God, in the cities of Judea and in the streets of Jerusalem, the sound of joy and the sound of celebration, the voice of a groom and the voice of a bride, the happy shouting of grooms from their weddings and young men from their feasts of song. Praised are you *Adonai,* who makes the groom and the bride rejoice together.

Praised are you *Adonai,* Our God, Sovereign of the Universe, who created the fruit of the vine.

Breaking the Glass

Mazal tov! You know a Jewish wedding is over when you hear the shattering of glass. This is perhaps one of the most well-known symbols of a Jewish wedding.

After sipping from the cup of wine at the conclusion of the *sheva berakhot,* the groom steps on a glass hard enough to break it. This practice has many different interpretations. One is that it serves as a reminder of the destruction of the Jerusalem temple. Even at times of great joy, the shattered glass reminds us of the sorrows that have defined the Jewish people.

Another interpretation is that the shattered glass is a reminder to the couple that there is much that is wrong with the world, so a priority of their relationship should be to work toward *tikkun olam,* "repair of the world."

Essential Takeaways

- The *shehecheyanu* is a prayer we use to express gratitude to God for enabling us to reach an important milestone.
- A newborn baby boy is welcomed into the covenant of the Jewish people with an ancient ritual called a *brit milah,* the covenant of circumcision.
- A newborn baby girl is welcomed into the Jewish people with ceremonies that have been created more recently, like *simchat bat, brit bat,* or a baby naming.
- A *bar* or *bat mitzvah* ceremony celebrates a Jewish child's coming of age in the eyes of Jewish law.
- The Jewish marriage ceremony establishes a covenant between two partners who have chosen to build a Jewish home together.

chapter 14

Prayers for Healing and Mourning

When a loved one is in need of healing

The *mitzvah* of visiting the sick

Mourning Jewishly

What you can do to help a family in mourning

Jewish tradition is a rich tapestry of customs that celebrate the wonders of life and help us understand what it means to be human. Judaism has endured for thousands of years in part because it gives voice to the widest range of human emotions. We can turn to Jewish prayer to express our deepest thoughts, in times of both joy and sadness.

The history of the Jewish people has not been easy. Jews have endured a great deal of suffering and persecution in the lands where they've lived. Yet against all odds, Judaism has survived. Jewish history, from the Bible forward, teaches us that life is a cycle that brings with it times of great prosperity and times less fortunate.

Jewish prayer allows us to access the emotional wisdom learned through the trials of Judaism's great and complex history. It's easy to connect with God when things are going well in our lives. But what about life's more difficult moments? What kind of comfort can Judaism provide when we're faced with the inevitable challenges life brings?

Reaching Out in a Time of Need

How do we cope with the reality of illness? Whether it's our own suffering or that of a friend or loved one, confronting illness can be a tremendous spiritual challenge. When we're healthy, it's so easy to take our physical well-being for granted and not give it a second thought. But when we're sick and in need of healing, our lives can start to feel out of our control.

Out of the depths I called out to God; God answered me by setting me free.

—Psalm 118

With all the amazing advances in modern medicine, illness is still full of mystery. Will medical treatments be effective? How long will it take to get better? Will I make a complete recovery? Will I suffer side effects? Why me, anyway?

Sometimes the hardest thing about coping with illness is the sense of helplessness that wells up in us. We're so used to being able to control every aspect of our lives. But when it comes to illness and recovery, we have no choice but to let go and learn to trust both our bodies and the health professionals we've chosen to care for us or our loved ones.

So what can Jewish prayer possibly offer at a time like this? In our day and age, isn't it naive to suggest that prayer has real healing power? I mean, it's one thing to suggest that prayer can have a positive impact on our own lives. But can we really hope to cure another person's suffering with words?

I recently received the terrible news that a close friend and colleague had been in a very serious accident. He survived, but it's uncertain whether he'll ever be able to walk again. Damage to his spinal cord makes it very likely he'll be permanently paralyzed from the waist down.

When I heard the news, the first thing I could think of doing was pray. I tried to imagine my friend in the hospital, receiving the best care possible, surrounded by concerned friends and loved ones. Although I was about 100 miles away, I tried to send him my deepest, most sincere wishes for a full recovery. Then I just closed my eyes and asked God to heal him.

In the biblical Book of Numbers, Miriam, Moses' sister, is stricken with leprosy. Afraid she might die from this terrible affliction, Moses cries out to *Adonai,* saying, "Please, God, heal her now." This simple prayer consists of only five Hebrew words: *El na refah na lah.*

Moses doesn't make a formal supplication before God. He doesn't offer sacrifices or address God with all sorts of flattering imagery. In an intense time of spiritual and emotional need, he gets right to the point: *God, please intervene and heal my beloved sister.*

A very trying time of need can open a door to genuine prayer. In difficult moments, it's very easy to shut down and close ourselves off from the world and those who care about us. But when we allow our care, our concerns, or even our fears to open our hearts instead, we allow the divine presence to come to us as a source of comfort.

There's recently been a great deal of research into prayer's power to impact the healing process. I'm not a medical researcher or psychologist, so I can't make any claim about whether prayer really "works." I can tell you, however, that in my own experience, prayer helps. And in difficult times when we're truly vulnerable, a little help can go a long way.

When my friend was ill, I felt powerless to change the situation. My prayer helped me feel connected to him and to the community of people who were concerned for his life. Prayer also helped me reach out to God for spiritual and emotional support. And although I'll never know for sure, I like to think that knowing my prayers were out there helped my friend feel a little less alone during what must have been a terrifying time.

Does prayer have the power to heal? I think it does. When we reach down into the depths of our being in search of God, we confront those places in our own souls in need of healing. Heartfelt prayer can strengthen us as we come to terms with illness, even if it's not possible to overcome it on a physical level. While prayer may not have the power to cure, it can most certainly fortify our hearts and give us the courage to contemplate our own mortality.

You don't have to wait for a formal synagogue service to pray for someone in need of healing. Try this healing meditation, which can be done in synagogue, at home, at work, or virtually any place when you have a quiet moment to yourself:

1. Close your eyes and take a few deep breaths. Bring to mind the face of the person in need of healing. If you can, imagine them healthy and active. Take a few breaths to meditate on this image.

2. When you feel ready, speak to the image in your mind, saying, "I wish you strength. I wish you healing. I wish you peace." Repeat these phrases until you feel you're saying them with complete awareness and integrity.

3. When you feel ready to end your meditation, pause for a moment, and say the following words out loud: "Please, God, heal _____ (*name of the person you're praying for*)."

4. Take a final breath and open your eyes.

Traditional Prayers for Healing

One of the many words the Jewish prayer book uses to describe God is *healer*. Even our ancestors called upon God to heal the sick. The ancient rabbis considered prayers for healing so important that they devoted one of the 18 benedictions of the *Amidah* to it and incorporated it into the blessings over the *Torah*.

Prayers for Healing in the Daily *Amidah*

Every single weekday, three times each day as part of the *Amidah,* the following prayer is recited:

> Heal us, *Adonai,* and we shall be healed. Help us and save us, for you are our prayer. Bring complete healing for all our afflictions.
>
> *R'fa-eynu Adonai v'neyrapay, hoshee-aynu v'nivasayah kee t'heelateinu atah. V'ha-alay r'fuah shlaymah l'kol makoteinu.*

This prayer is recited daily, even when you're not praying for the recovery of any particular individual. The rabbis included it as a daily affirmation of faith in God's healing and saving power.

If you want to pray for the recovery of a particular individual, the following paragraph is added to the *Amidah.* It's customary to include the person's Hebrew name in the prayer. It's also fine to use an English name if you don't know the Hebrew name, or if your prayer is for someone who isn't Jewish.

> May it be your will, *Adonai* our God and God of our ancestors, to send quick and complete healing of body and soul to _____ and all those who are ill among the people of Israel.
>
> *Yehee ratzon meel'fanekha, Adonai Eloheinu v'Elohay avoteinu, she-tishlakh m'hayra refuah shlaymah min ha-shamayim, r'fuat ha-nefesh u'refuat ha-guf, l'_____ ben/bat _____ b'tokh sh'ar kholei Yisrael.*

We then conclude the blessing with the following benediction:

> For you are a God who is sovereign over healing; you are faithful and compassionate. Praised are You *Adonai,* Healer of your people, Israel.
>
> *Kee El Melech rofeh ne'eman v'rahaman atah. Barukh atah Adonai, rofeh kholei amo Yisrael.*

Because the *Amidah* is recited silently, this prayer for healing can be a really meaningful time for daily reflection. Although it's customary to move through the text of the *Amidah* rather quickly, when I recite this paragraph, I try to slow down and take a minute to focus on the meaning of my prayers. I think of it as an opportunity to spend a few precious moments of a busy day to send healing wishes to someone I care about.

Mi-shebayrach and *Birkat ha-Gomel*

Two more opportunities to pray for healing within the fixed liturgy come during the *Torah* service, when the *Torah* is read publicly either on *Shabbat* or during the week.

The first is a prayer called the *mi-shebayrach,* and it's recited following an *aliyah* to the *Torah*. After the section of the *Torah* has been read, and after the concluding blessing has been recited, the prayer leader, or *Gabbai,* recites the prayer for healing:

> May the one who blessed our ancestors, Abraham, Isaac and Jacob, Sarah, Rebecca, Rachel and Leah, bless and heal _____. May the Holy, Blessed One who is full of compassion bring her/him strength and healing, and send a quick and complete recovery of both body and soul from all illnesses to her/him and to all who are ill among the people of Israel.

In many communities, individuals approach the reading desk to add to the prayer the names of friends and relatives who are in need of healing.

In some communities, this beautiful, spiritual moment is extended through singing. A number of popular melodies can be inserted into the *Torah* service to make the *mi-shebayrach* prayer more of a centerpiece during the reading. In my experience, this is one of the highlights of the *Torah* service. It's so moving to see people put themselves out there before the community and vocalize the names of those whom they love as they pray for recovery.

Birkat ha-Gomel is a prayer recited by a person who has survived a serious illness or life-threatening situation, or who has returned from a difficult journey. This prayer isn't so much a prayer for healing, but an expression of gratitude for our ability to overcome a difficult challenge.

The person reciting the blessing is called up to the *Torah* and says:

> Praised are You, *Adonai* our God, Sovereign of the Universe, who graciously bestows favor upon the undeserving, even as You have bestowed favor upon me.
>
> *Barukh atah Adonai Eloheinu, Melech Ha-Olam, ha-Gomel l'hayavim tovim, she-g'malani kol tov.*

The congregation then responds:

> May the One who has been gracious to you continue to favor you with all that is good.
>
> *Mee she-gmal'kha kol tov hu yig'malkha kol tov selah.*

These traditional prayers give us a structured way to pray for healing. They're part of the regular, daily liturgy, and they're important spiritual tools to have at our disposal. We may not need them on a daily basis, but when we do reach for them, they can help us make it through the tough times.

Healing Services

Although a traditional worship service includes several opportunities to pray for healing in the daily liturgy, formal healing services are becoming more and more popular in the Jewish community.

A relatively new innovation, healing services take many forms. The traditional liturgy might be interspersed with inspirational readings in English that focus on the theme of healing or wellness. Or sometimes a healing service includes meditation and singing, especially around the *mi-shebayrach* prayer. A more progressive model might incorporate Hebrew chant, deep breathing, and yoga postures.

Often a healing service embraces a broad view of healing, including not just personal prayers for the healing of body and soul, but also prayers that hope for a more comprehensive healing of the world.

The concept of *tikkun olam* (literally, "repairing the world") comes from an idea in Jewish mysticism that understands our physical universe as fundamentally shattered and in need of repair. Our role is to mend this state of brokenness through the performance of good deeds and *mitzvot*. In this way, our actions have the potential to bring about a kind of cosmic healing.

Healing services might also focus on emotional healing for those recovering from psychological trauma, addiction, or abuse. If you'd be interested in finding a healing service, inquire at local synagogues, a Jewish Community Center, or Jewish Family Service agency in your area. If you can't find one, consider organizing your own!

Finding Comfort in Psalms

The Book of Psalms is a remarkable collection of supplications and prayers, many of which are composed in the first person. These ancient poems, attributed to kings David and Solomon, were probably performed with musical accompaniment as part of the ceremonial worship in the ancient Jerusalem Temple.

Because the Psalms include petitions for personal salvation and healing, and because they address God primarily as a savior and liberator, they've been a source of comfort during trying times for many, many centuries.

Torah Tip

In some traditional communities, women gather regularly to recite the entire book of Psalms. Each participant recites a section of Psalms, and by the end, all 150 have been recited. This ritual, which often includes singing as well as social conversation, is a source of camaraderie and sisterhood. But it's also an important spiritual outlet for the women who participate. If someone in the community is ill, the gathering might be dedicated to praying for their recovery.

For generations, Jews have turned to the Psalms as a source of hope during times of challenge. Whether you're praying to get through difficult personal circumstances or praying specifically for healing, the Psalms are a vast repository of inspiration.

These are a couple of my favorites:

Psalm 102

Adonai, hear my prayer,
Let my cry come before You.
Do not hide Your face from me
In my time of trouble;
Turn Your ear to me;
When I cry, answer me speedily.
For my days have vanished like smoke
And my bones are charred like a hearth.
My body is stricken and withered like grass
Too wasted to eat my food
On account of my vehement groaning.
My bones show through my skin …
But You, *Adonai,* are enthroned forever,
Your fame endures throughout the ages.
You will surely arise and take pity on Zion,
For it is time to be gracious to her,
The appointed time has come.

Psalm 86

Incline your ear, *Adonai*,
Answer me,
For I am poor and needy.
Preserve my life, for I am steadfast;
You, my God
Deliver your servant who trusts in You.
Have mercy on me, *Adonai*,
For I call to you all day long;
Bring joy to Your servant's life,
For on You, *Adonai*, I set my hope.
For you, *Adonai*, are good and forgiving,
Abounding in steadfast love to all
who call on You.
Give ear, *Adonai*, to my prayer,
Heed my plea for mercy.
In my time of trouble I call You,
For You will answer me.

Visiting the Sick

The *Talmud* talks about the *mitzvah* of *bikur holim* (*bee-koor kho-leem*), visiting the sick, as an act of kindness that "yields immediate fruit and continues to yield fruit over time." If you've ever been ill, you know how easy it is to feel isolated by your illness. Whether you're recuperating at home or in a hospital, it's sometimes hard to be alone.

Rabbi Abba ben Hanina taught that a person who visits one who is sick takes away one sixtieth of the sick person's pain.

—*Babylonian Talmud*, Nedarim 39b

Practicing the *mitzvah* of *bikur holim* can be difficult. It's an emotional challenge to confront the reality of a loved one's suffering. But paying a sick call is truly one of the most meaningful things you can do for a friend in need.

While we may not be able to bring a full recovery to an ailing friend, a short visit can do wonders to elevate a person's spirits. Whether you bring nourishing food, straighten up the house, or just bring an open heart and a kind ear, your presence will mean a great deal. Sometimes the most valuable thing you can do is simply to be there to listen.

It's important to understand that *bikur holim* is a *mitzvah* in Jewish tradition—it's a sacred obligation. Of course, it's a nice thing to do, but in Jewish culture, it's our duty to serve the community in this way.

Your local community may have a *Bikur Holim* society, which organizes sick visits in local hospitals and nursing homes. If you think you might be interested in volunteering to visit individuals recovering from illness, see if a network exists in your area.

Torah Tip

When paying a visit to the sick, respect that the person you're visiting might be resting when you come. Don't sit on the bed, so as to respect a person's modesty and dignity. If possible, sit on a chair close enough to talk. If appropriate, bring a gift of nourishing food. Sometimes it's nice to have a break from hospital fare. If the person has a family at home, consider making a meal to bring to the house. Take the initiative of doing some light housekeeping in the room. Being in an orderly space can really impact morale. Don't worry about making small talk. Let the person you're visiting take the lead in conversation. Sitting in silence is okay, too. And be sensitive about the length of your stay. If your friend seems tired, it's time to leave.

Mourning and Loss

It should come as no surprise that, in a tradition that values life the way Judaism does, there are extensive rituals, prayers, and customs for marking life's end.

When a Jewish person dies, Jewish tradition has two central concerns. One is ensuring that the body of the deceased is treated with the utmost dignity and respect from the moment of death until the time of burial. The other is helping the mourners face the reality of death and come to terms with their own feelings of loss.

The Greatest Kindness

The *mitzvah* of caring for the dead and ensuring a proper burial is called *hesed shel emet,* a true act of mercy. Jewish tradition says that performing this *mitzvah* is the greatest kindness you can do for another human being because the dead can never say "Thank you."

A special communal institution called the *Hevra Kadisha* (*KHEV-ra ka-DEE-sha*), or Jewish burial society, generally takes responsibility for ensuring that the community's deceased receive a proper burial according to Jewish tradition. It's common to "outsource" this sacred work to professional funeral parlors, but many traditional communities still maintain a voluntary *Hevra Kadisha,* which enables lay people to experience this profound *mitzvah.*

Jewish Funerals

MISC. A few common burial practices are not part of a traditional Jewish funeral. For example, cremation is not a traditional Jewish practice. A Jewish funeral does not include a viewing of the body. Embalming is not encouraged and is permitted only under special circumstances.

The body of a deceased person is regarded with sanctity because it has been a vessel for the human soul. From the moment of death until burial, the body should not be left alone. An appointed person, whether professional or volunteer, must guard the body, even throughout the night, without sleeping. It's customary to read Psalms when one performs the act of guarding, or *shmirah.*

The body of the deceased is washed thoroughly from head to toe with warm water. This rite of purification is typically performed by members of the *Hevra Kadisha*. The body is then dressed in a white linen cloth or shroud, which is a symbol of equality in death. It's also Jewish custom to bury the dead in a plain wooden coffin, as another symbol that rich and poor are equals at the end of life.

wisdom of the sages

Kindness that is done for the dead is a true act of kindness, since one does it without expecting any repayment.

—Rashi

It's customary to bury the dead within 24 hours, although, of course, circumstances might require delaying a funeral by a few days. Carrying the coffin to the gravesite and filling the grave with earth are two more acts of kindness one can offer the deceased during burial. It's Jewish custom for guests at the gravesite to assist by shoveling dirt into the grave as a way of participating in this *mitzvah*.

However, to show our reluctance to perform this act, we do not hand the shovel to one another, but rather lay it on the ground for the next person to take a turn. Some people hold the shovel upside down to demonstrate their reluctance, and another custom is to stop seven times on the way to the grave to delay the process.

At the gravesite, mourners recite *kaddish*, a prayer that extols the sanctity and glory of God, as an expression of faith even in the midst of loss:

> Hallowed and enhanced may God be throughout the world of God's own creation. May God cause God's sovereignty soon to be accepted, during our life and the life of all Israel, and let us say: Amen.

> May God be praised throughout all time.

Glorified and celebrated, lauded and worshipped,
acclaimed and honored, extolled and exalted may
the Holy One be, praised beyond all song and psalm,
beyond all tributes which mortals can utter. And let
us say: Amen.

Let there be abundant peace from Heaven, with life's
goodness for us and for all the people Israel. And let
us say: Amen.

He who brings peace to the universe will bring peace
to us and to all the people Israel. And let us say:
Amen. (*Siddur Sim Shalom*)

Liturgy for a funeral also includes *El Malei Rahamim,* the prayer "God Is
Full of Mercy" (see Chapter 11), along with Psalms for comfort. Psalm 23
provides special comfort to mourners as they say good-bye to their loved
one:

Adonai is my shepherd, I shall not want.
God gives me repose in green meadows.
God leads me beside the still waters to revive my
   spirit.
God guides me on the right path, for that is God's
   nature.
Though I walk in the valley of the shadow of death,
I fear no harm, for You are with me.
Your staff and rod comfort me.
You prepare a banquet for me in the presence of my
   foes.
You anoint my head with oil; my cup overflows.
Surely goodness and kindness shall be my portion all
   the days of my life.
And I shall dwell in the House of *Adonai* forever.

Comforting Mourners

Consoling mourners through the *mitzvah* of *nihum aveilim* (*nee-KHOOM ah-vay-LEEM*) begins immediately after the burial. Guests at the funeral form two lines, and the mourners pass through them in a solemn procession. This is a gesture of support for the family as they begin the formal mourning process. As they leave the cemetery, they can see all the family and friends who are there to comfort them.

Torah Tip

It's hard to know what to say to a person who has just lost a loved one. Jewish tradition takes the guesswork out of that awkward moment with a special blessing you can offer to mourners. Of course, it's perfectly fine to say "I'm sorry" and offer condolences. But it's also customary to say:

May God comfort you among all the mourners of Zion and Jerusalem.

Ha Makom yinachem etchem b'toch sha'ar avilei tzion vi'yerushalayim.

Family and friends continue to show support to the bereaved family during the intense period of mourning called *shiva* (*SHIH-va*). *Shiva* is observed for one week following the burial of a loved one and usually takes place at the home of a family member.

It's customary for mourners to sit on stools that are lower in height than a normal chair to reflect their "low" spirits during this difficult time. Many Jews also cover all mirrors in the home to remind them that the mourning period is not a time for personal vanity.

During *shiva*, friends and neighbors can comfort mourners by bringing food to the home and helping serve meals to the family throughout the week. These meals of consolation are cathartic for both the mourners and those wishing to express condolences. Providing nourishing food to the family is a concrete task that shows the family they have support of the community during this sad time. It's really nice to be able to *do* something, when it's so hard to express how we feel when confronted by death.

At the *shiva* home, it's customary to convene a *minyan* twice daily so the mourners are able to recite *kaddish* each day. Mourners continue to recite *kaddish* each day for a period of 11 months following the death of an immediate relative. According to Jewish tradition, reciting *kaddish* for a loved one, and giving charity in their memory, elevates their soul and brings their eternal presence closer to God.

These acts also help a mourner come to terms with the loss of a loved one. The intense period of *shiva,* followed by a year focused on the recitation of daily *kaddish,* is meant to help the mourner gradually transition back into life.

Essential Takeaways

- Prayers for healing are a central part of daily Jewish liturgy.
- Visiting the sick is a very important *mitzvah* in Jewish tradition.
- When a person dies, assuring a proper burial is considered the greatest kindness one can bestow on another person.
- Providing comfort to mourners is also an important *mitzvah* in Jewish tradition.

Jewish Spirituality in the Synagogue and Beyond

Community is essential to the practice of Judaism, and the synagogue is the central institution of Jewish communal life. We turn to the synagogue to support our spiritual journey in so many ways. Worship services are the focal point of synagogue life, but synagogues are also gathering places for social activities and educational programs. In Part 4, I cover the ins and outs of synagogue-based spirituality. By taking a tour of the synagogue and its symbolism, you'll come to appreciate why this ancient institution has endured for centuries and what it can offer you today.

As important as the synagogue is to Jewish communal life, it's not the only arena for Jewish prayer. In Jewish tradition, the home is viewed as a microcosm of the Temple. Just as the ancient Temple in Jerusalem was a dwelling place for God, you can bring the divine presence into your home through a variety of traditional practices. Many basic human activities, from eating meals, to putting your kids to bed at night, can infuse a home with awareness of the sacred.

We can also draw God's presence into the wider world through acts of charity and kindness. Also in this part, I introduce the many avenues for finding spirituality, from the formality of the synagogue to the clamor of the soup kitchen, to the quiet waters of the ritual bath. We finish up with some practical tools for putting into practice all you've learned in the course of your reading.

chapter 15

The Synagogue as Sacred Space

What does it mean to "belong" to a synagogue?

The synagogue as a sacred community

Making sense of all the symbolism

Understanding the role of clergy

How to find a spiritual home

Throughout its long history, the synagogue has been a central institution in the Jewish community. *Synagogue* isn't a native Hebrew word; it actually comes from an ancient Greek word meaning "gathering" or "assembly." After the Romans destroyed the ancient Temple in Jerusalem in 70 C.E., these gathering places became the dominant focal point for religious and communal Jewish life.

Synagogues serve a variety of functions in the Jewish community. A synagogue is a house of study, a house of prayer, and a social center for Jews at every stage of life. While synagogues today may be very different from what they were long ago, they still provide an anchor for the Jewish people. There's a reason we refer to a synagogue as a "house" of worship. A synagogue is like a home for us—a home for prayer, study, a place for gathering, and a dwelling for the divine presence.

One of the ironies of American Jewish life in the twenty-first century is that the majority of Jews living in America today feel at home pretty much everywhere *except* synagogue. This is especially true for younger generations of Jews who have become very suspicious of organized religion and its institutional structures. In this chapter, we explore what synagogues have to offer in today's complicated spiritual marketplace and how you can find a spiritual community you can call home.

Belonging

When I was a teenager, my younger sister, Allison, was killed in a car accident. It's a day I remember with astonishing clarity, even though it happened more than 25 years ago. Needless to say, this sudden tragedy changed me forever. But the experience also taught me one of the most memorable lessons about how the Jewish community works.

When my sister died, our family didn't hold membership at a synagogue. So when we found ourselves in need of a rabbi to conduct the funeral, we had to rely on a stranger, someone who didn't know us at all, and who certainly had never met Allison.

A young rabbi from one of the area congregations came to our home to counsel us and learn about our family in preparation for his eulogy. I remember how awkward it felt to have this unfamiliar rabbi in our home. Without the context of a synagogue community to make sense of the Jewish mourning process, I had no idea what was going on. I felt like such an outsider, and the whole process felt humiliating at a time when we were suffering from intense grief.

This feeling was confirmed when, at a point in the interview, my mother asked the rabbi if she could purchase a memorial plaque at his synagogue to honor Allison's memory. The rabbi responded, apologetically, that those plaques were available to members only. This rejection made us all feel so alienated from the Jewish community, at the time when we needed community most.

I was only 17 at the time, but that memory really stayed with me through the years. Reflecting on it as I grew older, I came to realize that I had learned a profound lesson that day about what Jewish communal institutions are all about. Sure, as an unaffiliated family, we lacked access to specific Jewish "services" that "come with" membership dues, like memorial plaques and pastoral counseling. But more than that, the thing I felt most intensely was that we lacked a sense of true belonging. We had no communal framework for moving through the mourning process in a way that was both meaningful and Jewish. We had no mentor to guide us on our way.

Synagogues, in their ideal form, are sacred communities of belonging. They are gathering places that help us move Jewishly through the milestones of life, from the cradle to the grave. Whether it's the daily *minyan* there to support you when you're in mourning or the religious school that helps teach your children Jewish history and values, the synagogue joins people together with a sense of spiritual purpose.

Definition

A **synagogue** is a Jewish house of worship. In Hebrew, a synagogue is called *beit k'nesset,* or "house of assembly." While some Jews use the term *temple* to refer to a Jewish house of prayer, more traditional Jews avoid this term, out of respect for the ancient Temple in Jerusalem and in the hope that it will one day be rebuilt. Ashkenazi Jews use the Yiddish term *shul,* which means "school," reflecting its historic role as a house of study.

In the ancient Temple, the priests would worship God through the service of ritual sacrifice. One of several names for ritual sacrifice is *avodah* (*ah-voh-DAH*), from the same *Hebrew* root as the word for "labor." The labor of sacrifice was a means of serving God in Temple times. Today prayer is our service of the heart, or *avodat ha-lev* (*ah-voh-DAT ha-LEV*), and synagogue is a sacred space where we serve God with the offerings of our lips.

Any Jewish person can attend synagogue, and you don't have to be a member to participate in worship services during the year. Becoming a member of a synagogue is a step you take when you're ready to make more of a commitment to the synagogue community. Your membership dues help support the physical infrastructure of the synagogue and other operating expenses.

Synagogues typically charge membership dues on an annual basis, and sometimes charge an additional fee for participation in High Holy Day services. Because they're nonprofit organizations, synagogues rely on additional philanthropic dollars to support their payroll and operating expenses, so they often run lots of fund-raising events to help keep the doors open.

Torah Tip

What happens if you want to join a synagogue but you don't have the financial resources to pay membership dues? While synagogues rely on membership dues for their financial solvency, most communities won't turn away a Jewish person in financial need. Don't be ashamed to speak privately with the spiritual leader of the community to request a dues reduction. You might even be able to volunteer your time in exchange for membership.

But belonging to a synagogue is about more than just meeting a set of financial obligations. When you belong to a synagogue, your presence matters. You become part of a community where people care about your well-being and are there for you in times of struggle. When you attend services regularly, bring your children to religious school, or participate in adult education courses, you become part of a community of like-minded people joined in the common pursuit of meaning.

How does a synagogue community infuse its members' lives with Jewish meaning? Five key functions of the synagogue help make this happen:

Spiritual leadership: Jewish clergy model engagement with Jewish practice and provide inspirational leadership through sermons, classes, and pastoral counseling.

Prayer: By participating in communal worship, "service of the heart," members move through time with one another, affirming the core principles of Jewish tradition.

Community: Synagogue members mark milestones together like Sabbaths and festivals, birthdays, anniversaries, graduations, and weddings in a way that cultivates an atmosphere of care and connection.

Torah *study:* Studying *Torah* together creates a community of learners who challenge each other to grow both spiritually and intellectually.

Social action: Doing a social justice project that reflects Jewish values can foster a deep sense of partnership and purpose within a congregation.

It's a mistake to show up at synagogue one day and expect it to change your life immediately. It takes time to become part of a spiritual community, and it's not at all a one-way street. To reap the benefits of belonging, you have to invest your time. Attend services regularly for a while, take a class after work, or help out with the food drive. The synagogue provides the framework, but you are ultimately responsible for helping build the community you want to be a part of.

Feeling at Home in the Synagogue

The synagogue can be a little intimidating at first. The formality of the services and the grandeur of the architecture are supposed to be spiritually inspiring, but they can also wind up making you feel self-conscious and uncomfortable. And if you don't know Hebrew or haven't been to services in a while, you might feel a little disoriented.

That's the way I felt when I first started attending synagogue regularly. I wasn't even sure which book was the *siddur* and which was the *chumash!* After I figured that out, I had an impossible time keeping up with what page we were on. I was perpetually lost. I wasn't sure when to sit or when to stand, yet it seemed like second nature to everyone else there.

Over time, however, I gradually learned the ropes so that now, anywhere in the world I might travel, I can feel at home in a synagogue of any denomination. And it's not because I'm a scholar of Jewish tradition! You can read all the books in the world about synagogue worship, but none of them can teach you as much as you can learn from doing it. Participating in synagogue services, I came to appreciate the spiritual rhythm of the year and slowly learned about all the different facets of synagogue life.

We are meant to feel at home in the synagogue. Yes, as a house of worship, its architecture is intended to inspire awe and reverence. But it's also supposed to be a sanctuary—a place where we can open our hearts and souls to the divine presence. After all, how can we do that important spiritual work if we're not 100 percent at ease? In this next section, I explain how a typical Jewish house of worship is organized and why.

Turning Toward Jerusalem

Since ancient times, it's been Jewish custom to face the holy city of Jerusalem during prayer. This is done out of reverence for the site of the ancient Temple, which was God's dwelling place, and also because Jerusalem is the spiritual home of the Jewish people. For us in the United States, this means directing our prayers toward the east.

Because of this custom, synagogues are typically built with the focal point of the sanctuary, the *bimah* (*BEE-mah*) and the ark facing eastward. If for some reason a house of worship is oriented in a different direction, some congregations turn to face east during certain points in the prayer service, like the *amidah*.

I find the idea of Jews throughout the world over turning to face Jerusalem in prayer three times each day to be a powerful image. It's certainly the case that our prayers are effective no matter which way we face. But the notion that Jews everywhere keep Jerusalem and the ancient Temple in mind each day with this physical gesture is a very touching symbol of unity that links Jews in the past, present, and future.

Elements of Sacred Space

Synagogue architecture draws on the symbolism of the ancient Temple to create an inspiring space for prayer, infused with Jewish history. As with all Jewish customs, there's tremendous variation in style among synagogues. Some synagogues are very ornate, with stained-glass windows and elaborate fixtures, while some are modest structures that perform their function with humility.

But all synagogues have a few key elements in common.

The Ark

The first thing you'll notice when you enter a synagogue is the *aron ha-kodesh (ah-RONE ha-KO-desh)*, or the Holy Ark, which holds the sacred scrolls of the *Torah*. The ark is the centerpiece of the sanctuary and is usually fixed on the eastern wall. The ark actually takes its name from the biblical description of the holy ark of the covenant, which contained the tablets of the 10 commandments as the Israelites encamped in the desert.

Torah Tip

Upon entering a synagogue, it's customary to recite a special biblical passage from the Book of Numbers. It's the blessing the prophet Balaam uttered when he looked out in admiration at the encampment of the ancient Israelites:

> How good are your tents, Jacob; your dwelling places, O Israel!
>
> *Mah tovu oha-aleicha Ya'akov; mishkenotekha Yisrael!*

The ark is typically rectangular, with doors or a curtain across the front. It's often decorated with key symbols relating to the *Torah,* like the 10 commandments or a tree, symbolizing the Tree of Life. Sometimes the ark is embellished in a way that recalls the tabernacle, with cherubim embroidered on the curtains. A small lamp called the eternal light, or *ner tamid (NAIR tah-MEED)*, sits at the very top of the ark. This lamp is perpetually illuminated as a sign of God's enduring presence among us.

During worship services, the ark is opened at key points to reveal the *Torah* scrolls. It's considered an honor for members of the congregation to open and close the ark during services. When the ark is open, it's customary to rise as a sign of respect before the *Torah* scrolls. There are also moments in the service when you bow before the ark as a sign of reverence and humility.

It's not that the scrolls themselves are being venerated. The *Torah* is a manifestation of the divine word, and as such, the scrolls represent God's presence in our midst. In this way, the ark is like the holy of holies— that inner sanctum of the ancient Temple that was the seat of God's concentrated presence in ancient Jerusalem. Today when we stand before the ark in prayer, we can imagine ourselves as priests entering God's inner sanctum.

The *Bimah*

Another focal point in the synagogue sanctuary is the reading platform, or *bimah*. The *bimah* is an elevated area situated at a central point in the room. Public, ritual reading of the *Torah* scrolls takes place on the *bimah*. It's also fairly typical for the prayer leader to stand at the *bimah* during worship services. The rabbi might also deliver the sermon from this point.

You'll find several different customs regarding the placement of the *bimah* in the sanctuary. In some synagogues, the *bimah* is placed in the very center of the room, with seating angled toward the center, so everyone in the congregation can hear equally well as the *Torah* is chanted. In other communities, the *bimah* is closer to the eastern wall, in front of the ark, with seating that's more theater style.

The *bimah* is elevated so congregants can see what's happening during the service. But the height of the *bimah* is also a symbol of spiritual ascent. When you approach the *bimah*, you elevate your spiritual status by coming closer to the divine presence. This is why we use the word *aliyah* (*ah-lee-YAH*), which means "ascend," when we talk about being called up to participate in the *Torah* service. Just as the Jerusalem Temple was situated on an elevated height, so ascending to the *bimah* is an opportunity for us to move to a higher spiritual plane.

Gender Segregation

If you attend services at an Orthodox synagogue, you might be surprised to learn upon entering that men and women are seated in separate areas of the sanctuary. In the context of secular American culture, where gender equality not only is the norm but, in many cases, is actually enforced by law, this experience can be a little jarring.

There are two main reasons for gender segregation in traditional synagogues. On the one hand, there's an issue of modesty behind this practice. Traditional Judaism upholds the idea that sexual tension between men and women can be a major distraction in the synagogue. Whether we're talking about a married couple or young singles in search of a mate, rabbinic authorities believed that men and women sitting together would distract from the intensity of one's prayer and from the quality of one's service.

There's also the issue of the different roles men and women have in the realm of the synagogue. As I discussed in Chapter 7, among Orthodox Jews, public prayer is considered the domain of men. Women are exempt from the obligation to pray in public with a *minyan* and, therefore, are not counted as part of the prayer quorum. Because women don't count in the *minyan* in these communities, they typically don't ascend the *bimah* during services. Therefore, women aren't really a part of what's happening on the *bimah* and really don't have to be there at all.

The physical partition that separates men from women in the synagogue is called a *mechitzah* (*meh-KHEE-tzah*). A *mechitzah* can be very strict, very liberal, or somewhere in between. A strict *mechitzah* might be an opaque curtain that entirely blocks the view of women. A more liberal *mechitzah* might be a low wall that stands only about waist height and allows women a full view of the *bimah*. A moderate *mechitzah* could be a sheer fabric curtain, a row of plants, or a panel made of latticework.

In some synagogues that make an effort to create an atmosphere that's inclusive of women, the room is divided equally down the middle, with men on one side and women on the other. In others, women sit in an elevated balcony, while men fill the entire room below. The Orthodox synagogue near where I live reserves seating in the center of the room for men, with two women's sections flanking each side, on the margins.

You might be wondering how any woman in the twenty-first century could tolerate sitting behind a *mechitzah*. Can this practice be viewed as anything but sexist and offensive to women and men alike? All the liberal denominations of Judaism have eliminated the *mechitzah*, in part because it seems so out of step with modern values. So if you visit any of the other denominations, men and women sit side by side, enabling families to sit all together during services.

However, many traditional women find spiritual and social value in the *mechitzah*. A lot of women enjoy the camaraderie and companionship of the women's section and use the time to socialize with their friends on *Shabbat* and Jewish holidays. Many men also agree that they can focus better on their prayers without the distractions of their spouse and noisy children nearby.

When I first started attending synagogue services, I actually enjoyed the anonymity of the women's section. It enabled me to participate in services, but as more of a spectator, so I could observe and learn quietly on my own. Over time, however, I gravitated toward an egalitarian community, where I could participate more fully in the service and in the reading of the *Torah*.

Every synagogue is different, and every Jewish person is different. Only you know what feels most comfortable for you.

More Ritual Objects

You might notice a few more items decorating the synagogue sanctuary. Many synagogues keep a *menorah* on the *bimah* as another symbol of the lamp stand that was lit in the ancient Temple.

In America, some synagogues raise flags of both the USA and the modern State of Israel. The American flag is a sign of national loyalty to the secular government and the founding ideas and principles of the United States. The Israeli flag is a symbol of solidarity with the Jewish homeland.

Many synagogues decorate their walls with memorial lamps in honor of loved ones who have passed away. These lamps are lit annually on the anniversary of the person's death as a reminder to recite *kaddish* for them.

Jewish Clergy

As I mentioned a few chapters back, it's the Jewish belief that human beings pray directly to God. There's no formal intermediary to absolve us of our transgressions or intervene on our behalf. The synagogue is a democratic community, in the sense that anyone with the appropriate knowledge can serve as a prayer leader, read from the *Torah,* or give a *d'var Torah.* You don't need any special ordination or certification to play these roles, and it's even possible for a synagogue to function without a rabbi at the helm.

This isn't to say, however, that there's no place for clergy in the Jewish community. Rabbis and cantors play a very significant role in Jewish life, especially in the United States. A rabbi is an expert in Jewish law and practice who serves as a spiritual guide, mentor, and role model for the community. A rabbi working in a congregation is responsible for setting the spiritual priorities in the community and teaching them regularly from the pulpit.

wisdom
of the
sages

Find yourself a Rabbi, and acquire for yourself a friend.

—Ethics of the Fathers

A cantor is typically a vocalist who is also an expert in Jewish liturgy. The cantor is responsible for overseeing all liturgical aspects of the worship services, including the public reading of the *Torah.* It's also the cantor's job to add beauty and flourish to the services.

In the classical tradition, the cantor is a performer who has been trained in an operatic vocal style, and many people would come to synagogue "to hear the cantor." In more recent generations, the role of the cantor has begun to change in favor of a more informal style. Some of the younger cantors today might use a guitar or keyboard to incorporate folk melodies that foster a participatory atmosphere. I've come to appreciate the technical expertise and grandeur of the classical cantorate, but I tend to love services that have a lot of opportunities for congregational singing.

Both rabbis and cantors play an important role in the community as spiritual advisers. In traditional communities, it's customary to consult the rabbi on specific matters related to Jewish law and practice. Rabbis and cantors also officiate at lifecycle events and provide pastoral counseling during times of need.

Jewish clergy are a great resource for you as you deepen your knowledge of Jewish tradition and your spiritual life. They're very learned and often very busy people, but rabbis and cantors are human beings. They typically love Jewish texts and traditions so much that they decided to make a career of studying and practicing Judaism. Don't be afraid to ask them questions. Connecting with a spiritual leader is an important step in your journey.

Synagogue Leaders

A Jewish prayer leader is called a *shaliakh tzibur* (*shah-LEE-akh tzee-BOOR*), meaning "one who is sent on behalf of the community." The *shaliakh tzibur* is the communal representative responsible for praying on behalf of the entire congregation. Although it's common for a cantor to serve as the *shaliakh tzibur,* any knowledgeable individual who is part of the *minyan* may perform this function. It's common for a *bar* or *bat mitzvah* to serve as *shaliakh tzibur* for part of the service on the day of their celebration.

Finding Your Spiritual Home

It can take a long time to find a Jewish community that feels like home. And once you've found one, you won't necessarily stay there forever. As we grow and our lives change, we bring different needs to the table. Here are some things to think about as you explore the options in your area:

- Do you find the worship services engaging?

- Do you connect with the rabbi's sermons? Do you find them thought-provoking? Inspiring?

- Are the congregants welcoming? If you show up as a newcomer on *Shabbat,* does someone acknowledge your presence? Invite you to sit with them at *kiddush* following services?

- Have you met people you can connect with?

- If you have children, have you met other families with kids of comparable ages?

- Do any synagogue activities outside of prayer services capture your interest, like a book club or social action committee?

- Do you feel like you can be your best and most true self when you're there?

A sacred community, in its ideal form, should be a place where you can be yourself. It should be an environment that fosters spiritual growth and increased learning. It should embody the values meaningful to you. In short, it should be a place where you feel like you belong.

Essential Takeaways

- A synagogue is a sacred community of individuals united in a desire to live a life of meaning, guided by principles of the *Torah.*
- Joining a synagogue is a financial commitment you make to the community that helps support its infrastructure.
- The sanctuary is a sacred space designed to foster meaningful, communal prayer.
- Any Jewish person with appropriate knowledge of the liturgy can lead services, read from the *Torah,* or deliver a teaching to the community.
- Jewish clergy are legal and ritual experts who serve as spiritual role models and teachers in the congregation.

chapter 16

The People of the Scroll

Understanding the art of chanting *Torah*

Why Jews practice this form of ritual reading

The sanctity of the *Torah* scroll

How to follow along in the *Torah* service

In Chapter 4, you learned some basic ideas about what the *Torah* is and why it's so precious to the Jewish people. In this chapter, we pick up where we left off. Here, I talk more specifically about the role the *Torah* plays in Jewish prayer and formal worship services.

One of the most profound components of Jewish spirituality is its deep reverence for study. After all, the entirety of Jewish religious tradition centers on a vision of God communicating with us through a holy text! That text, which is, of course, the *Torah,* is the inheritance of every single Jew. To claim that inheritance, Judaism places a high value on reading and study of the *Torah* as a spiritual practice.

There is no greater expression of the Jewish commitment to literacy and learning than the ritual of chanting the *Torah* in public worship. The whole ceremony surrounding the communal reading of the *Torah* scrolls is a fascinating and inspiring dimension of Jewish spirituality. In this chapter, I go over the ins and outs of the *Torah* service to help you appreciate what this ancient practice is really all about. Once you really understand what's going on, you'll get so much more out of it next time you experience it.

The *Torah* Service

During an ordinary week, the *Torah* is read publicly four times. The most elaborate and extensive reading takes place on *Shabbat* morning, embedded in the *shaharit* service. Shorter reading ceremonies also take place Saturday afternoon during the *mincha* service and on Monday and Thursday mornings during the *shaharit minyan*.

The *Torah* is also read in synagogue on holidays and festivals, including *Rosh Hodesh,* the celebration of each new month in the Jewish calendar. On major and minor fast days, the *Torah* is also taken out and read.

No matter when the *Torah* reading takes place, it's the high point of the worship service. It's an opportunity for many congregants to participate actively, by either chanting from the scroll, reciting the blessings before and after the readings, assisting the reader as *Gabbai,* dressing the *Torah,* opening and closing the ark, or sharing a *d'var Torah.*

At the start of the *Torah* service, the *Torah* is taken out of the ark and processed around the room with joyous singing and ceremonial flair. The reading of the scroll itself is an exercise in the value of community. The practice of reading *Torah* is different from reading any other book—you might say, "It takes a village."

Torah Tip

If you attend a service that includes a *Torah* reading, you may be invited to participate. An *aliyah* is a special *mitzvah* to include guests in the ceremony, and it's completely okay to ask for help if you're not sure what your job entails. If your Hebrew is a little rusty, most congregations have English transliterations of the blessings available, and many jobs don't require speaking at all.

Taking the *Torah* from the Ark

The *Torah* service begins at the conclusion of the *shaharit* service. While everyone is still seated, we recite a hymn that begins …

> None compare to you, *Adonai,* and nothing
> compares to your creation. Your sovereignty is
> everlasting. Your dominion endures throughout all
> generations. (*Siddur Sim Shalom*)

A person from the congregation then ascends the *bimah* to open the ark, by either sliding open a curtain or opening its doors. Once the ark is open, the entire congregations stands, out of respect for the sanctity of the *Torah* scrolls. We then recite the following verse, which draws on the image of God as a protector in battle:

> Whenever the Ark was carried forward, Moses
> would say, Arise, *Adonai!* May your enemies be
> scattered, may your foes be put to flight. For *Torah*
> shall come forth from Zion, and the word of *Adonai*
> from Jerusalem. Praised is the one who gave the
> *Torah* to the people Israel in holiness. (Adapted from
> *Siddur Sim Shalom*)

This verse explicitly connects the synagogue's ark to the biblical ark of the covenant, and its triumphal tone is meant to inspire pride among the community.

Standing before the open ark is a moment of tremendous spiritual potential on a personal level. Imagine yourself as a priest in the ancient Temple, entering the holy of holies—the most sacred place on Earth—to stand before the divine presence. In our day, standing before the ark is as close as we come to experiencing that level of holiness in our prayer. Use this moment to make a personal supplication to God. Close your eyes and try to feel the sacred energy of those scrolls, which have guided the Jewish people for generations.

After reciting a few more hymns before the open ark, a congregant who has been invited to receive the honor of carrying the *Torah* will come forward and take the *Torah* scroll from the ark. The scroll can be very heavy, so this is definitely a two-handed job. Sometimes the *Gabbai*, or the prayer leader, takes the *Torah* out of the ark for you and hands you the scroll. It's customary to hold the rolled side of the scroll facing out, with the top of the *Torah* resting on your right shoulder.

Holding the *Torah*

It's hard to describe what it feels like to hold a *Torah* scroll. In some respects, it's kind of like holding a sleeping child because you need to keep it upright, rest it on your shoulder, and manage its weight by embracing it with both arms. But the *Torah* also has symbolic "weight." The person carrying the *Torah* is symbolically carrying forward the weight of the tradition.

The person holding the *Torah* then faces the congregation, and the *Shema* is recited responsively. The prayer leader turns for a moment to bow toward the ark and says:

> Proclaim *Adonai's* greatness with me; let us exalt God together. (*Siddur Sim Shalom*)

Procession of the *Torah*

Next, the *Torah* procession begins. It's customary for the prayer leader to lead a procession around the room, giving everyone in the congregation an opportunity to touch and kiss the *Torah* scroll. During the procession, a festive and participatory hymn is chanted as the *Torah* is paraded around like royalty.

The procession usually includes the rabbi and cantor, which gives them an opportunity to circulate and greet everyone personally. If there's a family celebrating a *bar* or *bat mitzvah,* they might join in the procession as well, giving family and friends in attendance the opportunity to say "*Mazal tov!*"

When the *Torah* comes around to where you're sitting, it's appropriate to move toward the aisle so you can get within reach of the scroll as it comes around. When the procession stops, take the fringes of your *tallit* or the *siddur* you're holding and touch it to the *Torah*. Then kiss the fringes or the *siddur* as a sign of love and reverence for the *Torah*.

As the prayer leader passes by during the *Torah* procession, it's customary to touch the scroll with, and then kiss, a *siddur* or *tallit*.
(Photo by Jess Borba, courtesy of Camp Ramah in the Poconos)

The thing I love about the *Torah* procession is that it breaks down the barrier between those conducting the service and the congregation. When the clergy move through the congregation with the *Torah*, they're inviting all of us to join them in reading the *Torah* and honoring its sacred message.

When the procession stops, the *Torah* is then "undressed" at the reading desk. Its decorative mantle is removed, along with any ornaments that may adorn it. The reader then locates the place in the scroll that will be read and places a cover over the scroll temporarily so it's not sitting open during the preliminary blessings.

The Anatomy of a *Torah* Scroll

The wooden portion of a *Torah* scroll is called the *eytz hayim,* or Tree of Life. Because each scroll is wrapped around two wooden dowels, we use the plural form, which is *atzay hayim.*

Sometimes the *atzay hayim* are crowned with *rimonim,* or ornate silver embellishments that sit on top of the scroll when it rests in the ark. Silver ornamental breastplates also sometimes add decorative flourish to the *Torah* scroll. These are generally hung over the *atzay hayim* with a chain so the decorative breastplate lays across the front of the scroll.

The cloth used to tie the scroll securely when it's not in use is the *wimpel* or *gertel.* It's Jewish custom to make the *wimpel* out of the swaddling cloth from a *brit milah* ceremony. The cloth covering that slips over the *Torah* like a dress is the mantle. The mantle might be made of velvet, silk, or other fine fabrics. Sometimes the mantle is embroidered with designs like the 10 commandments, a Tree of Life, or the name of the person for whom the scroll had been dedicated.

Sometimes a silver pointer, called a *yad,* is also hung on the *Torah* scroll. A *yad* looks a lot like a pen with the shape of a human hand in the pointing position at the very tip. A *yad* is used to keep the reader's vision focused in the right place as the *Torah* is read. Using a *yad* protects against touching the ink with our hands, which could erode the ink.

Preserving the *Torah*

A *Torah* scroll is handwritten with quill and ink on real animal hide. The art of writing Jewish sacred texts is performed by a scribe, or *sofer.* Over time, *Torah* scrolls, and other sacred documents like *mezuzot* and *tefillin,* are checked to be sure the ink hasn't faded or chipped, compromising the integrity of the text. A *sofer* can be hired to inspect and repair documents that have become too worn for ritual use.

Ascending to the *Torah*

It's a great honor to participate in the reading of the *Torah,* whether you're actually reading the scroll itself or reciting the blessings before and after each section. We use the term *aliyah* to describe being "called up" to the *Torah.* On the literal level, the reading desk is usually on an elevated platform or on the *bimah.* On a metaphorical level, you are elevated spiritually as you approach this ancient, sacred scroll.

Sometimes it's nice to celebrate a special occasion with an *aliyah* to the *Torah.* It doesn't even have to be a religious occasion. People often have an *aliyah* to celebrate a birthday or anniversary, or to pray for a safe journey when they're going on vacation. It's customary to have an *aliyah* when you're commemorating a *yahrtzeit,* the anniversary of a death in the family. And it's tradition for the groom (and bride, in egalitarian settings) to have an *aliyah* to the *Torah* on the *Shabbat* prior to their wedding day.

The number of *aliyot* (plural of *aliyah*) in the service varies depending on the day. At regular weekday services, there are three *aliyot.* On *Shabbat* morning, there are seven, in celebration of the seventh day of creation. On *Rosh Hodesh,* the celebration of the new month, there are four. On most of the Jewish holidays, there are five, except for *Yom Kippur,* when there are six. On days when the *haftarah,* a section from the Prophets, is read, there is an additional *aliyah* called the *maftir.* This *aliyah* usually goes to the person who will be chanting the *haftarah.*

How to Have an *Aliyah*

If you are honored with an *aliyah* to the *Torah,* you'll be given a specific number—first, second, third, and so forth. In some congregations, the *Gabbai* distributes cards that tell you which *aliyah* is yours. It's important to pay attention so you know when it's your turn to go up to the *bimah.*

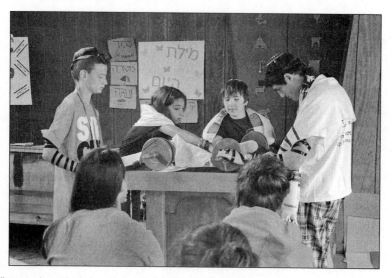

When you have the honor of an *aliyah* to the *Torah,* touch the *tallit* to the inside of the scroll and then kiss the *tallit.*
(Photo by Jess Borba, courtesy of Camp Ramah in the Poconos)

Many communities reserve the first *aliyah* for descendents of the *kohanim* (*ko-hah-NEEM*), who served as priests in the ancient Temple. The second *aliyah* is reserved for descendents of the tribe of Levi, known as Levites (*LEE-vites*), who also played a special role in ancient Temple worship. The remaining honors are open to anyone among the tribes of Israel. Some liberal congregations have done away with this distinction in the *Torah* service altogether.

In traditional synagogues, including Conservative congregations, it's customary to wear a *tallit* and a head covering when you have an *aliyah* to the *Torah.* In more liberal settings, this might not be an expectation. If you're not sure, you could bring along a *kipah* or a nice hat just in case.

When you're called up to the *Torah,* it's customary to use your Hebrew name as you approach the reading stand. The *Gabbai,* who should be standing to the right of the *Torah* reader, will announce, "*Ya'amod ...!*" (or "*Ta'amod ...!*" for women), which means "Stand up ...!" At this point, you should quietly whisper your Hebrew name to the *Gabbai,* who will then repeat it out loud. This is your special invitation to come forward and recite the blessings over the *Torah.*

> **Torah Tip**
>
> If you don't have a Hebrew name, you can still have an *aliyah* to the *Torah.* The *Gabbai* can simply call you up according to the number of the *aliyah* you are receiving. For example, *Ya'amod ha-shlishi!* means "Will the third *aliyah* please stand up!" In some congregations, this is actually the practice for calling everyone up to the *Torah.* It can sometimes be challenging for the *Gabbai* to repeat everyone's name accurately, so using numbers is a simpler method.

Once you've been summoned to the *Torah,* the reader opens the scroll and shows you the place in the text that's about to be read. You should take the fringes of your *tallit* in your hands and touch the scroll in that spot. Then kiss the fringes, release them, and take hold of the *atzay haim* as you recite the following blessing:

> Bless *Adonai,* who is Blessed.
>
> *Barekhu et Adonai ha-mevorakh.*

The congregation then responds:

> Bless *Adonai,* who is blessed for eternity.
>
> *Barukh Adonai ha-mevorakh l'olam va ed.*

Next, repeat the preceding line, and continue:

> You are blessed, *Adonai,* our God, Sovereign of the Universe, who has chosen us from among all peoples and given us your *Torah.* Blessed are you, *Adonai,* who gives the *Torah.*
>
> *Barukh atah Adonai, Eloheinu, Melech Ha-Olam, asher bahar banu mi-kol ha-amim, v'natan lanu et torato. Barukh atah Adonai, notein ha-Torah.*

Now the reader chants a passage from the *Torah,* using the *yad* as a guide. The *Gabbai* who called you up to the *Torah* will be following along in the printed text to be sure the reader doesn't make any mistakes. There's usually a second *Gabbai* to the left of the reader who is also checking for accuracy.

While the reader is chanting, take some time to glance at the beauty of the *Torah* scroll. Notice its calligraphy and the texture of the parchment. See how the reader moves through the columns of the text, and try to take in the beauty of the melody. This is your *aliyah*—the reader is chanting on your behalf, so try not to zone out or let your own self-consciousness take away from the moment. It's over before you know it!

The *Torah* reader uses a small pointer called a *yad* to keep the place in the text. The reader is assisted by a *Gabbai*, who follows along in a printed edition and checks for accuracy.
(Photo by Jess Borba, courtesy of Camp Ramah in the Poconos)

When the reader has finished reading the *aliyah*, they will show you the point in the text where the section ended. Once again, take the fringes of your *tallit* and touch them to the spot. Kiss the fringes, take hold of the *atzay hayim,* and recite the following blessing:

> You are blessed, *Adonai* our God, Sovereign of the Universe, who has given us the true *Torah* and has placed within our midst everlasting life. You are blessed, *Adonai,* who gives the *Torah.*

*Barukh atah Adonai Eloheinu, Melech Ha-Olam,
asher natan lanu torat emet, hayei olam natah be-
tokhaynu. Barukh atah Adonai, notein ha-Torah.*

At this point, your *aliyah* is technically over, but it's not time to go back to your seat just yet. You should stand now to the right of the reader as the next *aliyah* is called up. Remain standing at the *bimah* for the duration of the next *aliyah,* and return to your seat afterward.

There are some slight variations in the blessings for an *aliyah.* In Reconstructionist liturgy, the blessing omits the reference to the Jews as God's "chosen" people. A beautiful alternative translation of the traditional blessings before and after an *aliyah* appears in the Reform prayer book:

> Holy one of Blessing,
> Your Presence fills creation.
> You have enlightened this path
> With the wisdom of *Torah,*
> Giving it to the Jewish people
> As their particular way.
> Blessed are you, Merciful One,
> Who gives this *Torah* to the Jewish people.
>
> Holy one of Blessing,
> Your presence fills creation.
> This *Torah* is a teaching of truth,
> Whole and balanced,
> And from it comes eternal life
> For the people who embrace it.
> Blessed are You, Merciful One,
> Who gives this *Torah* to the Jewish people.
>
> —Mishkan T'filah

No matter what words you use, these blessings aim to make the moment of approaching the *Torah* into a sacred occasion.

Near the *Torah*

There's a tradition that we should rush to ascend the *bimah* when we're called for an *aliyah* but we should take our time coming down. We want the experience of being near the *Torah* to last as long as possible. So it's common to linger at the *bimah* as long as possible after an *aliyah*.

Chanting the *Torah*

The *Torah* scroll is written in Hebrew script without any vowels, punctuation, or line breaks. This means the reader, called in Hebrew a *ba'al koray*, has to be something of an expert in chanting the text. To read from the *Torah* scroll, the reader has to memorize the precise pronunciation of each word and breaks between verses.

The reader must also memorize the melody, or the *trop*. In the early Middle Ages, a group of scholars called the Masoretes developed an official version of the biblical text that became the standard in Jewish communities around the globe. The Masoretes also established a system of musical notation that standardized the way the text would be vocalized. This system of vocalization is called cantillation. Today printed copies of the *Torah* include vowels, punctuation, and cantillation marks to assist the reader in preparation for chanting from the scroll.

Learning to chant from the *Torah* scroll was an incredibly important part of my own personal spiritual growth. When you study a passage of *Torah* in preparation for chanting it in synagogue, you learn the text very intensively. The musical *trop* adds drama to your understanding of the text and sometimes helps bring out new interpretations. And because it's important to read every word correctly, it's a great opportunity to learn some of the finer nuances of biblical Hebrew.

But for me, the most important spiritual lesson of this practice is the way I felt it connected me to Jews everywhere, through both time and space. Bringing the words to life out of the sacred *Torah* scroll, and vocalizing them according to the melodies used by Jews for centuries, is a very powerful experience. Every single time I read in synagogue, I am moved by the idea of becoming a channel for the *Torah*. Through the *ba'al koray,* God's words are alive in the community, for us to study and probe for guidance and inspiration.

Many synagogues offer evening courses for adults who want to learn the art of *Torah* cantillation. If you know a little Hebrew and have a good musical ear, you will pick it up in no time. And even if those are not your strengths, don't be afraid to try it. If you never wind up chanting *Torah* yourself at the *bimah,* understanding how the *trop* works can really enhance your enjoyment of the *Torah* service overall. It's nice to be able to follow along and appreciate a really skilled *ba'al koray.*

Chironomy

Before printed copies of the Bible were readily available, the *ba'al ko-ray* was guided by a system of hand gestures known as *chironomy* (ky-RAH-no-mee). A *Gabbai* would assist the reader by using hand signals to indicate the *trop* pattern throughout the *aliyah.* Today it's rare to find someone who practices the art of chironomy, but these specialists do exist. Chironomy adds an interesting artistic element to the drama of the reading and looks almost like someone using sign language.

Returning the *Torah* to the Ark

After the *Torah* is read, and after the *haftarah,* if there's a section read from the prophets that day, it's time to return the *Torah* to the ark. This is done with the same pomp and circumstance we used to take it from the ark. Two individuals from the congregation are called up to the *bimah* to lift and dress the *Torah.*

After the *Torah* reading is complete, the scroll is lifted for the entire congregation to see.
This honor is called *hagbah*.
(Photo by Jess Borba, courtesy of Camp Ramah in the Poconos)

The honor of *hagbah* (*HOG-bah*) goes to someone who is able to take hold of both *atzay hayim*, lift the scroll, and turn around so the congregation is able to see at least three columns of text. When the *Torah* is lifted, the congregation says:

> This is the *Torah* that Moses placed before the children of Israel, given by *Adonai*, through Moses.
>
> *V'zot ha Torah, asher sam Moshe, lifnay b'nai Yisrael al pi Adonai, b'yad Moshe.*

The *hagbah* is then seated as another person honored with *g'lilah,* or wrapping and dressing the *Torah,* secures the scroll with the wimple and replaces the mantle and *rimonim.*

Hagbah is often given to a man, but I've been at many *minyanim* where women have had this honor. It's important that the person honored with *hagbah* be strong enough to support the entire weight of the *Torah.* If the *Torah* is dropped, all those who witness the fall are required to fast as an expression of mourning!

Following *hagbah,* the *Torah* then processes around the congregation once more and is returned to the ark. Before closing the ark, we sing one of the most beautiful hymns in Jewish liturgy:

> She is a Tree of Life for those who cling to her, and
> all her ways are just. Her pathways are pleasant, and
> all her paths are peace. Help us return to you, and we
> shall return. Renew our lives as you once did.

The ark is closed, the congregation is seated, and the service moves on to the next stage.

Essential Takeaways

- The *Torah* is read publicly four times each week, on holidays, and on fast days.
- Reading the *Torah* in synagogue is a ritual that expresses Judaism's high value on the transmission of our most sacred text.
- The *Torah* service is one of the most participatory aspects of Jewish worship.
- The *Torah* scroll is treated with utmost sanctity in Jewish tradition.
- If a *Torah* falls or is dropped, it's customary for those who witnessed the event to fast as an expression of their sorrow.

chapter 17

Jewish Spirituality at Home

Why the home is central in Jewish life

What it means to keep a kosher home

Ritual objects for the home

The *mikvah* and the idea of "family purity"

The synagogue is the focal point of public worship in the Jewish community. But it's certainly not the only place to cultivate a meaningful spiritual life. Many of the most important Jewish ritual practices actually take place at home. In fact, if you ask people to name their most meaningful Jewish memories, they'll probably talk about a *Shabbat* meal, a *seder,* or the *menorah* lighting at home among family and friends.

Home is where the Jewish heart is. The home is a fundamental building block of Jewish community because it's the primary place where Jewish values are instilled and lived. We've already seen how profoundly Judaism values the transmission of the *Torah* to the next generation. The home plays a major part in this process because, ideally, it's an environment where *mitzvot* are modeled and reinforced.

In Part 3, we saw the important role the home plays in the celebration of *Shabbat* and Jewish holidays. In this chapter, you learn about other Jewish traditions that can help you nurture a spiritual environment in your own home. You'll find a lot of information in these pages, but don't let it overwhelm you. The basic principle behind each of these practices is that they're there to help create an atmosphere for living that reflects the core values of the *Torah*.

A Small Sanctuary

The ancient rabbis taught that the home, like the synagogue, and like the Temple before it, is a dwelling place for the divine presence. Home-centered practices like the Jewish dietary laws and the laws that govern marital intimacy infuse even our most instinctive human behaviors with sanctity and make the Jewish home a vessel for holiness. In contrast to the kind of worship that takes place in synagogue, when we invite the divine presence into our homes, we can experience God in ways that are very private and deeply personal.

The primary and indispensible locus of Jewish life is undoubtedly the home, where the child receives his first impressions, and where he obtains the basic layer of his cultural and spiritual life. It is there that the principal Jewish habits and Jewish values should be transmitted from one generation to the other.

—Mordecai Kaplan, *Judaism as a Civilization*

The *Torah* says, "Build me a sanctuary that I may dwell within it." (Exodus 25:8) In antiquity, the Temple was God's dwelling place. But after the Jerusalem Temple was destroyed and Jews were dispersed throughout the Mediterranean, our homes became an anchor for Jewish religious life in the diaspora. Many of the rites that had been performed by the priests in the Temple were transformed into rituals of the home that could be practiced anywhere.

For example, the sacrificial cult that stood at the heart of Temple worship was, in its time, based on the metaphor of a meal shared between God and human beings. In the Temple, offerings of food were burned or roasted on the altar. And while the fragrant odors rose up to the heavens, the priests consumed the meat. Sacrifice was a way of affirming the relationship between God and the Jewish people and was the primary means of "drawing near" to the divine presence.

The whole institution of sacrifice ceased after the destruction of the Temple. But the idea of connecting with God through sacred meals continued. Instead of "dining" at the Temple altar, the dining table in our homes became a substitute for it. Today the table is a place to draw near to God with festive meals that are sanctified with Jewish foods and traditions.

As it says in the *Talmud*:

> At the time when the Temple stood, the altar used to make atonement for a person; now a person's table makes atonement for him. (*Babylonian Talmud*, Hagigah 27a)

If our dining table represents the temple altar, then by analogy, our home is like a temple. One of the interesting things about this idea is that it transforms housework into a sacred calling. After all, if the home is a temple, then who are the priests?

By traditional standards, women take on an elevated status within the domestic sphere because the home is their realm of ritual power. Orthodox women may not have much of a role in public Jewish life, but they certainly do reign supreme within the household! The work of creating and maintaining a Jewish home can be an important expression of piety for a traditional Jewish woman.

Yose ben Yoezer of Zeradah said, "Let your house be a meeting place for the wise." (Mishna Avot 1:4)

And even in more liberal and egalitarian communities, creating a Jewish home is considered sacred work, no matter who does it. Sharing the labor of making weekly *Shabbat* meals, or assisting with other preparations at home, is a great way to cement the bonds of marriage and lets both members of a couple share ownership of the process.

Marking Doorposts

I live in a Jewish neighborhood, and many Jewish families of all denominations live within a few blocks of my home. When I take a walk around the block, I can identify a Jewish home by the *mezuzah* that hangs on the doorpost. The *mezuzah* is a sign that says proudly, "This home governed by Jewish values." It's a symbol to the outside world, but also a reminder for those who enter of the importance of *Torah* and *mitzvot*.

Definition

A **mezuzah** (*meh-zoo-ZAH;* plural: *mezuzot*) is a small, handwritten parchment made of animal skin; the scroll is also called a *klaf*. It contains the verse of the first two paragraphs of the *Shema*. The *klaf* is tucked into a small, decorative box, which is then affixed to the top third of the doorway on the right side as you enter a room.

The commandment to affix a *mezuzah* to our doorposts comes from Deuteronomy 6:9, where the Israelites are instructed to inscribe the words of God "upon the doorposts of your homes and upon your gates." This text is actually part of the first paragraph of the *Shema,* which is written on the *mezuzah* itself.

We know the custom of affixing *mezuzot* is ancient because their remnants were found, along with *tefillin,* among the treasures of the Dead Sea Scrolls. Scholars believe that, in ancient times, the *mezuzah* was considered a kind of magical amulet that would protect the inhabitants of the home from evil spirits. Even today, many Jews believe the integrity of their *mezuzot* can impact their health and happiness. It's customary to check the text of a *mezuzah* twice in seven years to be sure none of the letters have become worn.

The idea of the *mezuzah* as an amulet of protection is probably connected to the story of Passover, when Jews were instructed to smear their doorposts with lamb's blood so the angel of death would "pass over" their homes on the night the plague of the firstborn took place. As a firstborn child, I vividly remember learning this story and feeling quite reassured that the family who lived in my house before us had left a *mezuzah* on my bedroom door!

Traditional Jews affix *mezuzot* to every doorway in their home, with the exception of the bathroom. (The bathroom is excluded because it's deemed inappropriate to have a sacred *klaf* close to the toilet.) When passing from room to room, we are continually reminded of the *Torah* and of God's presence in our homes. In less traditional communities, it's customary to have just one *mezuzah* on the front door.

Torah Tip

It's customary to kiss a *mezuzah* whenever you pass one. Touch your fingers to the *mezuzah*'s case and then kiss your fingers. This gesture helps create awareness as you enter a Jewish space.

When you move into a new home, you have approximately 30 days to put up your *mezuzot*, according to Jewish law. Some people choose to have a formal housewarming to celebrate, including a *mezuzah* ceremony to add a spiritual tone to the event. It's nice to invite friends and family over for a light meal and then put up the *mezuzah* and recite the blessings together.

A celebration of this kind is called a *hanukat ha-bayit*, or dedication of the home. If you noticed the similarity of the word *hanukat* to the festival of *Hanukkah*, you picked up on an important theme. Interestingly enough, this is the same word that was used to refer to the dedication of the ancient Temple.

Here's how to affix a *mezuzah*:

1. Facing the doorway as if you're entering the room, choose a spot in the top third of the door frame on the right side. Don't locate the *mezuzah* too high because you want to be able to see it and perhaps even touch it as you pass through the doorway.

2. Position the *mezuzah* case on a diagonal, with the top of the case pointing toward the room.

3. Secure the *mezuzah* with nails, screws, or any other adhesive.

4. Recite the following blessing:

> You are Praised, *Adonai* our God, Sovereign of the Universe, who has sanctified us with the commandment to affix a *mezuzah*.

> *Barukh atah Adonai Eloheinu, Melech Ha-Olam, asher kidshanu b'mitzvotav likboah mezuzah.*

5. If you're affixing the *mezuzah* as part of a housewarming celebration, also recite the *shehecheyanu* prayer:

> You are Praised, *Adonai* our God, Sovereign of the Universe, for granting us life, for sustaining us, and for helping us to reach this day.

> *Barukh atah Adonai Eloheinu, Melech Ha-Olam, shehecheyanu, v'kiyamanu v'higianu lazman ha-zeh.*

Torah Tip

Mezuzot can be purchased at any Judaica store. Hundreds of different styles are available from retailers online, both in the United States and in Israel. You can spend more than $100 on just a case alone! A word of caution: sometimes when you're shopping for a *mezuzah,* you're buying only the decorative case. When you're ready to buy, be sure the merchant sells you the scroll as well. It's not unusual for a high-quality scroll to cost around $50. Don't be fooled by a photocopied piece of paper that might be tucked into the case for display purposes. This is not a traditional, *kosher klaf.*

Sanctifying the Way We Eat

Food is central to Jewish life. And when I say that, I'm not just talking about the bagels and lox, the *matzoh* ball soup, and the pastrami on rye that have become synonymous with Jewish culture. In Jewish tradition, eating is a vehicle for connection, for celebration, and for sanctification. Every single meal is an opportunity to connect with God.

Long before the dining table was equated with the Temple altar, the dietary laws set forth in the *Torah* infused the act of eating with the potential for holiness. Observing these dietary laws, which are known as the laws of *kashrut* (*kosh-ROOT*), is another way to make your home a sacred dwelling place for the divine presence.

Four main sources in the *Torah* provide the basis for the laws of *kashrut*. The principles we find in the biblical text are elaborated by the rabbinic tradition, so the practices we follow today are actually much more strict than what we find in the *Torah*.

Separation of Meat and Dairy

One of the basic elements of the Jewish dietary laws is the prohibition against consuming meat and milk together. The *Torah* says, "You shall not cook a kid in its mother's milk." (Exodus 23:19) This law is generally understood to reflect an ethical concept—that killing a kid in the fluid that nurtured its life is cruel and perhaps morally wrong. From this principle, the rabbis developed the practice of separating milk and meat completely.

In a kosher kitchen, separate utensils are used for preparing and eating meat and dairy foods. This means a traditional kosher kitchen has two sets of pots and pans, two sets of dishes, two sets of flatware, and even two sets of sponges for washing them. Someone with a very large kitchen might even have two dishwashers, since *halakha* does not allow meat and dairy dishes to be washed on the same racks.

Neutral Foods

Foods that are neither meat nor dairy are considered neutral, or *pareve* (*PAHRV*) . *Pareve* foods can be eaten together with either meat or dairy dishes and include all vegetables, legumes, unprocessed grains and fruit, and eggs and fish. At one time, poultry was also *pareve*. This changed in the Middle Ages, and today poultry is considered meat.

Another aspect of this keeping kosher is that meat and dairy do not combine at any single meal. This means no cheeseburgers and no veal parmesan! Jewish cuisine has developed a whole repertoire of delicious dishes that are either meat *or* dairy, so it's really not all that limiting.

After eating meat, traditional Jews wait six hours before eating dairy. This means no ice cream for dessert after that steak! Fortunately, there are many *pareve* desserts, like sorbets, fruit, and dairy-free baked goods.

More liberal Jews observing *kashrut* have different customs about this waiting period. Some wait three hours, others wait one hour, and others don't wait at all. For some Jews, the waiting period is more of a symbolic gesture of separation in deference to the biblical principle.

Prohibition of Forbidden Animals

Another aspect of *kashrut* is making a distinction between permitted animals and prohibited animals. (Leviticus 20:25) The *Torah* includes a discussion of the kinds of animals Jews are permitted to eat. For a mammal to be kosher, it has to have a split hoof and chew its cud. Cows, sheep, and goats fall into this category. Pigs have a split hoof but do not chew their cud, so they're prohibited as food. This means all pork products are not kosher.

What about fish? Any fish with both fins and scales are permissible. This means shellfish like lobster, shrimp, and clams is not kosher.

The *Torah* also prohibits the consumption of birds of prey.

Kosher Slaughter

To be kosher, animals that fall into the permissible category must still be slaughtered in a particular way. Even a kosher animal, if it died naturally or was killed in some other way, is not fit for eating. The Torah states clearly that, "You must not eat flesh that has been torn by beasts" (Exodus 22:30) and "You shall not eat anything that died a natural death." (Deuteronomy 14:21)

Kosher slaughter is performed by a trained professional, called a *shokhet* (*SHO-kheyt*). Using a very sharp blade, the *shokhet* slaughters the animal with one swift cut to the neck that severs both the trachea and the esophagus. In the case of poultry, only one of these must be cut.

According to rabbinic tradition, this was considered the most compassionate method of slaughter. Their interpretation of the biblical verses listed at the start of this section was that the *Torah* is concerned with the suffering of animals, and precautions must be taken to procure meat for food in the most humane way possible.

Kosher Vessels

The strictest interpretation of the laws of *kashrut* requires that food be prepared and served in vessels that have been used only for kosher food. This means very observant Jews won't eat food cooked in a restaurant that's not kosher. Fortunately, in cities where large Jewish populations live, many kosher restaurants cater to the needs of the traditional community.

Traditional Jews also purify their pots, pans, dishes, and utensils by immersing them in the ritual bath prior to use. Once again, this practice stems from the analogy of the Temple and the dining table. Like the vessels used by the ancient priests in the Temple, those we use to prepare food for our table/altar must be ritually pure.

Here's the blessing we recite upon the immersion of dishes and utensils in the ritual bath:

> You are Praised, *Adonai,* our God, Sovereign of the Universe, who has sanctified us with your *mitzvot,* and commands us concerning the immersion of vessels.
>
> *Barukh atah Adonai, Eloheinu, Melech Ha-Olam, asher kidshanu b'mitzvotav, vetzivanu al tevilat ha-kaylim.*

Variations in Practice

Keeping kosher at the strictest level makes it hard for observant Jews to eat together with non-Jews. In fact, throughout Jewish history, *kashrut* has kept Jews rather insulated from the outside world. So why would anyone in today's multicultural world choose to separate themselves in this way?

Kashrut can be a deeply spiritual practice, especially nowadays, when it seems we can eat whatever we want whenever we want. By contrast, the Jewish dietary laws require that we consume with a measure of restraint. Before eating a meal, we have to think, *Where did this food come from? Is it from a permissible source? In the case of meat, how was it killed?*

For those who choose to eat only from kosher vessels, it feels important to know that food has never come in contact with food from a nonkosher source. Practicing this level of separation is one way of interpreting the idea that eating is a holy act. After all, human beings have to eat—it's necessary for our survival. But what differentiates us from animals is that we eat with awareness. In this respect, *kashrut* is a spiritual discipline that teaches mindfulness and restraint.

There are so many variations in the practice of *kashrut*. Some Jews maintain a kosher lifestyle both inside and outside the home. Others keep kosher inside their home but eat anything outside the home. Even among those Jews who consider their homes kosher, tremendous variations exist. Some have two dishwashers; others wash everything together. Some separate milk and meat but have only one set of dishes. Some use only food that was produced under rabbinic supervision, while others go by the ingredients listed on the label.

Nowadays, even very liberal Jews are engaging with the concept of *kashrut* in creative ways. While they may not want the dietary laws to segregate them from secular society, the spiritual discipline *kashrut* offers is very attractive.

Dovetailing with the broader local food movement that's emerged in American culture, there's a movement underway in American Judaism that connects *kashrut* with environmentalism. Are fruits and vegetables grown with harmful pesticides that run off into streams and rivers still "kosher"? According to traditional *halakha*, yes. But some see a conflict of ethical values in this scenario. If the *Torah* were written today, wouldn't God want us to consider the environmental impact of our farming practices?

Another important example is the proliferation of factory farming, a practice the ancient rabbis could never have imagined. Is kosher *shekhita* performed in the context of a factory farm still the most humane form of slaughter?

Because the *Torah* cares about what we consume and how we consume it, many Jews today are embracing a new definition of *kashrut* that speaks to these concerns.

Mealtime Blessings

Blessings at mealtime are another opportunity to draw divine holiness into our homes. It's Jewish tradition to recite blessings of gratitude both before and after eating.

How to Begin Keeping Kosher

The detailed laws of *kashrut* can be overwhelming. No one can adopt a kosher lifestyle overnight. If you're interested in experimenting with *kashrut,* start slowly. Try adopting one practice at a time and see how it feels. For example, if you're used to eating bacon every day for breakfast, try switching to turkey bacon or skipping the meat altogether.

Also, think of every meal as a choice. Every time you sit down to nourish your body with food, you make a choice about what you'll eat and how you'll eat it. Even if you try eating just one kosher meal a week, it's a step in the right direction.

It helps, too, to find a mentor. To really learn how *kashrut* works, it's critical to talk with people who live a kosher lifestyle. A mentor can be a rabbi or your best friend's grandmother.

Allow yourself to make mistakes. Taking on the *mitzvah* of *kashrut* is an evolving process. Every person who keeps kosher makes mistakes sometimes, so don't be too hard on yourself.

Blessings for a Formal Meal

When you're sitting down for a full meal at any time of the day, it's customary to wash your hands by pouring water over them three times on each side, and recite the blessing:

> You are Blessed, *Adonai*, Sovereign of the Universe, who has sanctified us with your *mitzvot* and commanded us concerning the elevation of the hands.
>
> *Barukh atah Adonai Eloheinu, Melech Ha-Olam asher kid'shanu b'mitzvotav v'tzeevanu al netilat yadayim.*

Following hand-washing, you recite this blessing over a piece of bread:

> You are Blessed, *Adonai*, Sovereign of the Universe, who brings forth bread from the earth.
>
> *Barukh atah Adonai Eloheinu, Melech Ha-Olam, ha motzee lekhem min ha-aretz.*

The peculiar thing about this blessing is that God actually does not bring forth bread from the earth. The most interesting explanation I've heard is that bread is created in partnership between God and humanity. God provides the raw materials, and human beings created the technology that turns grain into bread.

Sometimes the ritual hand-washing and blessing over the bread is performed individually by all present. In more liberal communities, it's customary for one person to perform these actions symbolically for the group.

Bentchers

When you're participating in a meal at the home of someone who is observant, the blessings before and after the meal can be found in a small book called a *bentcher.* A *bentcher* contains all the standard blessings for weekdays, *Shabbat,* and holidays, along with some traditional table songs for festive occasions. A *bentcher* is a popular party favor at traditional weddings and *b'nai mitzvah.*

When the meal is complete, a lengthy blessing called *birkat ha-mazon,* or "Grace After Meals," is given. When three or more people have eaten a meal together, it's customary to begin this blessing with an invitation to prayer called a *mezuman* (*meh-ZOO-mun*). It's formulated as a call and response, with one leader inviting the others to participate:

The leader begins:

> Friends, let us give thanks.

The others respond:

> May God be praised, now and forever.

The leader repeats the preceding line and then continues:

> With your consent, friends, let us praise the One of whose food we have eaten.

The others respond:

> Praised be the One of whose food we have eaten and by whose goodness we live.

The leader repeats the preceding line and then everyone says in unison:

> Praised is God, and praised is God's name.

Then everyone present joins in singing together:

> We praise you, *Adonai* our God, Sovereign of the Universe, who graciously sustains the whole world with kindness and compassion. You provide food for every creature, as your love endures forever. Your great goodness has never failed us; may Your great glory always assure us nourishment. You sustain all life and You are good to all, providing all of your creatures with food and sustenance. We praise You, *Adonai,* who sustains all life.

Following this opening blessing, several more paragraphs acknowledge God as a nourishing caretaker of humanity. There's a spot during the grace where you can specifically acknowledge your host by offering him and his family a special blessing.

Some people have the custom of singing the entire blessing out loud, which can take about 10 minutes. Others recite the rest of the blessings silently.

Blessings for Snacks and Lighter Meals

If you're not sitting down to a full meal with bread, the custom is to bless the specific foods you're eating individually.

For fruit that grows on a tree, we say:

> You are Praised, *Adonai*, our God, Sovereign of the Universe, who has created the fruit of the tree.
>
> *Barukh atah Adonai, Eloheinu, Melech Ha-Olam, boray pree ha-etz.*

For fruit or vegetables that grow in the ground, we say:

> You are Praised, *Adonai*, our God, Sovereign of the Universe, who has created the fruit of the earth.
>
> *Barukh atah Adonai, Eloheinu, Melech Ha-Olam, boray p'ree ha-adamah.*

For grains, or anything besides bread made with grains, such as cookies or crackers, we recite:

> You are Praised, *Adonai*, our God, Sovereign of the Universe, who has created all varieties of nourishment.
>
> *Barukh atah Adonai, Eloheinu, Melech Ha-Olam, boray minay mezonot.*

And for all other foods, even water or other beverages, we recite:

> You are Praised, *Adonai,* our God, Sovereign of the Universe, who brings all things into being with Your word.
>
> *Barukh atah Adonai, Eloheinu, Melech Ha-Olam, she-hakol n'hiyeh bi-d'varo.*

Niddah: Separation

A traditional Jewish home is governed by another set of ritual practices called *taharat ha-mishpakha,* or the laws of family purity. Just as the laws of *kashrut* sanctify our instinctive need to eat, the laws of family purity sanctify and regulate the human sexual drive in an atmosphere of mutual love and respect.

In a home where the family purity laws are observed, the intimate life of a couple is governed by a woman's menstrual cycle. According to *halakha,* when a woman is menstruating, she is in a state of *niddah (nee-DAH),* which means "separation."

During *niddah,* a husband and wife are prohibited from having sex. The rabbis believed that, in the ideal marriage, the sexual tension between a man and woman is so high that they created a safety net around this law. To ensure a couple would not be tempted, they prohibited all physical contact during *niddah.* In traditional families, it's customary for a couple to sleep in separate beds, refrain from holding hands, and avoid gestures of physical affection. Some couples avoid passing each other things, so as not to create any kind of unintended arousal through touch.

Niddah begins the moment a woman notices any sign of blood from the uterus. The period of separation continues through the duration of her menstrual flow, which is usually 5 to 7 days, and extends for 7 "clean" days after she stops bleeding.

This means that couples may not have intimate sexual relations for approximately 12 to 14 days out of each month. I know this probably sounds strange. Why would anyone want to abide by these restrictive, ancient customs? And doesn't this all sound like some sort of primitive blood taboo?

The truth is that for women who practice the laws of family purity, there's a tremendous amount of freedom and autonomy that comes with these restrictions. And according to Jewish tradition, they are the key to a healthy marriage. Think about it: by formulating these practices, Jewish tradition acknowledges that women might need some freedom from their husbands. This was probably especially important during the earlier periods in history, when wives were viewed as property. The practice of *niddah* determines when a woman is off limits and when she is available.

A lot of couples who observe the family purity laws say the monthly separation keeps their marriage fresh and exciting. For nearly two weeks of every month, a couple has to find ways to communicate that are not physical. This means they actually have to talk or engage in other activities together—what a great way to cultivate true intimacy in a marriage!

Mikvah

After the period of *niddah* is complete and a woman has had 7 consecutive days without any sign of blood from the uterus, she must immerse in a *mikvah,* a ritual bath, before resuming sexual relations with her husband.

A *mikvah* is a gathering of waters made up at least in part by water from a natural source, like rain or a stream. Any body of water open to the elements can serve as a *mikvah,* but most communities build dedicated baths for ritual immersion. A *mikvah* can be housed in its own building, or it might be connected to a synagogue, school, or community center.

A modern *mikvah* usually has a bathroom with a shower where you prepare for immersion, and the *mikvah* itself is a small pool built into the ground. In large cities, a *mikvah* might even have several preparation rooms and several immersion pools. But in most communities, a *mikvah* is a modest structure.

In my neighborhood, the *mikvah* is housed in a simple, residential home that was converted to a ritual bath. From the outside, it looks like a small, suburban house. I'm sure most of my neighbors have no idea what's inside!

According to tradition, immersing in the *mikvah* is not about physical cleanliness. Rather, it's about marking a spiritual transition from one status to another. Because menstruation is associated with the loss of potential life (after all, a woman ovulated and could have conceived a child), she needs to transition from the state of ritual impurity to purity in order to resume her marital relations.

Spa Night?

Many married women consider the evening they visit the *mikvah* to be something of a spa night. How often do you get to take a really long shower and take care of all your grooming needs without interruption? After taking time for themselves, women can feel really good returning home to their husbands for a physical reunion. Some women say it's like the wedding night all over again!

To make the transition back to the sacred state of marital union, a woman must fulfill the *mitzvah* of immersion. In preparation for the *mikvah,* she cleanses her body thoroughly, checking under her nails, removing any polish or bandages that might form a barrier between her body and the water.

Once she is physically clean, it's time to immerse in the *mikvah's* warm waters. A typical *mikvah* has a few steps down into a small pool. She immerses her entire body one time and recites the following blessing:

> Praised are you, *Adonai,* our God, Sovereign of the
> Universe, who has sanctified us with your *mitzvot*
> and commanded us concerning the immersion.
>
> *Barukh atah Adonai, Eloheinu, Melech Ha-Olam,*
> *asher kid'shanu b'mitzvotav, v'tzeevanu al ha-tevilah.*

After reciting the blessing, she immerses two more times and then takes a quiet moment for personal prayers. This is one of the most truly amazing spiritual moments, because you have the sense of being completely alone with God. Without even the protective barrier of clothing, in the *mikvah,* it's just you, the water, and God. The experience of immersion in the *mikvah* can feel very much like a spiritual rebirth.

Other Uses of the *Mikvah*

It's customary to immerse in the *mikvah* prior to your wedding day. Many men have the custom of immersing on the eve of *Shabbat* and *Yom Kippur* as a means of spiritual preparation for those holy days.

Immersion in the *mikvah* is also part of the traditional conversion process for both men and women, as a symbol of transition into the Jewish people. When a child is adopted into a Jewish family, even in infancy, the child is often immersed in the *mikvah* following her or his conversion.

Torah Tip

You can usually find a *mikvah* by looking in the phone book or checking with the synagogues in your area. Because ritual immersion is a practice that's highly personal, traditional communities go to great lengths to protect the anonymity of those who use the *mikvah*. You'll need to schedule an appointment, and it's customary to visit the *mikvah* only after nightfall, when your anonymity can be protected.

Today new rituals surrounding the *mikvah* are on the rise, even among liberal Jews. For example, the *mikvah* can be used as part of a healing ritual when dealing with a serious illness like cancer. Some people use the *mikvah* to mark other life passages, like *bat mitzvah* or divorce. Figuring out how to incorporate *mikvah* into same-sex marriages is a hot topic of conversation in some liberal communities.

Although it has long been the practice for a woman to immerse in the *mikvah* following the birth of a child, women today are exploring the *mikvah* as a means of coping with infertility and miscarriage. I have even seen *mikvah* rituals that mark the end of the first trimester of pregnancy. How wonderful to find a uniquely Jewish way to express gratitude for making it through those precarious early weeks!

If you think about it, the family purity laws are an amazing concept. Centuries ago, the rabbinic sages developed them to increase the sanctity of marital intimacy. Today women who practice *taharat ha-mishpacha* are in touch with their bodies' rhythms and learn to speak frankly about their cycles. Viewing sex as a healthy and holy part of marriage, these customs establish limits that aim to increase its sanctity.

Essential Takeaways

- The home is just as central to Jewish spiritual life as the synagogue.
- A *mezuzah* hangs on the doorposts of a Jewish home to remind those who enter that the household is governed by Jewish values.
- A kosher home is one that observes the Jewish dietary laws. These laws help sanctify the process of eating and foster a sense of mindfulness at every meal.
- Immersion in a *mikvah* is a powerful ritual for adding sanctity to the intimacy of marriage.

chapter 18

Charity, Ethics, and Social Justice

Why social justice is so central to Judaism

The noblest form of giving

How to cultivate generosity as a spiritual practice

Expressing your spirituality through service

I recently learned a memorable lesson about charity from a friend who had been traveling in India. She was on a hike, accompanied by a professional guide and a teenage boy from the local region. By the end of the hike, my friend noticed that the boy's shoes were terribly worn with holes and barely protected his feet from the ground below him. In a gesture of compassion, she gave him her own hiking boots, which were almost brand new. He put them on, saw that they fit, and ran off.

My friend was shocked that the boy would run off without saying thank you, and she felt offended that he appeared so ungrateful for her generosity. When she expressed her feelings to the guide, he said, "Miss, you are mistaken. In our culture, you are the one who should feel gratitude to the boy for providing you with the opportunity to give."

Ironically, although this story isn't about Jews or Judaism, I think it lends a beautiful perspective on the Jewish view of charity. In Jewish tradition, the ability to give is a gift. It doesn't matter whether you're giving of your time, your money, or your possessions. Generosity and compassion are two of the most important spiritual qualities we can cultivate because they are divine qualities. For many Jews, a commitment to charity and social justice represents the very essence of Judaism. In this chapter, we explore the spirituality of giving.

Biblical Foundations

The centrality of social justice to Jewish tradition is rooted in the Bible. In the words of the Prophet Michah, "God has told you, O humanity, what is good, and what *Adonai* requires of you: Only to do justice and to love goodness and to walk modestly with your God." (Micah 6:8)

The *Torah* is deeply concerned with the ethical treatment of those on the margins of society, especially the poor. In some respects, you might even say the *Torah* is a blueprint for the creation of a just and compassionate society. It's clear that many of the precepts found in the *Torah* are grounded in an ethical imperative to help those in need.

The Book of Deuteronomy actually acknowledges that the Israelites will undoubtedly encounter poverty as they establish themselves in their new home:

> For there will never cease to be needy ones in your
> land, which is why I command you to open your
> hand to the poor and needy kinsman in your land.
> (Deuteronomy 15:11)

Recognizing the persistent reality of poverty, the *Torah* commands that we must do something to alleviate suffering. It's not just a suggestion or something we "should" do, but a *mitzvah*, a sacred duty.

The mandate to help those in need connects powerfully to the Jews' own history of oppression. Even in the Bible, God often reminds the Israelites that they must care for the stranger and those in need because they themselves know the experience of slavery and oppression. And to this day, many Jews think of Judaism as a practice that, above all, teaches how to live ethically in a world that has been less than kind to the Jewish people.

You shall not wrong or oppress a stranger, for you were strangers in the land of Egypt. You shall not ill-treat any widow or orphan.

—Exodus 22:20–23

The *Torah* is particularly concerned with the need for economic justice. In its pages, we see countless laws and practices that express concern for the orphan, the widow, the slave, and the stranger. A classic example is the practice of the sabbatical year, which provided for the full release of all debts every seven years. Every seven years, debts were completely forgiven, and even slaves were released from their bond:

> Every seventh year you shall practice remission
> of debts. This shall be the nature of the remission:
> every creditor shall release what he has loaned to
> his neighbor; he shall not dun his fellow kinsman,
> for the remission proclaimed is of *Adonai*.
> (Deuteronomy 15:1–2)

But knowing the sabbatical year is coming should not discourage you from being generous:

> If there is a needy person among you, one of your
> kinsmen, in any of your settlements in the land
> which the Lord your God is giving you, do not
> harden your heart and shut your hand against
> your needy kinsman; rather, you must open your
> hand, and lend him sufficient for whatever his
> need. Beware lest you harbor the base thought in
> your heart, saying, "The seventh year, the year of
> remission, is approaching," so that you are mean to
> your needy kinsman, and give him nothing; he will
> cry out to *Adonai* against you, and you will incur
> guilt. (Deuteronomy 15:7–9)

During the sabbatical year, land is also given a release from its burden. In a remarkable concept known as *shmittah* (*shmee-TAH*), land ordinarily used for farming would lie fallow for the entire year, as it was prohibited to plant or to reap. During that time, whatever would grow on its own in the fields would be collected by those in need.

Produce left in the fields after a harvest, because it either fell to the ground or grew on its own during the *shmittah* year, is called "gleanings." Even when it wasn't a *shmittah* year, the *Torah* establishes gleaning as a practice to enable those in need to benefit from the bounty of landowners:

> When you reap the harvest of your land, you shall
> not reap all the way to the edges of your field, or
> gather the gleanings of your harvest. You shall not
> pick your vineyard bare or gather the fallen fruit of
> your vineyard; you shall leave them for the poor and
> the stranger. (Leviticus 23:22)

Helping Those in Need

Misc.

Project SHARE is an active food pantry in my town that provides groceries to needy families every week. During the fall growing season, volunteers for Project SHARE go out to local farms for gleaning, collecting vegetables from the fields and bringing them back to the food pantry for distribution to those who can't afford fresh produce. Sometimes my husband takes our kids to Project SHARE on a Saturday morning to help distribute the groceries. It may not be a traditional way to observe *Shabbat*, but for them, it's meaningful to know they're helping people who are really struggling.

The mandate that farmers leave some of the produce behind also serves as a reminder to the landowners that the bounty of their fields is a gift from God and does not belong entirely to them.

Prayer in Action

So how do all these ideas about generosity and social justice in the Bible connect with Jewish prayer today? The truth is, in Judaism, the moral imperative to bring justice to the world is deeply intertwined with prayer.

Prayer connects us with God and community through words. But doing kind acts is a *mitzvah* and brings us close to God and community through our actions. In our prayers, we ask God to heal the world and end poverty and injustice. But when we go out and perform acts of charity, we're actually doing something to make that happen.

The *Torah* reminds us that Jewish spirituality is not just about talking with God in isolation. Living Jewishly is just as much about conducting our lives in a way that brings sanctity into the world. We have to take the prayer dialogue we have with God out into our communities and do something with it. And for lots of Jews, serving God through action is the most meaningful spiritual practice there is.

Perhaps you're the kind of person for whom sitting in synagogue feels too passive—or maybe you love synagogue worship, but also want to engage the *Torah's* teaching in a more hands-on way. Wherever you are, Judaism is a tradition that affirms the power of human beings to change the world for the better. Think of prayer as a guide to help set your social action agenda. By taking our spiritual energy out of the synagogue and actually doing something to help someone in need, we embody the spirit of *Torah* and become agents of the divine will.

Cultivating Generosity

Jewish tradition has several ways of thinking about generosity. On one hand, there's the kind of giving we're required to do. This obligatory giving is called *tzedakah* (*ts'da-KAH* or *tse-DUH-kuh*), and it's a *mitzvah,* a sacred duty to perform. On the other hand, the *Torah* also values a more organic kind of giving, which comes straight from the heart and not from a sense of obligation. This kind of giving is called *nedivut* (*neh-dee-VOOT*) and means a kind of open-heartedness.

There's also another *mitzvah* of generosity called *gemilut hasadim* (*g'mee-LOOT kha-sah-DEEM*), which means "acts of lovingkindness." *Gemilut hasadim* generally refers to the gift of one's time and strength to help those in need.

In an ideal situation, our desire to give *tzedakah* or do acts of lovingkindness is aligned with a sense of *nedivut*. But for most people, this is a big challenge, for many reasons. If it were easy to give straight from the heart, we wouldn't need to be commanded to give! Let's take a look at these ideas more carefully.

Giving from the Heart

In a scene in the *Torah,* God instructs Moses to command the Israelites to build a sanctuary for the divine presence:

> *Adonai* spoke to Moses, saying, "Tell the Israelite
> people to bring Me gifts; you shall accept gifts for me
> from every person whose heart so moves him ....
> And let them make me a sanctuary that I may dwell
> among them." (Exodus 25:1–2, 8)

The phrase "whose heart so moves him" is interpreted to mean that the Israelites brought their gifts out of a deep feeling of open-heartedness and generosity. In Jewish tradition, this episode becomes the model for the quality of generosity we should all strive toward—one where we give without any hesitation whatsoever, from a place deep within our souls.

How do we cultivate open-hearted generosity? There's no question it's a struggle. So many things close off our hearts to the needs of others. Most of the time, fear prevents us from giving. We're afraid of not having enough for ourselves, or afraid of doing without. Sometimes we're afraid to face the reality of need in the world. Coming to grips with the extent of poverty and social injustice can be simply overwhelming, and we may want to close ourselves off from that reality, out of fear that our guilt and helplessness will be too much to bear.

The Jewish value of *nedivut* asks us to peel away these layers of fear from our hearts and strive toward a generosity of spirit that's godly. God gives abundantly without receiving anything in return. So when we give in such a way that it's so automatic, so natural, and completely without hesitation, we embody that divine quality.

Here's an exercise to help you cultivate *nedivut:*

1. During prayer, or at any quiet time when you have a few minutes to yourself, close your eyes, relax, and take several deep breaths.

2. Feel how the air fills your lungs, and enjoy this felling of fullness. Notice the way you can control your breath as you exhale—letting just a little air out very slowly or forcing the air out all at once.

3. As your chest rises on the inhale, think about abundance and try to tap into a feeling of gratitude for all the gifts you enjoy in life.

4. As your chest falls, think of all you have to offer the world. And notice that when your lungs are empty, there's abundant air to fill your lungs again.

Repeat this breathing exercise as you reflect on the idea of abundance. Learning to appreciate the gift of your own life is the first step in opening your heart to generosity.

Tzedakah: Obligatory Giving

Tzedakah is an interesting word. It's usually translated to mean "charity," but this translation doesn't really capture what *tzedakah* is all about. In Hebrew, *tzedakah* is related to the word *tzedek* (*TSEH-deck*), which means "just" or "righteous." A person who is extraordinarily pious and righteous is called a *tzadik* (*tsah-DEEK*) in Jewish tradition.

So the word *tzedakah,* while it's used to describe the act of giving charity, also conveys a sense of justice or fairness in making the world right, if you will. It's not just about opening your hand to help another; it's also about playing a role in making society more just.

wisdom of the sages

The spiritual is higher than the physical, but the physical needs of others are an obligation of my spiritual life.

—Rabbi Israel Salanter

Obligatory giving in Jewish tradition can take many forms. The standard formula, based on the biblical principle of tithing, is that a person should give a minimum of 10 percent and a maximum of 20 percent of his or her income to *tzedakah* each year. Even a poor person who receives *tzedakah* is required to give in some way.

The great Jewish scholar, philosopher, and rabbi Moses Maimonides, who lived approximately 800 years ago, outlined eight levels of *tzedakah*. These levels are still taught today as a Jewish model for fulfilling the commandment to give.

Here are Maimonides' eight levels, going from the lowest level to the highest:

- A person gives unwillingly.

- A person gives cheerfully, but not enough.

- A person gives enough, but not until asked.

- A person gives before being asked, but directly to the poor person.

- The poor person knows from whom he or she takes, but the giver does not know who is receiving.

- The giver knows to whom he or she gives, but the receiver does not know the giver.

- Fully anonymous giving—the giver does not know to whom he or she gives, nor does the poor person know from whom he or she receives.

- The very highest form of *tzedakah* is to strengthen the hand of the poor by giving a loan, or joining in partnership to help a person become independent.

Maimonides' "ladder" of *tzedakah* presents an interesting framework for thinking about how we give. He starts with the premise that we must give because we're commanded to do so. But our manner of giving fulfills the *mitzvah* in different ways.

It's very clear from Maimonides' framework that we must make every effort not to shame the recipient of our gift. And the high value he places on anonymity suggests that our giving should not be motivated by a desire for self-aggrandizement. Maimonides also writes that it's important to give to causes that help those in need outside the Jewish community as well.

There's an idea in Jewish folk wisdom that if someone is on their way to perform a *mitzvah,* they enjoy the special protection of the divine presence. When someone you know is going on a significant trip, it's customary to give them a few dollars to give to someone in need at their destination. The idea is that, as a *shaliakh mitzvah,* someone sent to do a *mitzvah,* that person will return safe and sound.

Although giving *tzedakah* is a *mitzvah,* there's no traditional blessing to recite upon completing an act of charity. Doesn't it seem strange that in a tradition where there's a blessing for every conceivable occasion, a commandment as central as *tzedakah* goes without one?

The reasoning is simple: when someone is in need, we don't want to hesitate even for a moment if we can provide relief. Pausing to recite a blessing would delay this act of generosity, which, ideally, should come spontaneously from the heart. And although giving *tzedakah* is a *mitzvah,* the reality of poverty and suffering is not something we want to bless God for.

Although there's no traditional blessing for giving *tzedakah,* the reform movement has developed a new blessing that can be used to sanctify a moment of giving. This beautiful blessing is based on a verse from Deuteronomy, "Justice, Justice, you shall pursue" (Deuteronomy 16:20):

> Blessed are You, Eternal our God, Sovereign of the Universe, You hallow us with Your *mitzvot* and command us to pursue justice.
>
> *Baruch Atah Adonai, Eloheinu, Melech Ha-Olam, asher kid'shanu b'mitzvotav v'zivanu lirdof tzedek.*

There is so much need in the world, both in the United States and abroad, and so many opportunities to help others. If you're not already in the habit of giving *tzedakah,* now is a great time to get started with a cause that means something to you.

One relatively painless way to start is to begin with spare change. Every time you empty your pockets or change purses, take your pennies and other loose coins and put them in a *tzedakah* box or another small bank. You'll be amazed at how quickly your spare change adds up. Whenever you find change around your house, make a point of dropping it in the jar.

When you're lighting candles on Friday nights for *Shabbat,* it's customary to put a bit of money in the *tzedakah* box. In just two or three months, you could very well have a sizeable amount of cash in there! When the box feels full, count up the change and bring it to a local food bank or homeless shelter, or donate it to an organization that will direct your gift where it's needed most.

Living a Jewish life means joining a cause that is greater than ourselves. It means contributing to the betterment of the world, what some in the Jewish tradition have called *tikkun olam* (repairing the world). It means taking the secret of our soul and joining it to others who believe in redeeming the world through goodness and spiritual passion.

—Rabbi David Wolpe, *Why Be Jewish?*

Gemilut Hasadim: Acts of Lovingkindness

Tzedakah is a *mitzvah* that requires us to reach into our pocketbooks to help those in need. But acts of lovingkindness represent an even higher level of giving because they require us to give of ourselves. For many of us, our time is even more valuable than our money.

When we perform an act of compassion, we must focus on the needs and situation of someone outside our own immediate sphere of need. Sometimes this means leaving our comfort zone for the sake of lessening someone's pain.

How do we know that if we see someone drowning in a river, or a wild beast dragging someone off, or bandits attacking someone, we must try to save the person? Because it is said, "You shall not stand idly by the blood of your neighbor." (Leviticus 19:16)

—*Babylonian Talmud,* Sanhedrin 73a

One of the first volunteer experiences I ever had was to go with a synagogue group to visit residents in a nursing home on the afternoon before *Shabbat*. We sang songs for them, enjoyed some snacks together, and just sat and talked. I'll never forget the woman I sat with. Her name was Zipporah, and she must have been in her 90s. I was absolutely terrified of her because she was so old and sickly, but I struggled to overcome my fear.

At one point, she reached out for my hand and held it for a moment. I noticed tears well up in her eyes, and I was so moved by how grateful she was for my company. This visit was a tremendous gift to me, and I remember vividly the powerful emotions I felt that day.

Tzedakah benefits the poor. But compassionate acts of kindness have the potential to benefit everyone, regardless of their social status. Everyone gets sick, so everyone can receive the *mitzvah* of *bikkur holim*. Everyone experiences loss, so paying a *shiva* visit is a way of comforting mourners at any station in life. The *mitzvot* of *hevra kadisha,* ensuring a proper burial, is a way of doing *gemilut hasadim* even for the deceased.

Because Judaism places such a high moral value on deeds of kindness, acts of charity, and the giving of *tzedakah,* Jewish communities tend to have a very strong culture of volunteerism and community service. As I discussed in the chapter on the synagogue as a sacred community (see Chapter 15), being part of a Jewish community means getting involved.

Getting Involved

A life informed by Jewish prayer and practice can inspire you to get out into the world to do your part to make it better. But sometimes it works in the opposite way. In my own life, I've certainly had the experience of finding deep spiritual meaning in a service project that means a lot to me.

The experience of really making a difference in someone's life can be a catalyst for seeking out new ways to connect to God and to the community through prayer.

A good place to start looking for volunteer opportunities is the synagogue. Many congregations have a social action committee that organizes volunteer projects like food drives and other service projects. Children studying for *bar* or *bat mitzvah* usually prepare a year-long "*mitzvah* project" that focuses on some area of service to the broader community, and you might be able to help out in some way.

Another great resource for finding service opportunities is the local Jewish Federation, Jewish Community Center, or Jewish Family Service. These agencies provide many different services to the local community as well as communities abroad. People working in these organizations might also be able to help you find opportunities to get involved outside the Jewish community.

A number of national Jewish organizations provide volunteer opportunities throughout the world. You can volunteer on a farm, build houses for the homeless, feed the hungry, help rebuild after a natural disaster, or provide aid to soldiers in combat—all through Jewish agencies whose mission is to alleviate suffering in the world. (You can find a list of these in Appendix B.)

As you continue on your journey into deeper Jewish prayer and spirituality, I hope you will explore the depths of Jewish wisdom and tradition by finding a community in which you can continue to learn and grow. Living a meaningful Jewish life is a process—no one does it perfectly, but the goal is to strive to be the best person you can be by making the most of this sacred and holy life.

I'd like to close with an excerpt from a beautiful poem known as "The Traveler's Prayer." It's traditionally recited at the start of a journey:

> May it be your will, Eternal One, our God and the God of our ancestors, that You lead us toward peace, steer our footsteps toward peace, guide us toward peace, and help us reach our desired destination for life, gladness, and peace ….

> May You send blessing for all of our projects, and grant us peace, kindness, and mercy in your eyes and in the eyes of all who see us. May you hear the sound of our prayer, because you are the God who hears prayer and supplication. Praised are You, Eternal One, who listens to prayer.

> Amen!

Essential Takeaways

- Because Jews have historically known oppression, the *Torah* insists that we live compassionately and generously.
- *Tzedakah,* the Hebrew word for "charity," comes from the same root as the word for "justice." Giving charity to those in need is part of our mandate to create a more just society.
- Social justice work is a powerful spiritual outlet for Jews of all denominations.

Glossary

Adonai (*ah-doh-NAHY*)   Hebrew meaning "My Lord." This is just one of many names used to address God in prayer.

Aggada (*ah-ga-DAH*)   Hebrew meaning "narrative" or "telling." This term refers to the rabbinic interpretations of biblical stories.

aliyah (*ah-lee-YAH* or *a-LEE-yah*)   This term literally means "going up" to the *bimah* to receive the honor of blessing the *Torah* during services. This same word is used to describe migration to the modern state of Israel.

Am Yisrael   The people of Israel. This phrase is used to describe the unity of the Jewish people.

Amidah (*ah-mee-DAH*)   Literally, the "standing prayer." This is the high point of each daily prayer service in Jewish liturgy. It is a collection of 19 blessings, also called the *Shmoneh Esrei*.

Aramaic   The ancient vernacular of the Jewish people. Several prayers, including the *Kaddish* and *Kol Nidrei*, are recited in Aramaic to this day.

Ashkenazic   A term used to refer to Jews of Eastern and Central European descent.

b'racha (*bra-KHA*)   A Hebrew term for blessing.

bar mitzvah   A Jewish boy who has reached the age of legal majority according to Jewish law, which is 13. This term is also used to refer to the ceremony that marks the rite of passage from youth to adulthood.

Barechu (*bar-KHOO*)   A call to prayer that marks the formal start of prayer services.

bat mitzvah   A Jewish girl who has reached the age of legal majority according to Jewish law, which is 12 to some authorities and 13 to others. This term is also used to refer to the ceremony that marks the rite of passage from youth to adulthood.

bimah (*BEE-mah*)   An elevated platform that's the focal point for Jewish worship services. The *bimah* is usually at the front of the ritual space, but it's sometimes in the center of the room.

birkat ha-mazon (*beer-COT hama-ZOHN*)   A collection of blessings also called "Grace After Meals."

bris   A covenant.

brit milah (*breet mee-LAH*)   A covenant of circumcision.

chametz (*KHA-Mets*)   Leaven and other related foods prohibited during Passover.

Conservative   A centrist movement in American Judaism that originated in Western Europe but flourished in the United States during the twentieth century.

covenant   A pact established between God and the Israelite nation.

d'var Torah (*da-VAR to-RAH*)   Literally, "word of *Torah*." This is a short teaching from the *Torah* that can be shared at the dinner table or during synagogue services.

daven (*DAH-ven*)   Yiddish verb for "prayer."

egalitarian   The public worship services that include both men and women as equal participants.

Elul (*Eh-lool*)   The sixth month of the Jewish calendar. *Elul* marks the beginning of the High Holy Day season.

etrog (*EH-trog*)   A citron fruit used for ritual purposes during the festival of *Sukkot*.

Gabbai (*GAH-by*)   A synagogue functionary responsible for overseeing parts of the *Torah* service. Any knowledgeable Jew can serve as a *Gabbai*.

Haftarah (*haf-tah-RAH* or *haf-TOE-rah*)   A section from the Prophets chanted on *Shabbat* mornings following the *Torah* reading.

haggadah (*ha-ga-DAH* or *ha-GAH-da*)   A ritual text of the Passover *seder*.

halakha (*ha-la-KHAH*)   From the root for "walking." This term refers to the body of Jewish law that has guided Jewish life for centuries.

Hanukkiyah (*ha-noo-kee-YAH*)   The technical term for the nine-branched candelabra that's lit during the festival of *Hanukkah*. It's also commonly referred to as a *menorah*.

Hasidism   A pietistic sect of Judaism originating in the eighteenth century under the charismatic leadership of the Baal Shem Tov.

havdalah   A ceremony for marking the end of the Sabbath. The ritual includes a multiwicked candle, fragrant spices, and wine.

k'lal yisrael   "The community of Israel." This term refers to the unity of the Jewish people.

kaddish (*KAH-dish*)   A prayer recited by mourners in honor of relatives who have passed away. The *kaddish* does not mention death at all, but rather celebrates the many glorious attributes of the Divine. *Kaddish* derives from the Hebrew root meaning "holy."

kashrut (*kash-ROOT*)   A system of Jewish dietary laws. Foods that conform to these laws are called *kosher*.

kiddush (*kee-DOOSH*)   A blessing recited over wine. This term also derives from the Hebrew root meaning "holy."

kipah (*kee-PAH*)   A ritual head covering, worn traditionally by men, but also by women in some communities.

kofa (*KOH-fah*)   A ritual head covering traditionally worn by women.

Kol Nidre (*kol nee-DRAY*)   A solemn service that begins the *Yom Kippur* holiday.

lashon hara (*lah-SHON ha-RAH*)   Literally meaning "evil tongue," this term refers to the sin of gossip, which is considered a serious transgression in Judaism.

lulav (*loo-LAV*)   A palm branch used in the ritual observance of the festival of *sukkot*. Together with willow branch, myrtle branch, and *etrog*, this makes up the four species mentioned in the *Torah*.

Maariv (*ma-ah-REEV*) An evening service recited as part of the daily liturgical cycle of Jewish prayer.

mahzor (*makh-ZOHR*) A special prayer book used during services on the High Holy Days.

matzah (*mah-TSAH*) Unleavened bread eaten during the festival of Passover.

mezuzah (*meh-zoo-ZAH*) A small parchment scroll, handwritten with biblical passages from the Books of Deuteronomy and Numbers, affixed to the doorposts of a Jewish home. A *mezuzah* is usually encased in a decorative case to protect the small scroll.

midrash (*mee-DRASH*) A rabbinic tradition of textual interpretation.

mikveh (*MIK-vah*) A Jewish ritual bath.

mincha (*min-CHA* or *MIN-cha*) An afternoon service that's part of the daily liturgical cycle in Jewish prayer.

minyan (*MIN-yan*) A prayer quorum of 10 adult Jewish males (or females, in egalitarian communities) required to recite certain prayers.

Mishna (*MISH-na*) A collection of rabbinic commentary on the *Torah*, transmitted orally and compiled in the second century. The *Mishna* organizes its discussion of the *Torah*'s laws by subject, making it more of a user-friendly guide to *halakha*.

mitzvah (*meets-VAH* or *MITZ-vah*) A sacred obligation. Sometimes translated as "good deed" or "commandment" of the *Torah*.

mitzvot (*meets-VOTE*) Plural of *mitzvah*.

Mohel (*moil* or *MO-hel*) A professional who is trained to perform ritual circumcision.

monotheism Theological belief that God is One.

Musaf (*MOO-sahf*) An additional service traditionally recited on *Shabbat* and festivals.

negel vasser Literally, "nail washing." This is a ritual washing of the hands performed first thing in the morning before setting one's feet on the ground.

Neilah (*neh-ee-LAH* or *ne-EE-lah*)   The concluding service during the *Yom Kippur* holiday. The ark remains open throughout the service, which is recited in a standing position.

ner tamid (*nehr tah-MEED*)   Literally "eternal flame." This refers to a small lamp above the ark holding the *Torah* scrolls in synagogues. It's never extinguished and symbolizes God's eternal commitment to the Jewish people.

niggun (*nee-GOON*)   A melody sung without words. This musical style became popular in the Hasidic movement as a form of prayer both in synagogue and at the dining table. Because you don't need to know the words, it's easy to hum along to a *niggun,* so this is a style of prayer that encourages participation on any level.

olam ha-ba (*oh-LAM ha-BAH*)   Literally, the "World to Come." This term is used in rabbinic literature to refer to the messianic era.

Old Testament   The Christian term for the Hebrew scriptures. Jews prefer to use the term *Hebrew Bible* or *Hebrew Scriptures.*

Omer (*OH-mer*)   A period of 7 weeks between Passover and *Shavuot* that marked the progress of the annual barley harvest. It's also understood as a "countdown" from the liberation of the Exodus to the revelation at Sinai.

Oral *Torah*   A body of interpretive tradition and commentary on the Written *Torah.* Traditional Jews believe the Oral *Torah* and Written *Torah* were revealed together at Mount Sinai.

Orthodox   A term for the most traditional denominations of Judaism.

P'sukei d'Zimra (*peso-KAY de-zim-RAH*)   Literally "verses of song." These provide a spiritual "warm-up" during morning prayer services.

Pesach (*pay-SAKH*)   The Hebrew name for the festival of Passover.

pikuach nefesh (*pee-KOO-akh NEH-fesh*)   Literally "saving a soul." This term refers to the *mitzvah* of caring for human life above all things.

rabbi   Literally "my teacher." This is an honorific title held by a person who is learned in Jewish law. In modern times, *Rabbi* has become an official title bestowed upon "ordination."

Reconstructionist The youngest of the formal Jewish denominations, and the only one to develop entirely in America. Reconstructionism was founded by Rabbi Mordecai Kaplan. The movement values traditional practice but rejects the notion of a God who is supernatural. Another hallmark of Reconstructionist theology is the rejection of the doctrine that the Jews are a chosen people.

Reform A progressive denomination that developed in Germany and later flourished in the United States. The Reform movement developed as an effort to make Judaism more meaningful to modern Jews by translating the *siddur* into the vernacular (German) and adapting ritual practices so the style of worship was more in line with Protestant practices of the time.

Rosh HaShanah The celebration of the Jewish New Year. *Rosh HaShanah* takes place on the first of the month of *Tishrei,* which is actually the seventh month in the Hebrew calendar.

Secular Humanist A contemporary, liberal movement within that views Judaism primarily through the lens of culture and values.

seder A ritual meal central to the celebration of the Passover festival. *Seder* literally means "order." At the *seder* table, symbolic foods are used as prompts to tell the story of the Jews' liberation from Egyptian slavery.

Sephardic A term used to describe Jews of Spanish and Portuguese descent. Sometimes Jews of North Africa and the Middle East are also called Sephardic.

seudah shleesheet (*soo-DAH shlee-SHEET*) The third festive meal celebrated in the late afternoon toward the end of the Sabbath day.

seudat mitzvah (*soo-DAT meets-VAH*) The festive meal to accompany any Jewish celebration.

Shaharit (*sha-kha-REET*) A morning service recited daily as part of the Jewish liturgical cycle.

Shavuot (*sha-voo-OAT*) A pilgrimage festival that celebrates the revelation of the *Torah* at Mount Sinai, along with the offering of first fruits.

shehecheyanu (*she-he-khay-YAH-nu*) A prayer expressing gratitude for any special milestone or unique occasion.

sheitel   A wig worn by traditional Jewish women who observe the laws of modesty or *tzniut*.

Shema (*she-MAH*)   Recited each morning and evening, the *Shema* is the central affirmation of Jewish faith in the unity of God.

Shiva (*SHIH-va*)   The seven-day period of mourning following the death and burial of an immediate relative.

shmoneh esrei   Literally, "eighteen." This is an alternate name for the *Amidah*.

shofar   A ram's horn, sounded daily during the month of *Elul* and on *Rosh HaShanah* as a call to repentance during the Days of Awe.

siddur   The Jewish prayer book.

simchat bat (*seem-KHAT BAHT*)   The ritual celebration welcoming a new daughter into the Covenant of the Jewish people.

Sukkot (*soo-COAT*)   The Feast of Tabernacles, an autumn pilgrimage festival that celebrates God's protection during the 40 years of wandering in the desert. Hospitality and fall harvest are two major themes of this holiday.

taharat ha-mishpacha (*ta-ha-RAT ha-meesh-pa-KHA*)   Literally, "family purity." This term refers to the Jewish laws and practices governing marital intimacy.

Tal (*TAHL*)   A prayer for dew recited annually on the second day of Passover.

tallit (*tah-LEET*)   A four-cornered garment adorned with *tzitzit,* or fringes, symbolic of the 613 *mitzvot*. A large *tallit* is worn on top of the clothing during prayer services. A small *tallit* is an undergarment worn throughout the day.

Talmud   A vast compendium of legal commentary on the *Mishna*. Although the *Talmud* is predominantly a legal document, it contains discussions that help us understand the cultural world of the ancient rabbis as well.

tashlikh   A ritual performed during *Rosh HaShanah* in which crusts of bread, symbolizing our sins, are cast into a body of water.

tefillin (*te-FILL-in*)   A ritual object worn during weekday morning prayers. *Tefillin* are small leather boxes containing hand-written excerpts from the *Torah*. The *tefillin shel yad* is affixed to the arm, and the *tefillin shel rosh* is affixed to the head. *Tefillin* are often called "phylacteries" in English.

Teshuvah   A process of repentance that can take place all year round but is a special focus of the High Holy Day season.

tzedakah (*tze-dah-KAH*)   From the Hebrew root meaning "justice." Refers to the *mitzvah* of giving charity.

tzitzit (*tseet-TsEET*)   Fringes tied with special knots and affixed to the corners of a *tallit*. They serve as a physical reminder of the *mitzvot*.

ushpizin (*oosh-pee-ZEEN*; feminine: ***ushpizot***, *oosh-pee-ZOAT*)   Mystical ancestors from biblical times who are welcomed nightly into the *sukkah* during the festival of *sukkot*.

yad (*YAHD*)   A pointer used for ritual reading of a *Torah* scroll. The *yad* helps the reader keep his or her place and protects the scroll by keeping hands away from the ink.

Yamim Noraim (*yah-MEEM no-rah-EEM*)   The Days of Awe, the period from *Rosh HaShanah* to *Yom Kippur,* also known as the High Holy Days.

yarmulke (*YAH-muh-kuh*)   A ritual head covering worn by men and some women as a symbol of reverence for God.

Yizkor (*YIZ-kor*)   A special service for mourning the loss of loved ones who have passed away recited on the morning of *Yom Kippur* but also during the festivals of Passover and *Shavuot*.

Zohar (*ZOH-har*)   A classic work of Jewish mysticism that focuses on esoteric interpretations of the *Torah*. It's attributed to the ancient rabbinic sage Rabbi Shimon bar Yohai. However, modern scholars have determined that the *Zohar* was composed in Spain during the Middle Ages by Rabbi Moses DeLeon and his disciples.

Resources

The chapters in this book have provided the basic tools you need to embark on your journey toward a richer, more fulfilling inner life. But what you've learned here is just the beginning. So many resources are available to help you grow as you venture forward. But with all the books and websites available, sometimes it can be difficult to know whom to trust. In this appendix, I've compiled a list of my absolute favorite resources. You'll find here some of the books, websites, institutes, and applications I turn to time and again for information, advice, and inspiration.

Recommended Reading

Jews are known as the People of the Book for a reason: we love to read! This is just a small sampling of the many books available to teach you about Jewish history, culture, beliefs, and practices.

Accessible Introductions

Diamant, Anita, and Howard Cooper. *Living a Jewish Life: Jewish Traditions, Customs and Values for Today's Families.* New York: HarperPaperbacks, 2007.

Donin, Hayim H. *To Be a Jew: A Guide to Jewish Observance in Contemporary Life.* New York: Basic Books, 1991.

Dosick, Wayne D. *Living Judaism: The Complete Guide to Jewish Belief, Tradition and Practice.* New York: HarperOne, 1998.

Greenberg, Blu. *How to Run a Traditional Jewish Household.* New York: Simon & Schuster, 1983.

Scheindlin, Raymond. *A Short History of the Jewish People: From Legendary Times to Modern Statehood.* New York: Oxford University Press, 2000.

Shenker, Lois S. *Welcome to the Family: Opening Doors to the Jewish Experience.* Ashland, OR: White Cloud Press, 2001.

Siegel, Richard, et al. *The First Jewish Catalog: A Do-It-Yourself Kit.* Philadelphia: Jewish Publication Society, 1965.

Wylen, Stephen M. *Settings of Silver: An Introduction to Judaism.* New York: Paulist Press, 2000.

Jewish Holidays

Greenberg, Irving. *The Jewish Way: Living the Holidays.* Northvale, NJ: Jason Aronson, 1998.

Lew, Alan. *This Is Real and You Are Completely Unprepared: The Days of Awe as a Journey of Transformation.* New York: Little, Brown and Co., 2003.

Reimer, Gail, and Judith A. Kates. *Beginning Anew: A Woman's Companion to the High Holy Days.* New York: Touchstone, 1997.

Waskow, Arthur. *Seasons of Our Joy: A Modern Guide to the Jewish Holidays.* Boston: Beacon Press, 1991.

Classics of Jewish Thought

These titles are a little more challenging to read, but if you're inclined to push yourself, they represent classic works of Jewish philosophy.

Buber, Martin. *I and Thou.* New York: Touchstone, 1996.

Gillman, Neil. *Sacred Fragments: Recovering Theology for the Modern Jew.* Philadelphia: Jewish Publication Society, 1990.

Heschel, Abraham Joshua. *The Sabbath*. New York: Farrar, Straus & Giroux, 2005.

———. *God in Search of Man: A Philosophy of Judaism*. New York: Farrar, Straus & Giroux, 1976.

Plaskow, Judith. *Standing Again at Sinai: Judaism from a Feminist Perspective*. New York: HarperOne, 1991.

Soloveitchik, Joseph B. *The Lonely Man of Faith*. New York: Doubleday, 2006.

Steinsaltz, Adin. *The Thirteen Petalled Rose: A Discourse on the Essence of Jewish Existence and Belief*. New York: Basic Books, 1985.

Contemporary Spirituality

Comins, Mike. *Making Prayer Real: Leading Jewish Spiritual Voices on Why Prayer Is Difficult and What to Do About It*. Woodstock, VT: Jewish Lights Publishing, 2010.

Hoffman, Lawrence A. *The Way into Jewish Prayer*. Woodstock, VT: Jewish Lights Publishing, 2004.

Korngold, Jamie S. *The God Upgrade: Finding Your 21st-Century Spirituality in Judaism's 5,000-Year-Old Tradition*. Woodstock, VT: Jewish Lights Publishing, 2011.

Matlins, Stuart M., ed. *The Jewish Lights Spirituality Handbook: A Guide to Understanding, Exploring and Living a Spiritual Life*. Woodstock, VT: Jewish Lights Publishing, 2004.

Morinis, Alan. *Everyday Holiness: The Jewish Spiritual Path of Musar*. Boston: Trumpeter, 2008.

Slonim, Rivkah. *Bread and Fire: Jewish Women Find God in the Everyday*. Jerusalem: Urim Publications, 2008.

Strassfeld, Michael. *A Book of Life: Embracing Judaism as a Spiritual Practice*. Woodstock, VT: Jewish Lights Publishing, 2006.

Wolpe, David. *Why Be Jewish?* New York: H. Holt and Co., 1985.

———. *Why Faith Matters.* New York: HarperOne, 2008.

Bibles and Commentaries

Hundreds of Bibles are out there, but most of them are published for a Christian readership. Jewish translations and commentaries interpret the Hebrew text in a way that's in keeping with Jewish theology.

The Jewish Bible: Tanakh: The Holy Scriptures—the New JPS Translation According to the Traditional Hebrew Text. Philadelphia: The Jewish Publication Society, 1985.

Berlin, Adele, et al., eds. *The Jewish Study Bible.* New York: Oxford University Press, 2004.

Eskenazi, Tamara C., and Andrea Weiss. *The Torah: A Women's Commentary.* New York: Union for Reform Judaism, 2007.

Katz, Michael, and Gerson Schwartz. *Swimming in the Sea of Talmud: Lessons for Everyday Living.* Philadelphia: Jewish Publication Society, 1997.

Lieber, David, et al., eds. *Etz Hayim: Torah and Commentary.* Philadelphia: The Jewish Publication Society, 2001.

Plaut, Gunther W., and David Stein. *The Torah: A Modern Commentary.* New York: Union for Reform Judaism, 2005.

Scherman, Nosson. *The Stone Edition Chumash.* Brooklyn: Artscroll/Mesorah Publishers, 1993.

Prayer Books

Feld, Edward. *Mahzor Lev Shalem.* New York: The Rabbinical Assembly, 2010.

Frishman, Elyse D. *Mishkan T'filah: A Reform Siddur.* New York: CCAR Press, 2007.

Harlow, Jules. *Siddur Sim Shalom: A Prayerbook for Shabbat, Festival sand Weekdays*. New York: The Rabbinical Assembly, 1985.

Scherman, Nosson. *The Complete ArtScroll Siddur*. Brooklyn: Mesorah Publications, 1990.

Teutsch, David. *Kol ha-Neshamah (Shabbat v'hagim)*. Wyncote, PA: Reconstructionist Press, 1996.

Finding a Jewish Community Near You

Contact the organizations listed here to locate Jewish communities and institutions in your area.

Reconstructionist Judaism

Jewish Reconstructionist Federation
jrf.org

Reform Judaism

Union for Reform Judaism
urj.org

Orthodox Judaism

Orthodox Union
ou.org

Conservative Judaism

United Synagogue of Conservative Judaism
uscj.org/index1.html

Jewish Federations of North America
jewishfederations.org

Society for Humanistic Judaism
shj.org

Torah on the Web

So much information is available about Judaism online. This list compiles the most content-rich sites out there. But remember, *Torah* study is most meaningful when it happens in partnership and in community. Use these sites as a reference and a starting point, but then take what you've learned and find a partner to study with you!

Sites for Exploring Orthodox Spirituality

Aish
aish.com

Chabad
chabad.org

Jewish Orthodox Feminist Alliance
jofa.org

Drisha Institute for Jewish Education
drisha.org

Liberal Sites for Information and Inspiration

Beliefnet
beliefnet.com

InterfaithFamily.com
interfaithfamily.com

MyJewishLearning.com
myjewishlearning.com

Jewish Outreach Institute
joi.org

Online Resources for Jewish Prayer and Ritual

Ritualwell
ritualwell.org

The Open Siddur Project
opensiddur.org

Mechon Hadar
mechonhadar.org

Mayyim Hayyim—Living Waters Community Mikveh
mayyimhayyim.org

Instructional Videos for Putting on *Tefillin*

youtube.com/Y8r3QlF07Ac

youtube.com/cKdr50iLqf8

Resources for Online Study

Skirball
adultjewishlearning.org

Jewish Women's Archive
jwa.org

JewishGen
jewishgen.org

Jewish Virtual Library
jewishvirtuallibrary.org

Heritage: Civilization and the Jews
pbs.org/wnet/heritage

On1Foot: Jewish Texts for Social Justice
(American Jewish World Service)
on1foot.org

Daily/Weekly *Torah* Study

Daf Yomi
dafyomi.org

G-DCAST
g-dcast.com

Chabad Daily *Torah* Study
chabad.org/dailystudy/default_cdo/jewish/Daily-Study.htm

Online Cultural 'Zines

***Tablet* magazine**
tabletmag.com

The Jewish Daily Forward
forward.com

ZEEK: A Jewish Journal of Thought and Culture
zeek.forward.com

Jewcy
jewcy.com

Heeb
heebmagazine.com

Residential Opportunities for Adult Learning

National Havurah Committee
havurah.org

Elat Chayyim Center for Jewish Spirituality
isabellafreedman.org/jewish-retreats/elatchayyim

Pearlstone Conference and Retreat Center
pearlstonecenter.org

Best Jewish Prayer Apps

Technology makes Jewish prayer more portable than ever. Check out what these innovative applications for your smartphone or tablet can do for your spiritual practice!

Jewish iPhone Community
jewishiphonecommunity.org
This site has all the latest information about Jewish apps available for any iPhone and other smartphone platforms.

Totally Tanach
iPad application
Redlex and Davka Corporation
Browse, search, and study the Hebrew Bible! Includes full Hebrew text and English translation.

iBless Food
iPod Touch/iPad/iPhone application
Davka Corporation
Look up and study all the basic blessings over food or for any occasion.

Jewish Cal
iPod Touch/iPad/iPhone application
Crowded Road Publishers
The most comprehensive Jewish calendar tool available. Includes text from the prayer book, *minyan* finder, and daily learning resources.

iComfort
iPod Touch/iPad/iPhone application
Behrman House Publishers
Teaches all the Jewish traditions, rituals, blessings, and prayers for the mourning process.

iManishtana
iPod Touch/iPad/iPhone application
Behrman House Publishers
Learn the traditional Four Questions to prepare for the Passover *Seder.*

OmerCount 2.2
iPod Touch/iPad/iPhone application
David Cooper and Rabbi David Seidenberg
Keep track of the 49 days between Passover and *Shavuot* with Jewish mystical insights into the daily practice of counting the *Omer.*

Index